Magnetics 2019

Orlando, Florida, USA
23 - 24 January 2019

ISBN: 978-1-5108-8106-8

Printed from e-media with permission by:

Curran Associates, Inc.
57 Morehouse Lane
Red Hook, NY 12571

Some format issues inherent in the e-media version may also appear in this print version.

Printed by Curran Associates, Inc. (2019)

For permission requests, please contact TWST Events
at the address below.

TWST Events
622 3rd Ave, 34th FL
New York, NY 10017
USA

twstevents.com

Additional copies of this publication are available from:

Curran Associates, Inc.
57 Morehouse Lane
Red Hook, NY 12571 USA
Phone: 845-758-0400
Fax: 845-758-2633
Email: curran@proceedings.com
Web: www.proceedings.com

TABLE OF CONTENTS

New Standards for Permanent Magnets 1
M. Devine

Magneto-Optical Inline Scanner for Measuring and Characterization of Permanent Magnets 16
R. Holzhey

Selecting Optimal Lamination Materials 31
S. Constantinides

Magnetic Answers for Market Driven Needs 46
J. Whalen

Rare Earth Magnets: Yesterday, Today And Tomorrow 59
J. Ormerod

Rare Earth Magnets Alternates? 89
S. Narasimhan

Reducing the Rare-Earth Content of Strong Permanent Magnets 115
D. Parker

Tunable Quadrupole Magnets for Next Generation Electron Ion Colliders 130
J. Liu

Significant Weight Reduction of Three-Phase Transformers through Advancements in Core Construction and Materials 147
K. Furmanczyk

Comparison of Numerical and Analytical Methods for the Design of Permanent Magnets 155
T. Schliesch

Anisotropic Injection Moulding of Multipole Radial Rotors for IPM 173
M. Ohm

Impact of New Tariffs and a Looming Trade War 186
M. Miller

Accurate 3-Axis Magnetic Field Measurements 209
R. Ughini

Rare Earth Recycling to Increase Supply Security 230
D. Naumann

Author Index

New Standards for Permanent Magnets

MICHAEL DEVINE
SENIOR APPLICATIONS ENGINEER

ADAMS MAGNETIC PRODUCTS

Why Do We Need a New Standard?

- Yet ANOTHER standard? What gives?
- A lot of things are taken for granted:
  - Alnico 5 & 8 – So many sub-grades
  - Ceramic 8 – Dozens of sub-grades
  - SmCo22 – Is that 1:5 or 2:17?
  - NdFeB - Who came up with & governs the letter designations?

ADAMS MAGNETIC PRODUCTS

BH Curves for Cast Alnico 8

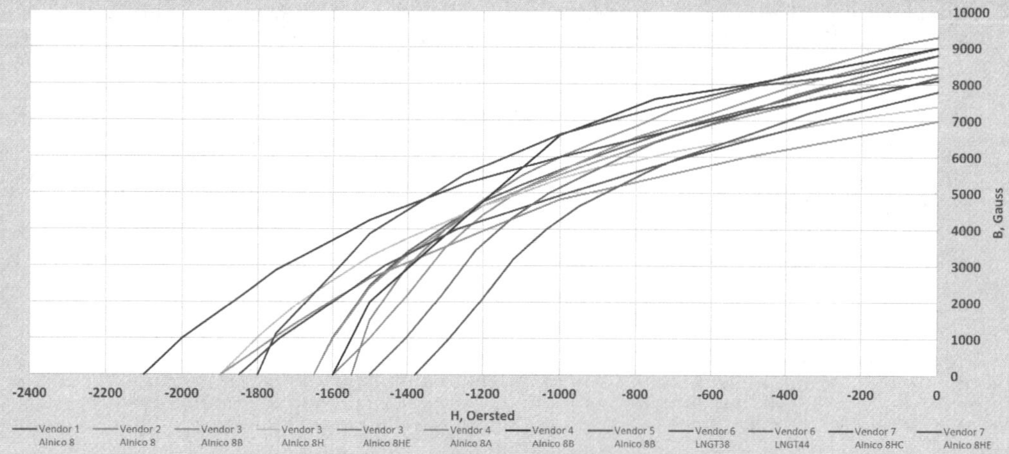

ADAMS MAGNETIC PRODUCTS

Imagine a world without standards

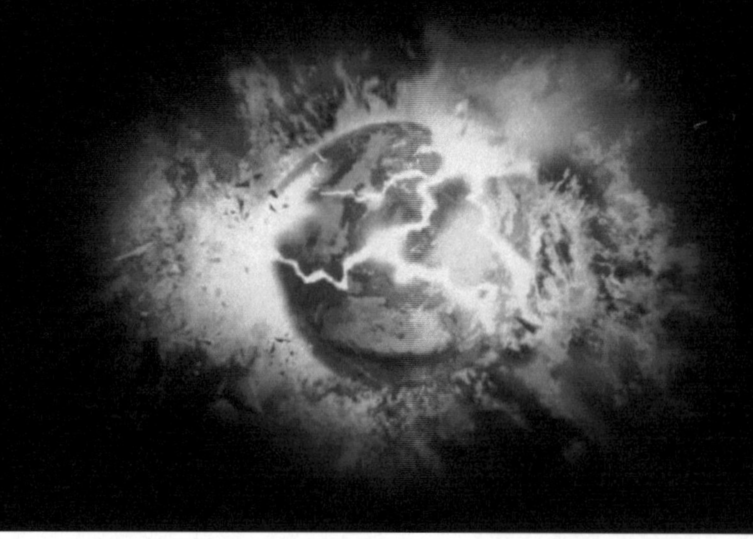

How are magnets specified now?

- Some specifications are regional
- Some are outdated

ADAMS MAGNETIC PRODUCTS

MMPA Standard

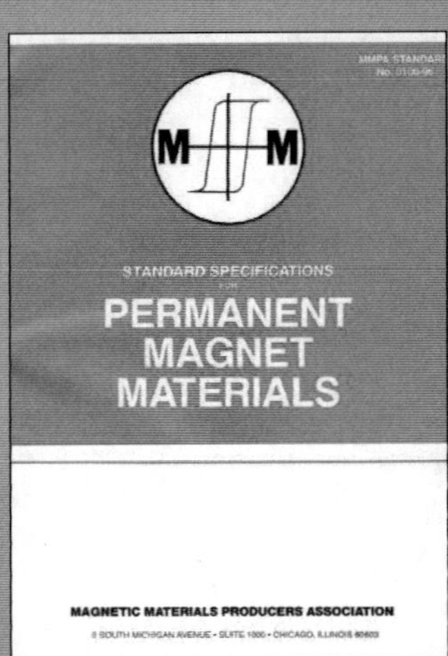

- Popular in USA
- First released in 1966
- Managed by magnet producers
- Last update in 2000

ADAMS MAGNETIC PRODUCTS

IEC Standard

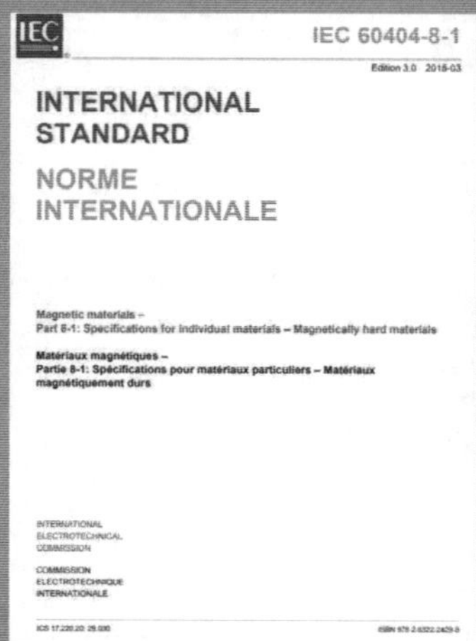
IEC 60404-8-1

Edition 3.0 2016-03

INTERNATIONAL STANDARD

NORME INTERNATIONALE

Magnetic materials –
Part 8-1: Specifications for individual materials – Magnetically hard materials

Matériaux magnétiques –
Partie 8-1: Spécifications pour matériaux particuliers – Matériaux magnétiquement durs

INTERNATIONAL ELECTROTECHNICAL COMMISSION

COMMISSION ELECTROTECHNIQUE INTERNATIONALE

- Popular in Europe
- First released in 1979
- Managed by magnet producers
- Last update in 2016

ADAMS MAGNETIC PRODUCTS

Japanese Standard

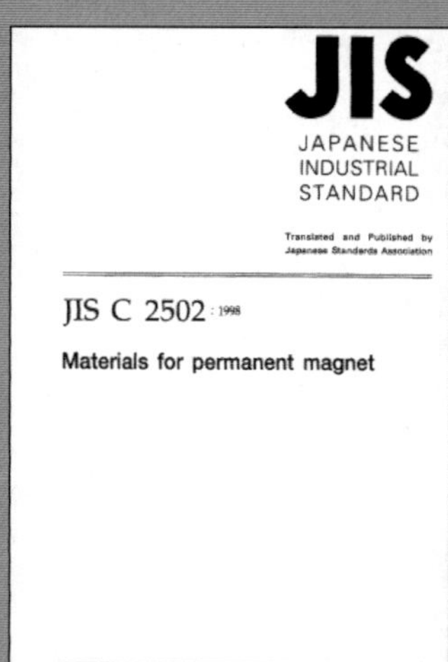
JIS

JAPANESE INDUSTRIAL STANDARD

Translated and Published by Japanese Standards Association

JIS C 2502 : 1998

Materials for permanent magnet

- First released in 1954
- Managed by Ministry of International Trade and Industry
- Last update in 1998, but reaffirmed in 2013
- Based on IEC 60404-8 with some additions for the Japanese market

ADAMS MAGNETIC PRODUCTS

Chinese Standard

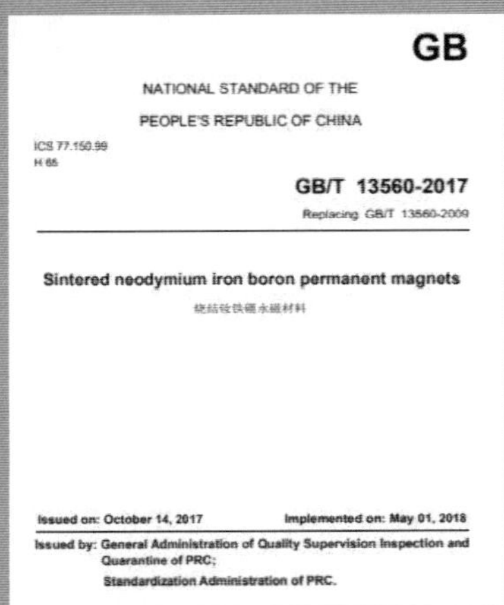
GB

NATIONAL STANDARD OF THE

PEOPLE'S REPUBLIC OF CHINA

ICS 77.150.99

H 65

GB/T 13560-2017

Replacing GB/T 13560-2009

Sintered neodymium iron boron permanent magnets

Issued on: October 14, 2017 **Implemented on: May 01, 2018**

Issued by: General Administration of Quality Supervision Inspection and Quarantine of PRC;

Standardization Administration of PRC.

- Some vendors call out SJ 285-77, created in 1977
- SJ/T 10410-2016 Permanent ferrite materials
- Managed by Standardization Administration of China
- N, M, H, SH, UH and EH indicate:
  - Low coercivity
  - **M**edium coercivity
  - **H**igh coercivity
  - **S**uper-**H**igh coercivity
  - **U**ltra-**H**igh coercivity
  - **E**xtremely **H**igh coercivity
  - etc

ADAMS MAGNETIC PRODUCTS

Inconsistencies among standards: Cast Alnico 5

MMPA 0100-00
- One type
- Nominal values
- Br: 12,800 Gauss
- Hc: 640 Oe
- (BH)max: 5.5 MGOe

IEC 60404-8-1
- Two types
- Minimum values
- Br: 11,800 & 12,000 Gauss
- Hc: 615 & 665 Oe
- (BH)max: 4.6 & 5.5 MGOe

China
- Two types
- Minimum values
- Br: 11,800 & 12,000 Gauss
- Hc: 615 & 665 Oe
- (BH)max: 4.6 & 5.5 MGOe

Japan
- Two types
- Minimum and Nominal values
- Br: 11,800 & 12,000 Gauss (minimum)
- Br: 12,300 & 12,500 Gauss (nominal)
- Hci: 716 & 766 Oe (minimum)
- Hc: 615 & 665 Oe (nominal)
- (BH)max: 4.6 & 5.5 MGOe (minimum)
- (BH)max: 5.1 & 6.0 MGOe (nominal)

ADAMS MAGNETIC PRODUCTS

Inconsistencies among standards: Hard Ferrite 5

MMPA 0100-00
- One type
- Nominal values
- Br: 3,800 Gauss
- Hc: 2400 Oe
- Hci: 2500 Oe
- (BH)max: 3.40 MGOe

IEC 60404-8-1
- One type (S1-1-6)
- Minimum values
- Br: 3700 Gauss
- Hc: 2890 Oe
- Hci: 3260 Oe
- (BH)max: 3.2 MGOe

China
- Two types (Y30H-1 & Y30H-2)
- Range of values
- Br: 3800 to 4150 Gauss
- Hci: 2950 to 4200 Oe
- (BH)max: 3.4 to 4.1 MGOe

Japan
- One type (S1-1-6)
- Minimum & Nominal values
- Br: 3700 & 3900 Gauss
- Hc: 2890 & 3440 Oe
- Hci: 3260 & 3570 Oe
- (BH)max: 3.2 & 3.5 MGOe

ADAMS MAGNETIC PRODUCTS

Inconsistencies among standards: SmCo 22 MGOe

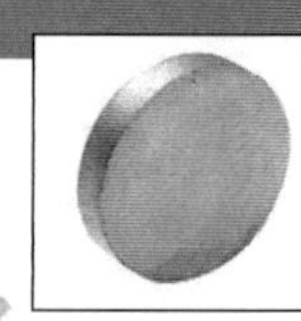

1:5 Type

MMPA 0100-00
- One type
- Nominal values
- Br=9500 Gauss
- Hci=15,000 Oe

IEC 60404-8-1
- One type
- Minimum values
- Br=9300 Gauss
- Hci=8800 Oe

China
- One type
- Minimum values
- Br=9300 Gauss
- Hci=8800 Oe

Japan
- One type
- Minimum and Nominal values
- Br=9300 Gauss
- Hci=8800 Oe

ADAMS MAGNETIC PRODUCTS

Inconsistencies among standards: SmCo 22 MGOe

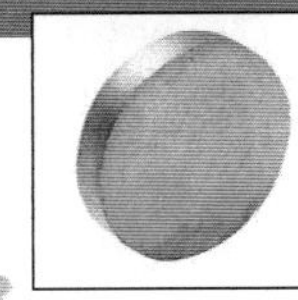

2:17 Type

MMPA 0100-00
- None listed
- 0100-96 lists:
  - Br=9600 Gauss
  - Hci=12,000 Oe

IEC 60404-8-1
- One type
- Minimum values
- Br=9400 Gauss
- Hci=8800 Oe

China
- One type
- Minimum values
- Br=9400 Gauss
- Hci=8800 Oe

Japan
- One type
- Minimum & Nominal values
- Br=9400 Gauss
- Hci=8800 Oe

ADAMS MAGNETIC PRODUCTS

Inconsistencies among standards: NdFeB

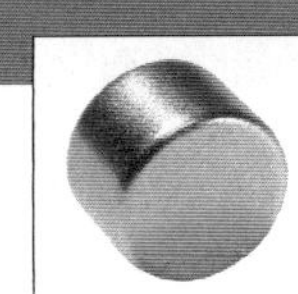

MMPA 0100-00
- 19 grades
- Nominal values
- Highest grade is 50 MGOe
- Br: 14,100 Gauss
- Largest value for Intrinsic Coercivity is 41,000 Oe

IEC 60404-8-1
- 16 grades
- Minimum values
- Highest grade is 50 MGOe
- Br: 14,200 Gauss
- Largest value for Intrinsic Coercivity is 30,000 Oe

China
- 16 grades
- Minimum values
- Highest grade is 48 MGOe
- Br: 14,200 Gauss
- Largest value for Intrinsic Coercivity is 30,150 Oe

Japan
- 16 grades
- Minimum & Nominal values
- Highest grade is 45 MGOe
- Br: 14,000 Gauss (Nominal)
- Largest value for Intrinsic Coercivity is 30,150 Oe

ADAMS MAGNETIC PRODUCTS

About ASTM

- 12,500+ Standards
- 30,000+ Volunteer Members
- 140+ Participating Countries
- 120 Years of Operation

- Strategic Objectives
  - Global Technical Expertise
  - Standards and Technical Content Development
  - Services Provider
  - Organizational Vitality

ASTM INTERNATIONAL

Committee A06 on Magnetic Properties

- Formed in 1903
- Covers Soft & Hard Magnetic Material
  - Material specifications
  - Test Methods
- Currently 50 members
  - Producers
  - Users
  - General Interest
- Currently 52 active standards
  - Hysteresis testing Low Coercivity Materials (A773)
  - Hysteresis testing High Coercivity Materials (A977)
  - Specification for Low-Carbon Magnetic Iron (A848)
  - Test Method for Evaluating Hygrothermal Corrosion Resistance of Permanent Magnet Alloys (A1071)

ADAMS MAGNETIC PRODUCTS

ASTM Standards

- Alnico
- Ceramic (Hard Ferrite)
- SmCo
- NdFeB

Designation: A1070 – 16

Standard Specification for
Cast and Sintered Alnico Permanent Magnets[1]

Designation: A1054 – 16

Standard Specification for
Sintered Ferrite Permanent Magnets[1]

Designation: A1102 – 16

Standard Specification for
Sintered Samarium Cobalt (SmCo) Permanent Magnets[1]

Designation: A1101 – 16

Standard Specification for
Sintered and Fully Dense Neodymium Iron Boron (NdFeB) Permanent Magnets[1]

ADAMS MAGNETIC PRODUCTS

What the new standards will/can do

- Guarantee a minimum level of magnetic performance
- Provide a common language between customer and supplier
- With 5-year renewal cycle, will always be up to date
- Clearly identify the type and amount of technical and quality information required for an order
- Clarify the magnet condition
  - Full magnetization
  - Stabilization
  - Not magnetized
- Clearly defined workmanship, finish and appearance criteria

ADAMS MAGNETIC PRODUCTS

Format of Specification

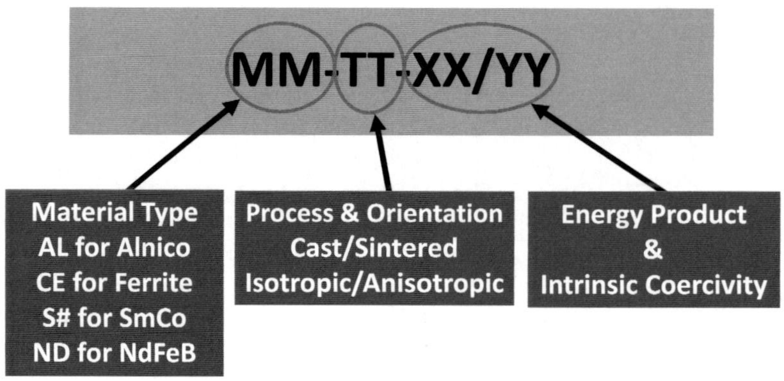

ADAMS MAGNETIC PRODUCTS

ASTM Alnico Standard (A1070)

- Cross reference with MMPA 0100-00 (Original & Brief) & IEC 60404-8-1 (Brief designation & Code number)
- 31 grades of material
- Designation format is MM-TT-XX/YY
  - MM = Material Type, AL for Alnico
  - TT = Processing & Orientation (Cast/Sintered, Isotropic/Anisotropic)
  - XX = Energy product (in kJ/m^3)
  - YY = Intrinsic coercivity (in kA/m)
- Cast Alnico 5, Low end: AL-CA-37/49
- Cast Alnico 5, Mid range: AL-CA-39/49
- Cast Alnico 5, High end: AL-CA-44/53

ADAMS MAGNETIC PRODUCTS

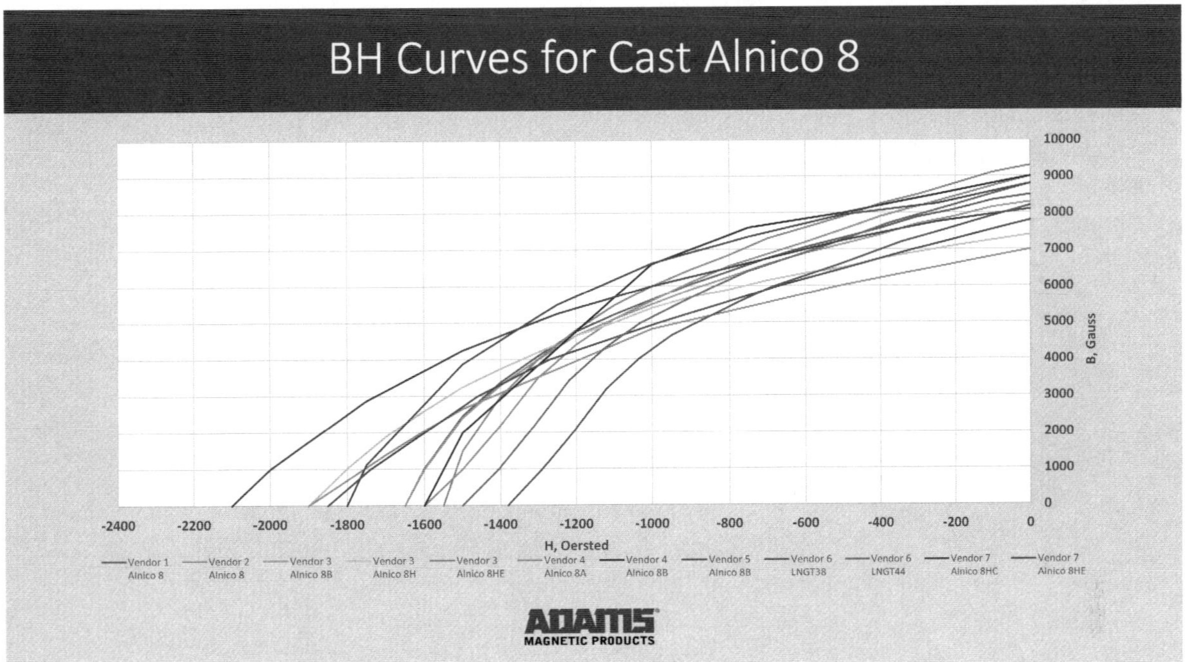
BH Curves for Cast Alnico 8
10000
9000
8000
7000
6000
5000
4000
3000
2000
1000
0
B, Gauss
-2400
-2200
-2000
-1800
-1600
-1400
-1200
-1000
-800
-600
-400
-200
0
H, Oersted
Vendor 1 Alnico 8
Vendor 2 Alnico 8
Vendor 3 Alnico 8B
Vendor 3 Alnico 8H
Vendor 3 Alnico 8HE
Vendor 4 Alnico 8A
Vendor 4 Alnico 8B
Vendor 5 Alnico 8B
Vendor 6 LNGT38
Vendor 6 LNGT44
Vendor 7 Alnico 8HC
Vendor 7 Alnico 8HE
ADAMS
MAGNETIC PRODUCTS

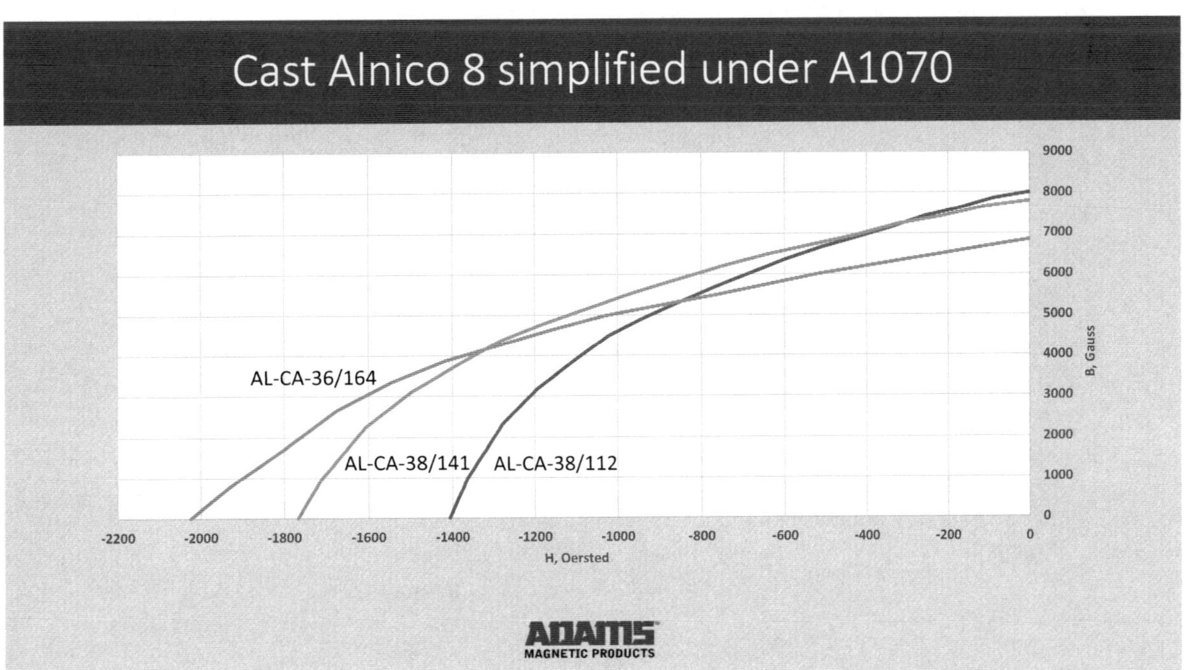
Cast Alnico 8 simplified under A1070
9000
8000
7000
6000
5000
4000
3000
2000
1000
0
B, Gauss
AL-CA-36/164
AL-CA-38/141
AL-CA-38/112
-2200
-2000
-1800
-1600
-1400
-1200
-1000
-800
-600
-400
-200
0
H, Oersted
ADAMS
MAGNETIC PRODUCTS

ASTM Samarium Cobalt Standard (A1102)

- Cross reference with MMPA 0100-00 & IEC 60404-8-1 (Brief designation & Code number)
- 9 grades of 1:5 material
- 26 grades of 2:17 material
- Designation format is MM-TT-XX/YY
  - MM = Material Type, S1 for 1:5 type, S2 for 2:17 type
  - TT = Processing & Orientation (Sintered, Isotropic, Anisotropic)
  - XX = Energy product (in kJ/m^3)
  - YY = Intrinsic coercivity (in kA/m)
- SmCo 22 MGOe (1:5 type): S1-SA-160/1200
- SmCo 22 MGOe (2:17 type): S2-SA-160/700

ADAMS MAGNETIC PRODUCTS

ASTM NdFeB Standard (A1101)

- Cross reference with MMPA 0100-00 & IEC 60404-8-1 (Brief designation & Code number)
- 60 grades of material
- Designation format is MM-TT-XX/YY
  - MM = Material Type, ND for Neodymium Iron Boron
  - TT = Processing & Orientation (Sintered, Isotropic, Anisotropic)
  - XX = Energy product (in kJ/m^3)
  - YY = Intrinsic coercivity (in kA/m)
- Neo 4811: ND-SA-370/875
- Neo 4812: ND-SA-370/955
- Neo 4814: ND-SA-370/1114
- Neo 4817: ND-SA-370/1353

ADAMS MAGNETIC PRODUCTS

ASTM Hard Ferrite Standard (A1054)

- Cross reference with MMPA 0100-00 & IEC 60404-8-1
- 13 grades of material
- Designation format is MM-Y-##
  - MM = Material Type, CE for Ceramic ferrite
  - Y = Processing & Orientation (Isotropic/Anisotropic)
  - ## = Numeric Grade designation
- Ceramic 8A, 'The Standard': CE-A-08A
  - (BH)max: 3.5 MGOe; Hci: 3050 Oe
- Ceramic 8B, Higher energy: CE-A-08B
  - (BH)max: 4.1 MGOe; Hci: 2960 Oe

ADAMS MAGNETIC PRODUCTS

Maximum Recommended Working Temperature

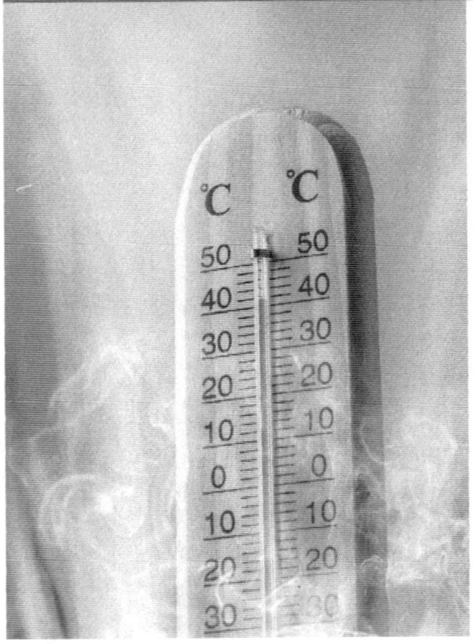

- Discourages use of 'Maximum Operating Temperature'
- Recommends accounting for magnetic circuit, not just magnet grade
- The 'Maximum Recommended Working Temperature' has a variety of interpretations:
  - Maximum temperature at which the normal hysteresis loop is linear in the second quadrant
  - In a less demanding interpretation, the normal loop must be linear on to the maximum energy operating point on the normal hysteresis loop.
- Alnico: 450°C to 550°C
- Ferrite: Not specified
- SmCo: 250°C for 1:5; 350°C for 2:17
- NdFeB: 80°C to 230°C

ADAMS MAGNETIC PRODUCTS

Workmanship, Finish and Appearance

- Magnets should be free of adhered magnetic particles and surface residue which may interfere with assembly or proper device function
- Chips shall be acceptable if no more than 10% of any surface identified as a magnetic pole is removed
- No visible cracks

ADAMS MAGNETIC PRODUCTS

Magnetic Condition – Stabilized, Calibrated, Knocked down

- A Stabilized magnet is exposed to heat or a magnetic field so that subsequent exposure will cause minimal to no additional demagnetization
- A Calibrated magnet is exposed to a reverse magnetic field so its magnetic field output fits within a narrow tolerance range
- A Knocked-down magnet is either partially or totally demagnetized

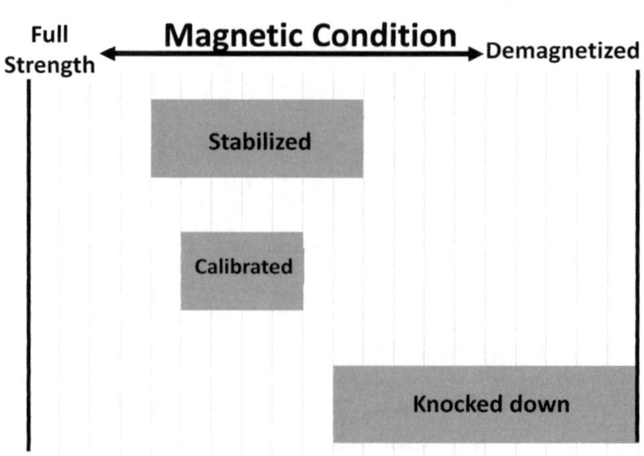

ADAMS MAGNETIC PRODUCTS

How to Cite an ASTM Spec

Reference String:

- Base Designation / Edition -Version / Title / Publisher/ Publisher City / Publisher State, Province / Publication Year/ DOI / Publisher Website

Examples:

Referencing Standards with Year of Approval:

- ASTM Standard A1054, 2016, "Standard Specification for Sintered Ferrite Permanent Magnets," ASTM International, West Conshohocken, PA, 2016, DOI: 10.1520/A1054-16, www.astm.org

Referencing Standards (reapproved):

- ASTM Standard A1054, 2016 (2021), "Standard Specification for Sintered Ferrite Permanent Magnets," ASTM International, West Conshohocken, PA, 2006, DOI: 10.1520/A1054-16R21, www.astm.org

ADAMS MAGNETIC PRODUCTS

Conclusion

ADAMS MAGNETIC PRODUCTS

INNOVENT Technology Development • Industry research facility • Founded 1994

Member of ZUSE-GEMEINSCHAFT

Magneto-Optical Inline Scanner for Measuring and Characterization of Permanent Magnets

Surface engineering • Biomaterials • Magnetic and optical systems • Analytics

5 RESEARCH DEPARTMENTS

Main fields of development

INNOVENT

Surface engineering
Head of department: Dr. Bernd Gruenler, Dr. Arnd Schimanski
Flame coating – Plasma technologies - Electrochemical processing - Sol-gel technique - PVD - Parylene coating- Surface functionalization – Surface characterization and analytics - Mechanical construction – Prototype construction

Primer and chemical surface treatment
Head of department: Dr. Joerg Leuthaeusser
Adhesion promoter/Primer – Functional surfaces – Hybrid injection moulding – Joining technologies: Bonding, Painting, Casting – Electro/Gas Phase silicatization – Composite materials – Corrosion/Durability – Cleaning/Activation

Magnetic and optical systems
Head of department: Rocco Holzhey
Magnetism – Optics – Crystal growth – Simulation – magnetic Nanoparticles – composites – Single crystals – Epitaxial films – Magnetic measurement techniques – Magneto-optical sensors – Optical measurement methods – Simulation software

Biomaterials
Head of department: Dr. Matthias Schnabelrauch
Synthesis - Characterization - biological Analysis - resorbable Polymers and Composites - Glycosaminoglycane - Polysaccharids – Bone repair materials - Polylactids - magnetic Nanoparticles - bioactive Coatings - Electrospinning

Analytic and material testing
Head of department: Dr. Katrin Pawlik
Polymers - Plastics - Oligomers - Additive Substances - Adhesives - Coatings - Paints - Bulk Analysis - Surface Analysis - Separation Technologies - Process Monitoring - Failure Analysis

Department MOS (Magnetic and Optical Systems)

Divisions of MOS

Fundamental and application oriented research in the fields of magnetic, optics and crystal growth in 4 divisions.

1. **Simulation & Software:** computer simulation of different physical systems
2. **Magnetic Systems:** generating, measuring and shielding of magnetic fields
3. **Optical Systems:** build up and optimization of optical systems (stray light based)
4. **Crystalline Materials:** growth and qualification of monocrystalline materials

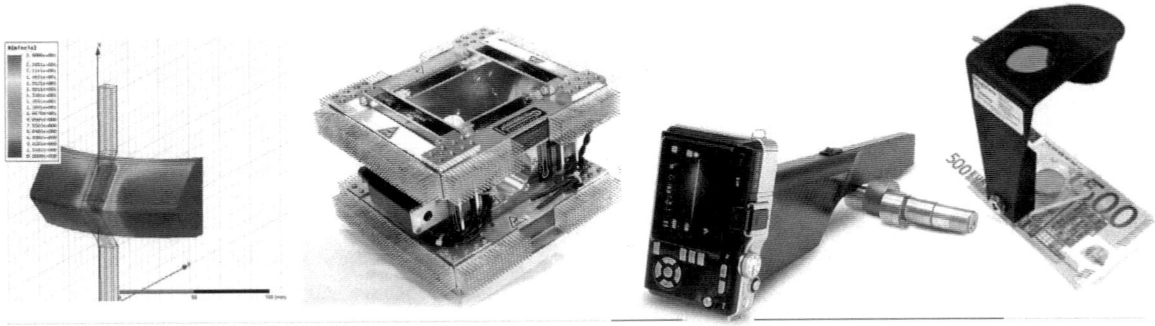

1/22/2019 M.Sc. Rocco Holzhey © INNOVENT Technology Development www.innovent-jena.com 5

STAFF

INNOVENT currently has 140 employees

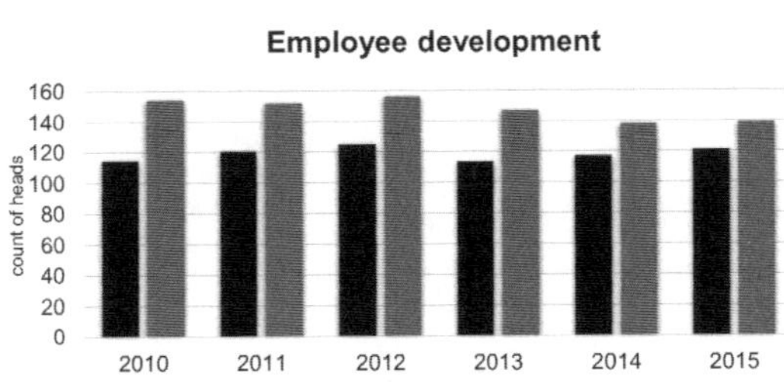

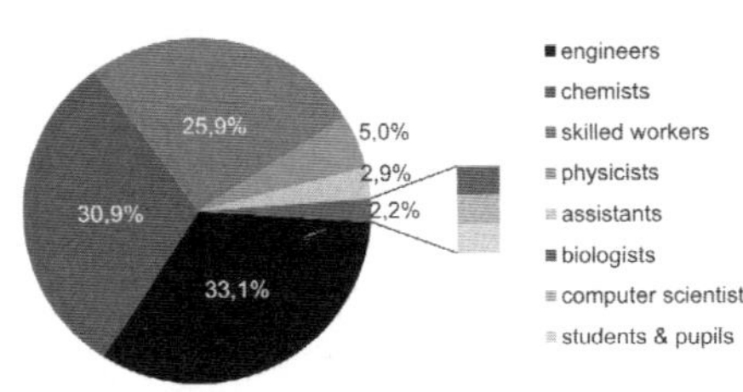

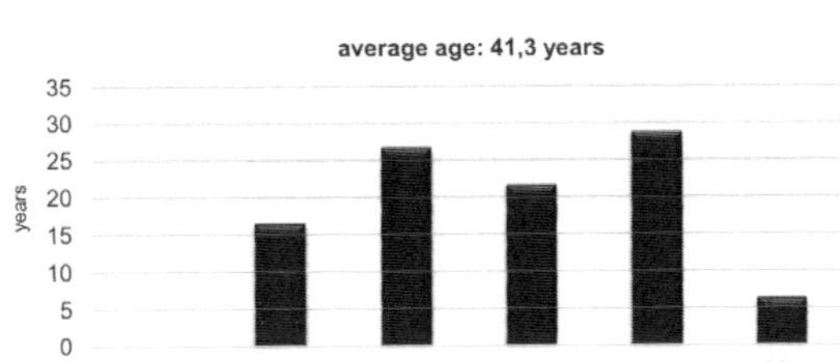

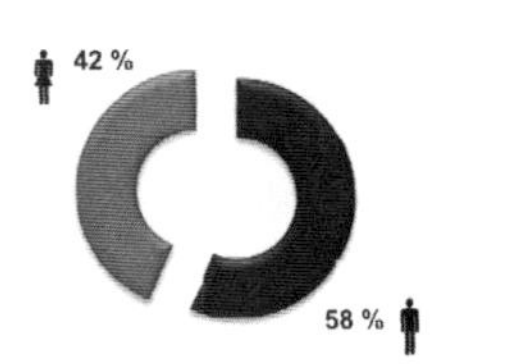

(effective date: 31st December 2015)

1/22/2019 M.Sc. Rocco Holzhey © INNOVENT Technology Development www.innovent-jena.com 6

SENIS
magnetic & current measurement

- Magnetic field and current measurements
- Sensors, Instruments and Services
- 3D Hall Sensor Development and Production

INNOVENT

R & D in the fields of
- Magnetic and optical Systems
- Surface engineering
- Primer and chemical surface treatment
- Biomaterials
- Analytics and material testing

spin-off
matesy
Magnetic Technologies & Systems

- Magnetic Technologies and Systems
- magnetic, magneto-optic and optical solutions

SURA INSTRUMENTS spin-off
Your Professional Partner for Surface Technologies

- pre-treatment and activating surfaces
- improving adhesion of paints, varnishes, inks and glues

spin-off
AXON
INNOVATIONS

- Software Development
- Embedded Systems
- Scientific Instrumentation
- Industrial Image Processing
- Robotic

Magneto-Optical Inline Scanner for Measuring and Characterization of Permanent Magnets

INNOVENT

Outline

- **Why measure magnets?**
  - near and far field of permanent magnets - What does it mean?
  - Technologies and Systems for far and near field
- **Build up Magneto-Optical Inline Scanner**
  - Measuring head
  - Test stand
  - Measurements
- **Magneto-Optics – How does it work?**
  - Liquid Phase Epitaxy (LPE)
  - Sensor types
  - Application examples
- **3D Hall Sensors**
- **Further activities**

Why measure magnets?

example: sensing magnet for industrial application (far field measurement)

- **Magnet typ:**
  - 12035 Hard Ferrite Magnets
  - Production: isostatic single pressing
  - Volume [mm³]: 153.9
  - **max. angle [°]: 2.0**
  - min. open remanenz [mT]: 370

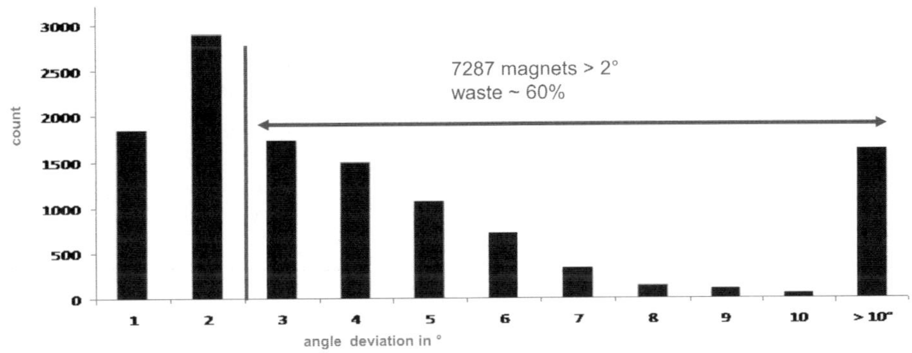

Why measure magnets?

example: 1. disk magnet / 2. micro magnet (near field measurement)

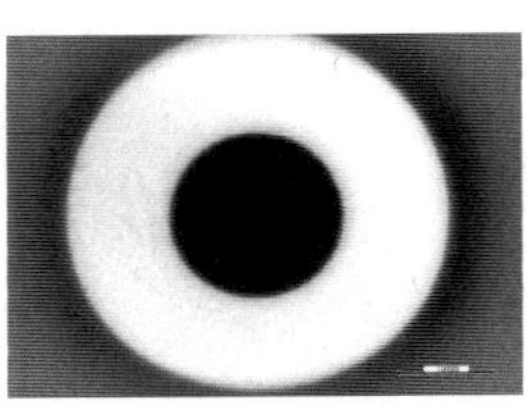

Fully magnetized good quality magnet

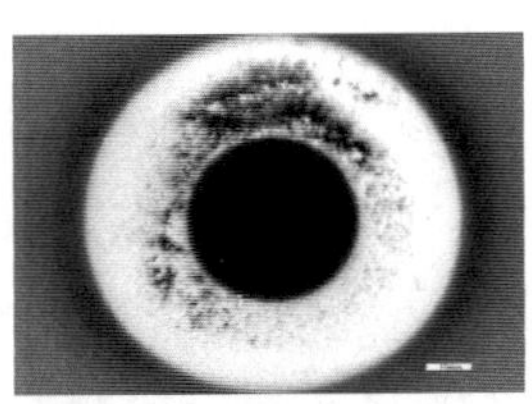

Fully magnetized bad quality Magnet with non-magnetic areas (dark)

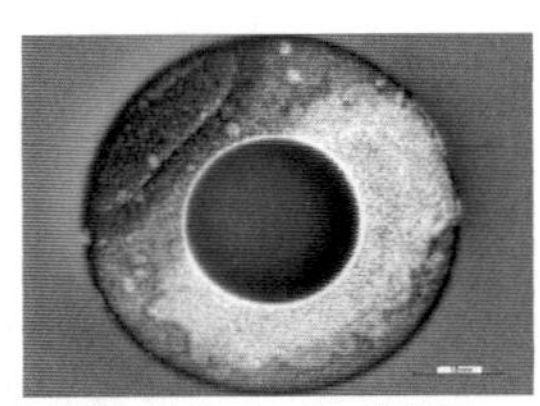

Fully magnetized and partially Demagnetized for visualization of material structure of a good quality magnet

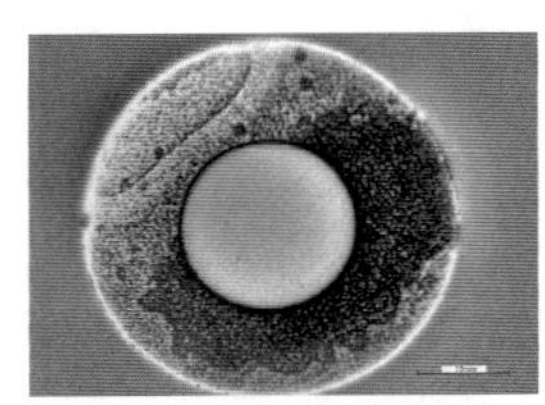

Fully magnetized and partially Demagnetized with reverse polarity

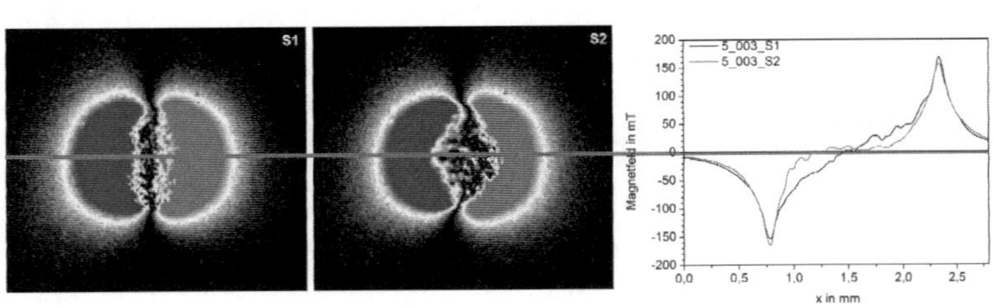

Micro magnet (watch industry):

- Diameter: 2mm
- Height: 0.8mm
- Production: isostatic single pressing
- Material: SmCo

Why measure magnets?

near and far field of permanent magnets - What does it mean?

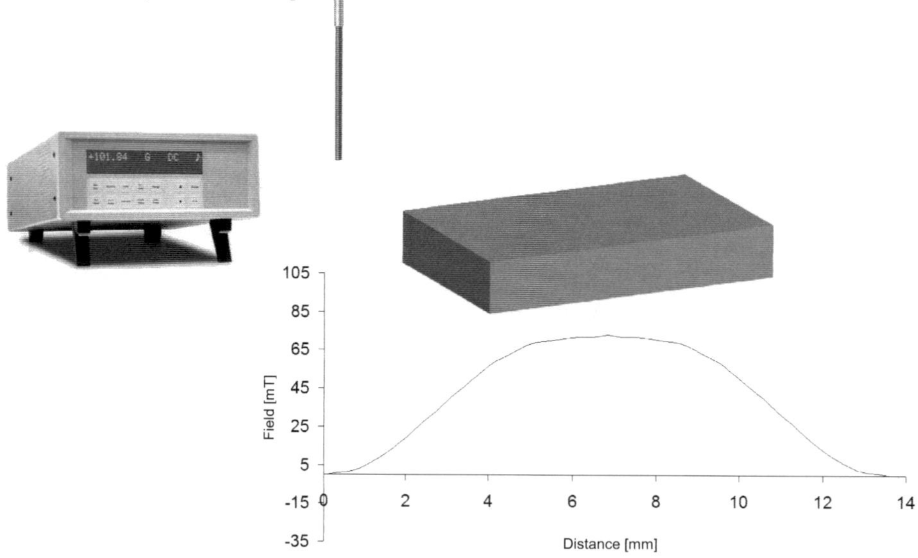

Why measure magnets?

near and far field of permanent magnets - What does it mean?

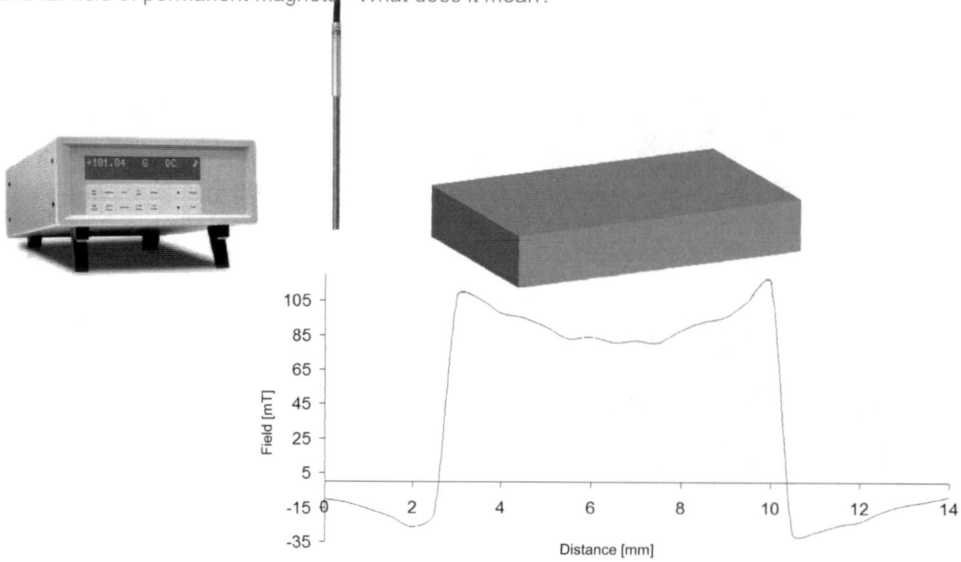

Why measure magnets?

near and far field of permanent magnets - What does it mean?

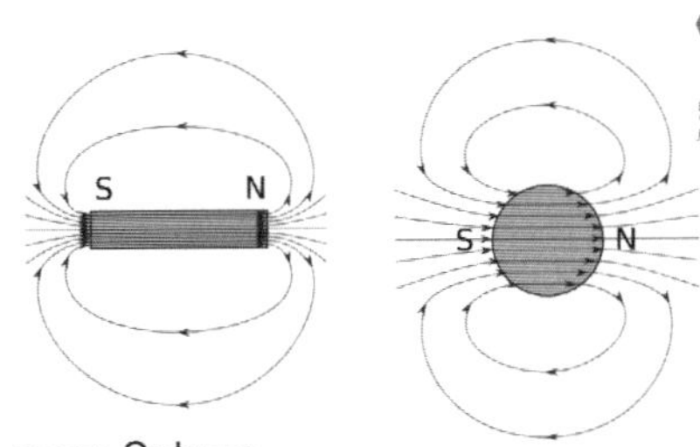

Defined by the geometry of the magnet

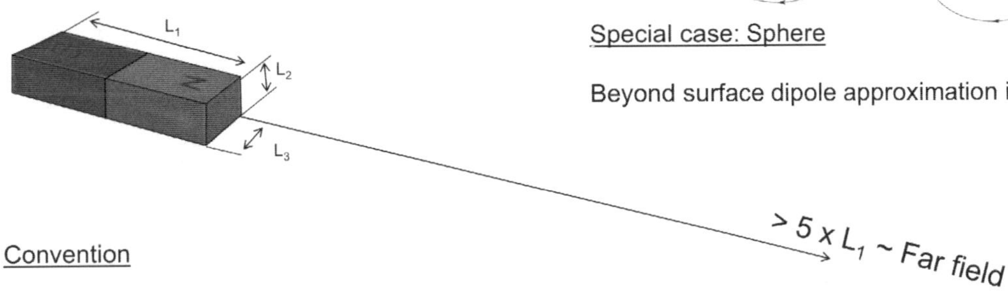

Special case: Sphere

Beyond surface dipole approximation is possible

Convention

$> 5 \times L_1$: far field: dipole approximation with small errors possible

$< 5 \times L_1$: near field: field is defined by geometry, magnetization and material inhomogeneity

Why measure magnets?

Technologies and Systems for far and near field

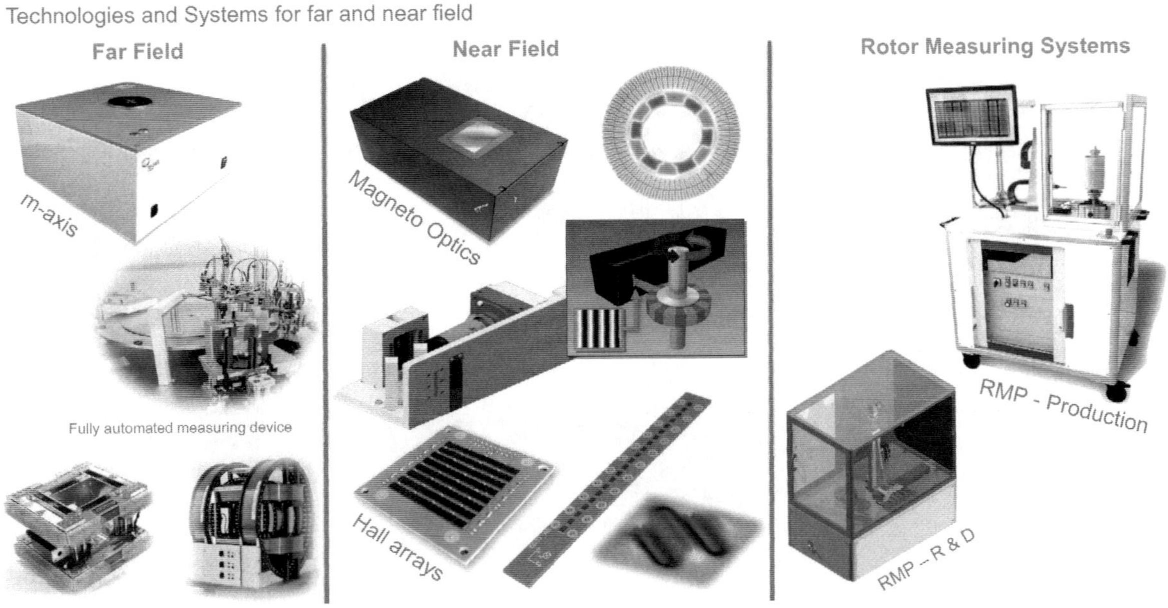

Build up Magneto-Optical Inline Scanner

Measuring Head

Idea

- combination of magnetooptical sensor and hall sensors
- position triggered System – specimen moving necessary
- magnetooptical sensor: high lateral resolution - µm area
- 3D hall sensor: precise field measurement of all 3 field components
- Detection of polarity, inhomogeneity's, pole geometries, cracks, scratches, missed magnetization

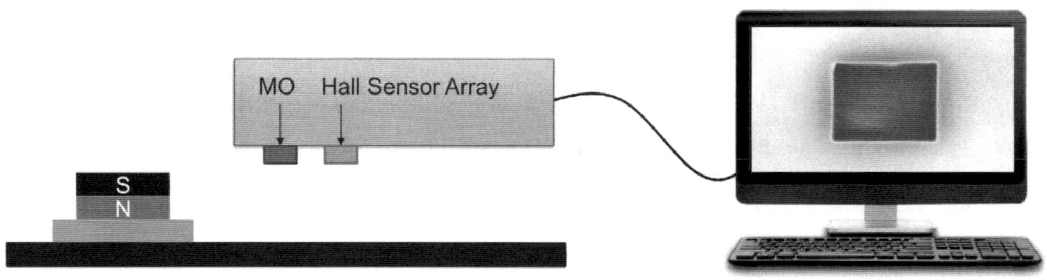

Build up Magneto-Optical Inline Scanner

Measuring Head

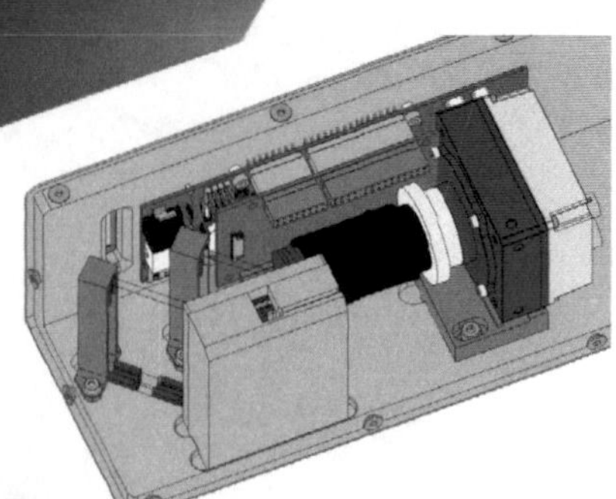

Magneto-optical Module

- 35mm Magneto-optical Sensor (30mm usable)
- GigE line camera with 2048 pixel @ 12bit
- Lateral resolution @ 30mm: 15µm
- Triggered measurement 4 kHz (up to 50kHz)

Hall Sensor Module

- 64 x 3D Hall sensor triplets (192 channels)
- Real x, y and z sensors
- x, y, z sensors in an area of $0.1mm^3$
- Up to 300Hz
- Shifted in rows
- Lateral resolution 0,6mm

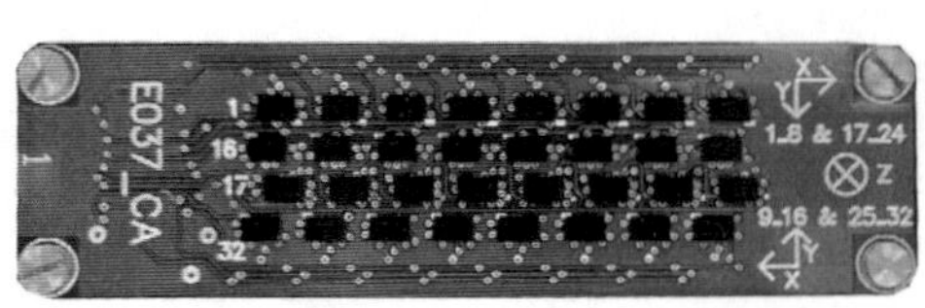

Build up Magneto-Optical Inline Scanner

Test Stand

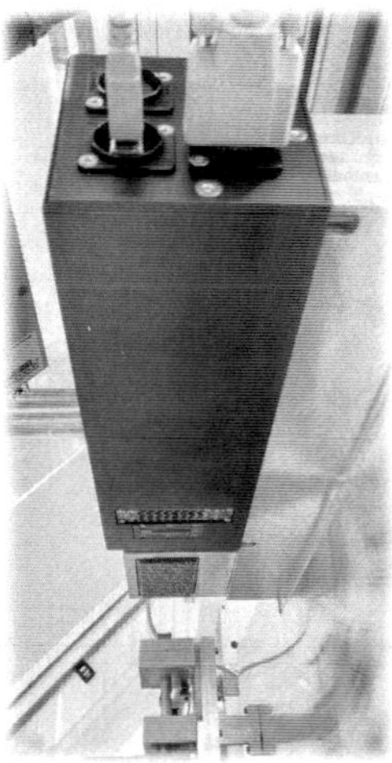

Y Axis: SMAC moving coil actuator

- programmable in force, acceleration and velocity
- with Soft-Land function
- bidirectional accuracy 1µm

X Axis: Steinmeyer LTP80 / 550mm

- bidirectional accuracy 7.5µm
- Positioning speed 130mm/sec

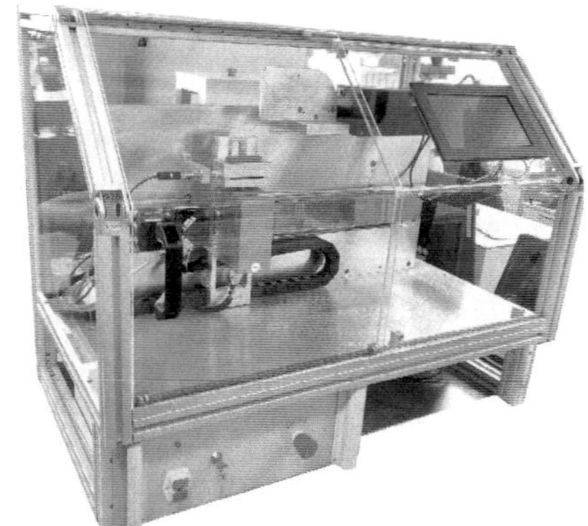

Build up Magneto-Optical Inline Scanner

Test Stand

Build up Magneto-Optical Inline Scanner

Measurement

Multipolar Ring (angular encoder)

- Plastic bonded magnet
- 20 poles (10 periods)

Combination of the magento-optical measurement with a high lateral resolution (15µm) and the precise 3D Measurement in all room axis (x,y,z)

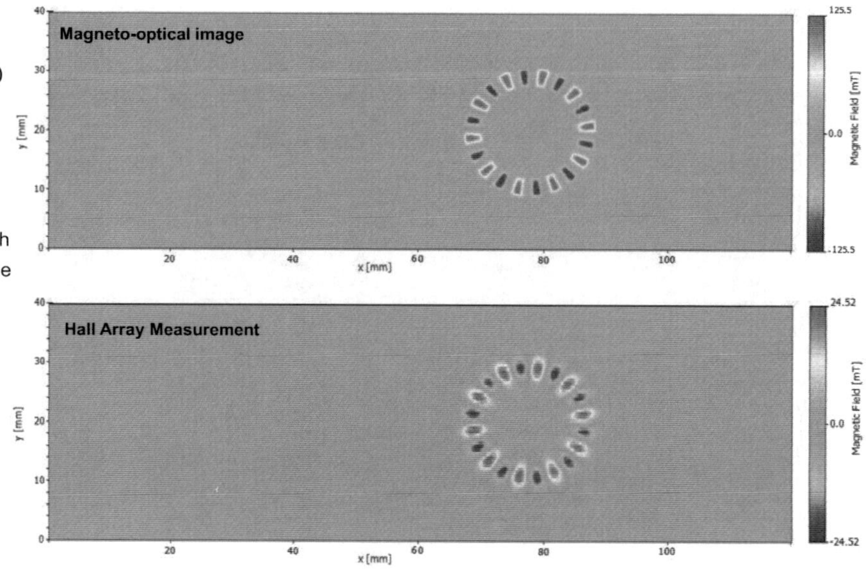

Magneto-Optics – How does is works

Faraday effect in reflection mode

Principle and properties of magneto-optical sensors

Basic principle:	Faraday effect in reflection mode
Optical contrast:	Field dependent
Main investigation:	Near field analysis
Different sensor types:	A, B, C, D
Faraday rotation:	5 to 12 degree
Magnetic field range:	0.05 to 180 kA/m
Lateral resolution:	1 to 75 µm
Working wavelength (VIS):	Warm white, 590 nm
Sensor chip sizes:	60 x 45 mm, 20.5 x 15.5 mm, 8 x 8 mm
Working temperature:	25°C ± 10 K

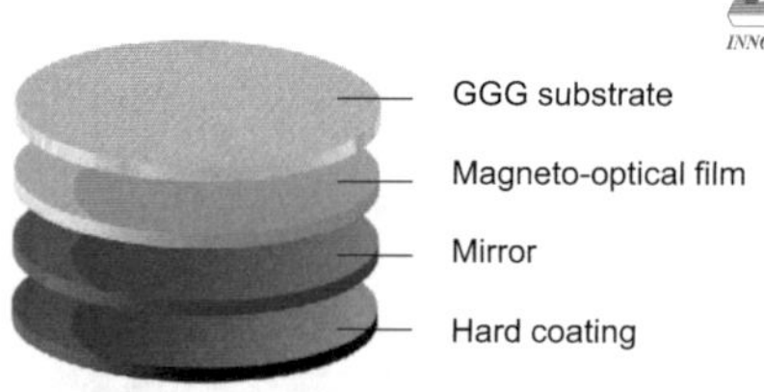

MO Sensor design

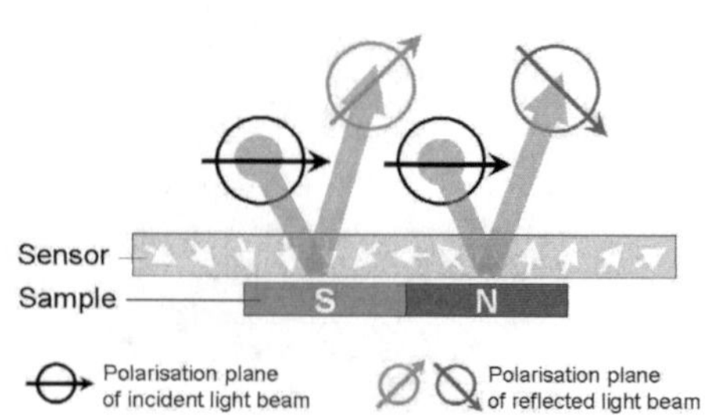

Magneto-Optics – How does is works

Liquid Phase Epitaxy (LPE)

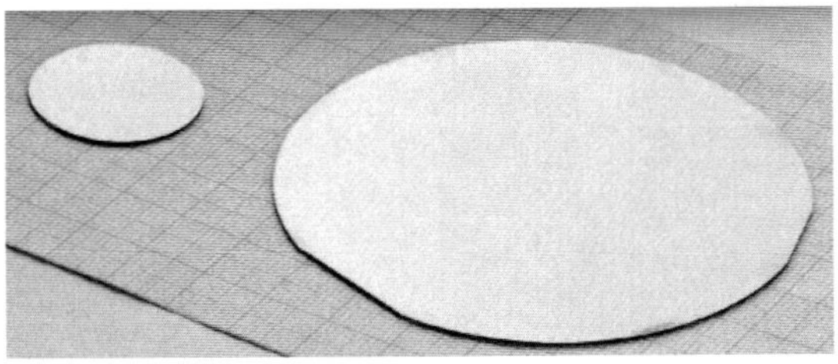

3 inch LPE process

- Effective epitaxy due to 3 inch substrate size
- Precise temperature management
- Production capacity 100 Wafers / year

Garnets:	$\{C\}_3\,[A]_2\,(D)_3\,O_{12}$
Bi-RE-IG:	$RE_{3-x-y}Bi_xRE_yFe_{5-z}Ga_zO_{12}$

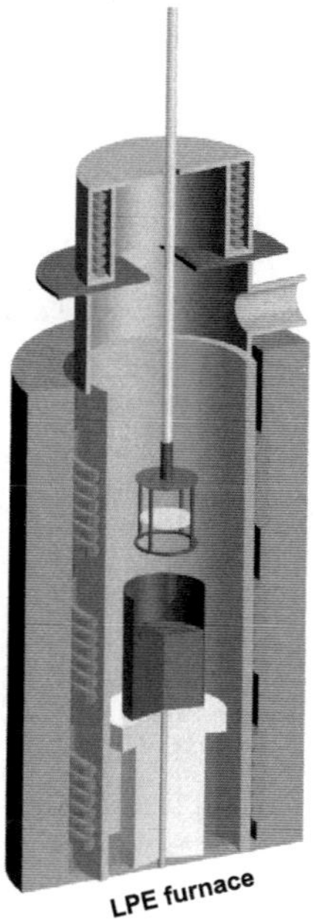

Magneto-Optics – How does is works

Sensor types

Imaging behaviour using sensors with different magnetic easy axis

Magnetic out-of-plane anisotropy

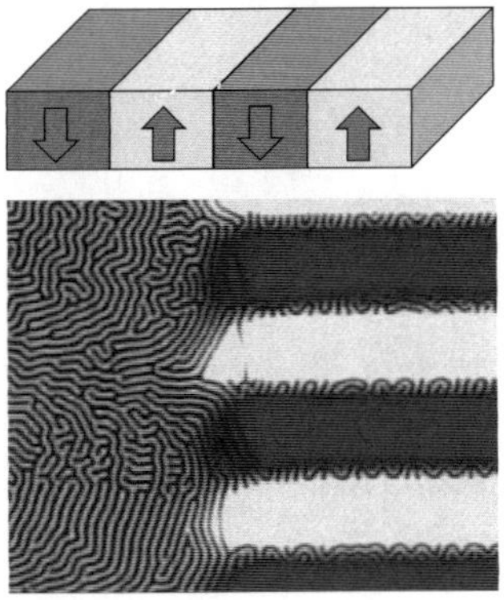

Magnetic in-plane anisotropy

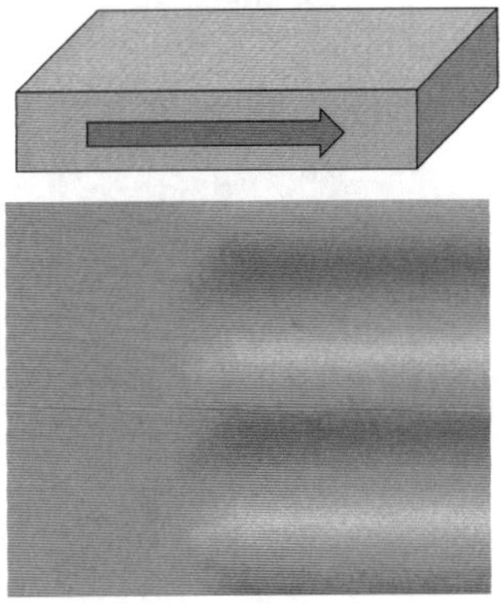

Magneto-optical images (750 μm x 750 μm) of a debit card made with different sensor types

Magneto-Optics – How does is works

Application examples – hard magnetic ink

Magneto-optical image

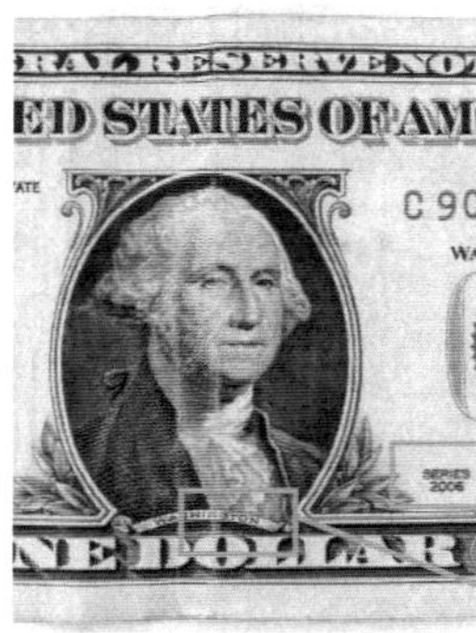

Optical image

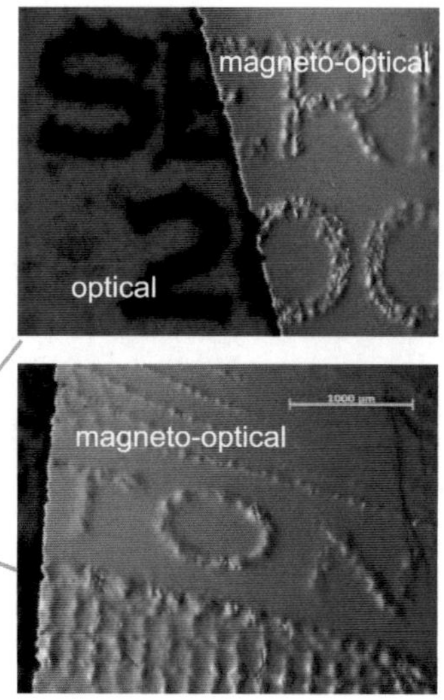

Magneto-Optics – How does is works

Application examples – soft magnetic ink

Optical image

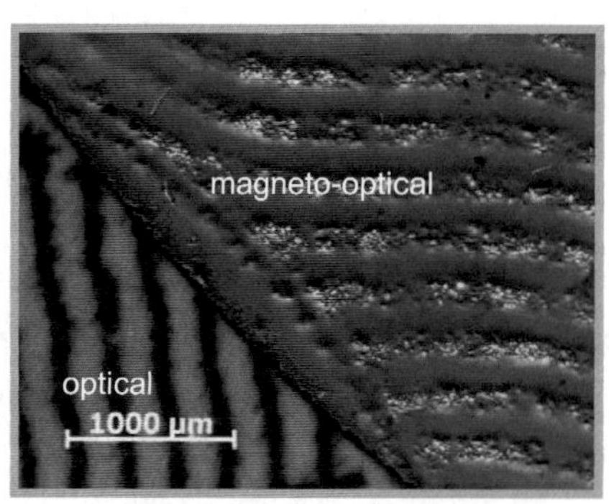

Magneto-optical visualisation of the structure in bias field

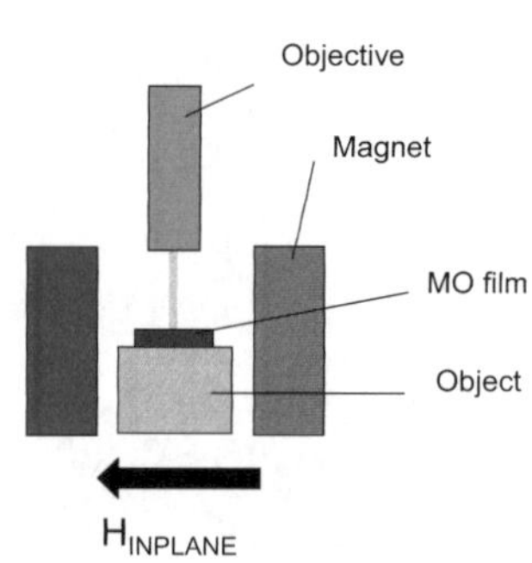

Magneto-Optics – How does is works

Application examples – Mobjective – MO adapter for microscope

Very high-resolution examination of structures in micrometer range

Hard disc with 200 MB as example to demonstrate the lateral resolution

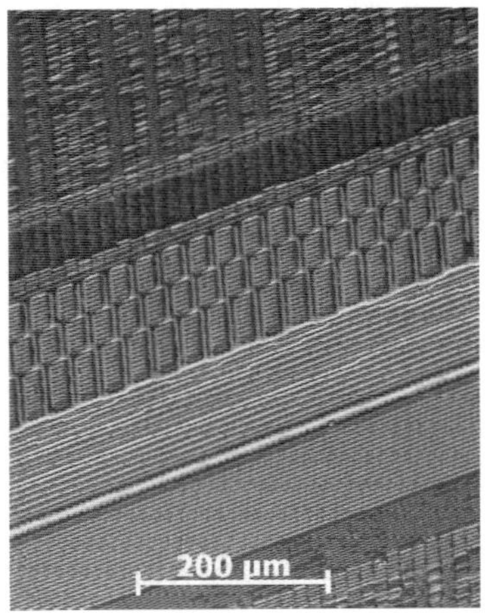

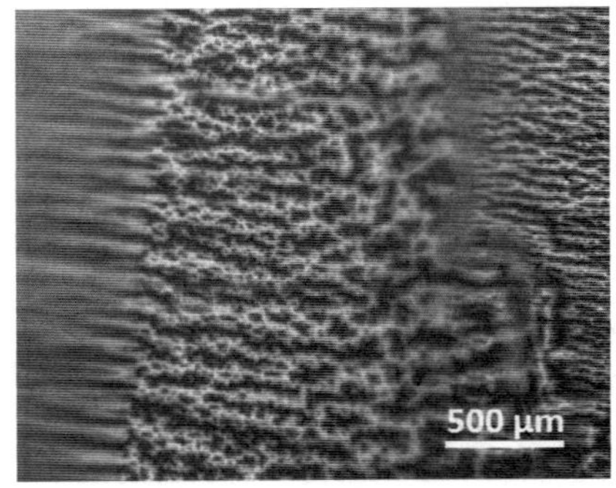

Domains of a shape memory alloy

Magneto-Optics – How does is works

Application examples – MagView – handheld device

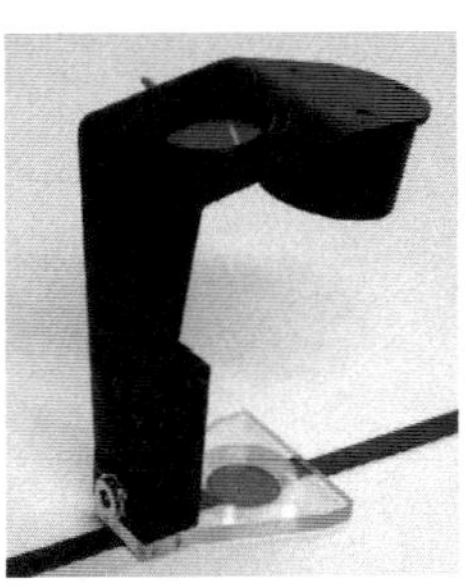

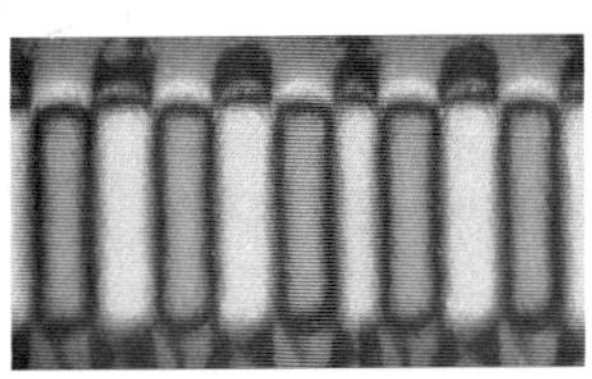

Magneto-optical visualization of a magnetic linear encoder

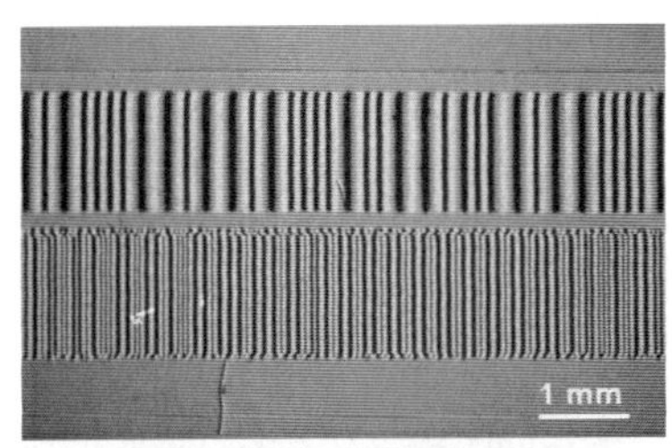

magnetic information of magnetic stripe card

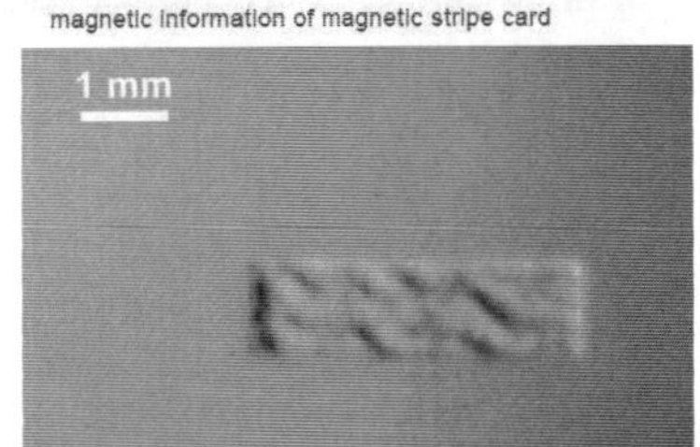

magnetic signature of a banknote

Magneto-Optics – How does is works

Application examples – systems with camera

- Detection of magnetic pole widths,
- Repeatability of angular measurements 0,02°
- Rotation encoders up to 38 mm diameter possible,
- Calibrated measurement range: ± 125 mT,
- Lateral resolution up to 60 µm

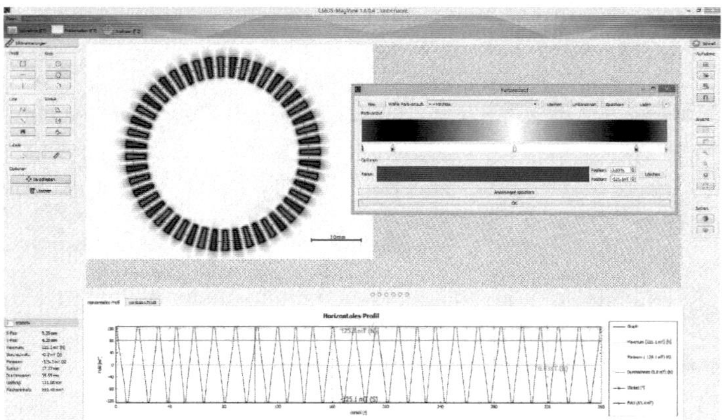

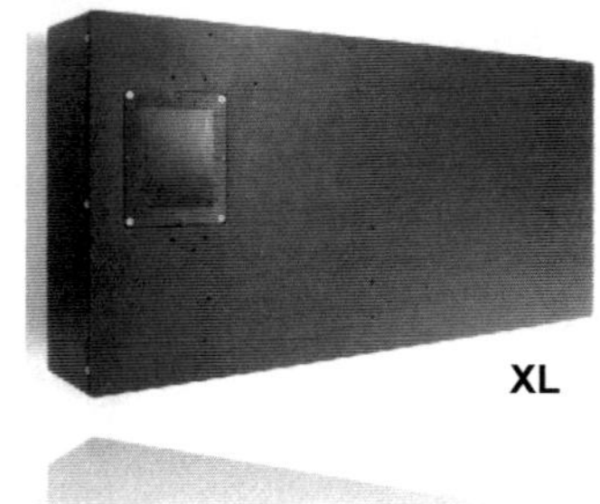

3D Hall Sensor

Build up

- 2 x 3D hall elements (6 hall channel in one IC)
- Integrated temperature sensor
- Measurement rate 1 kHz / 1Pixel
- Array build up is possible
- Internal EEPROM for calibration data and configuration
- Fully calibrated offsets
- Four different measurement modes for sequential measurements of different magnetic field components
- Chip Scale Package (CSP) – Measurement close to the surface possible

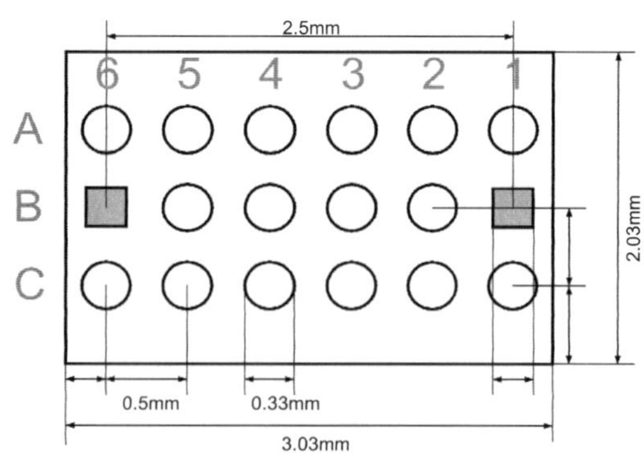

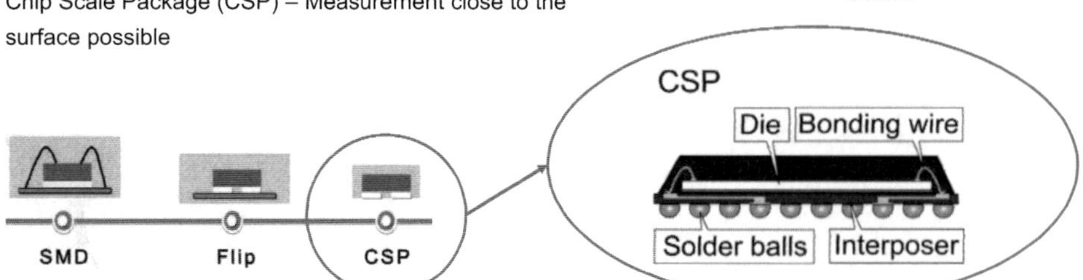

3D Hall Sensor

Example Hall Arrays

- 16 x 16 sensor triplets
- Real x, y and z sensors
- x, y, z sensors in an area of 0.1mm³
- Up to 300Hz
- USB connection
- Plug and play

Measurement Range	±100 mT	±400 mT	±1200 mT
Resolution	20 µT	100 µT	300 µT
Noise (RMS)	30 µT	50 µT	140 µT
Offset Error	±50 µT	±50 µT	±100 µT
Gain Error	1%	1%	2%

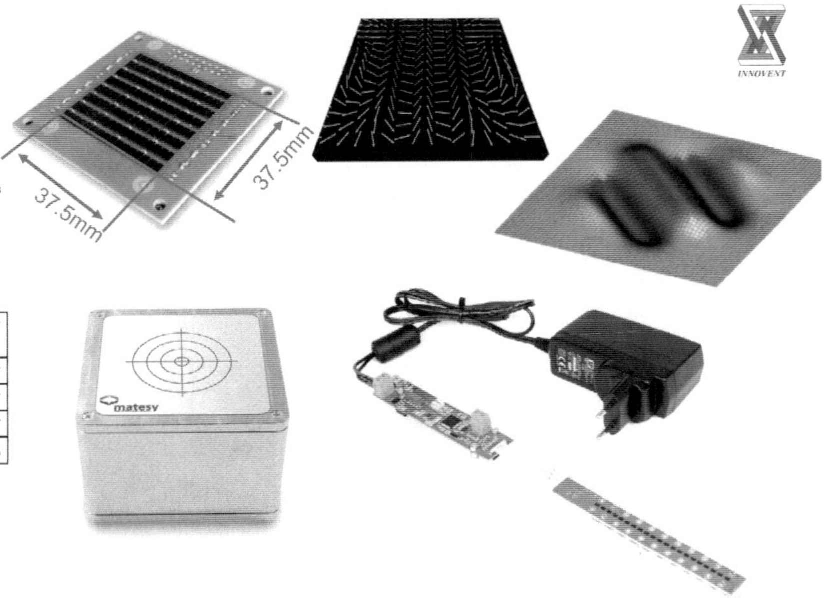

Special developments and further activities

New magnet measuring system for small magnets

nano-maxis

0.0001Am² – 0.03Am²

Combination of MO Sensor and dipolar measurement

big-mag

4Am² – 100Am²

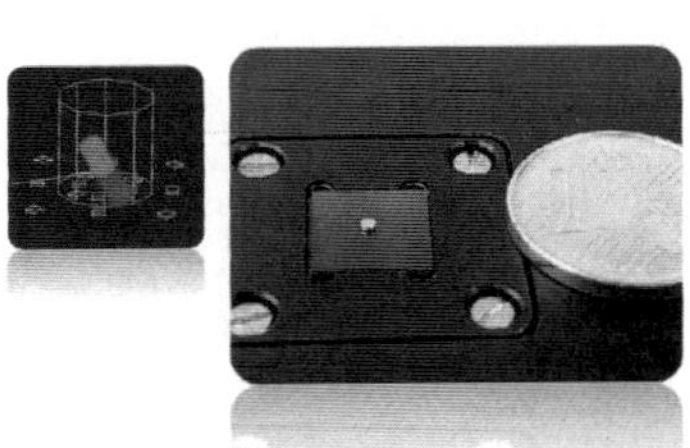

m-axis

0.01Am² – 10Am²

Magneto-Optical Inline Scanner for Measuring and Characterization of Permanent Magnets

Further information

http://www.matesy.de/en/home

matesy
magnetic technologies & systems

Products & Systems

Control - May 07 – 10 in Stuttgart
CWIEME - May 21– 23 in Berlin
SENSOR+TEST - June 25 – 27 in Nuernberg

INNOVENT

Research and Development

Magnetics Conference - January 23 – 24 in Orlando, FL (USA)
MR Symposium - March 19 – 20 Wetzlar
EDPC - December 2019

http://www.innovent-jena.de/en

Thank you very much for your attention

INNOVENT

Selecting

Optimal Lamination Materials

Steve Constantinides

Magnetics 2019

Orlando, Florida, January 23, 2019

Magnetics & Materials LLC

Why...

Why is the selection of soft magnetic material important?

- Limits device performance
- Affects product cost
- Constraints on material availability
- Product efficiency to meet increasingly more stringent standards

Key Figures of Merit

- High permeability: initial (μ_0) and maximum (μ_{max})
  - Ease of magnetization
- High saturation magnetization (M_S, J_S)
  - Flux carrying capability
  - Relates to required product size
- Low coercivity (H_{cB})
  - Relates to hysteresis energy loss
- High resistivity (ρ)
  - Relates to eddy current energy loss
- Hysteresis loop shape
  - Complex hysteresis energy loss factor

Key Figures of Merit (Other)

Other

- Usable temperature range
- Small magnetization change with temperature (RTC)
- Corrosion resistance
- Compromise of physical strength and malleability
  - Bend, form, stamp and press but with adequate yield strength to resist deformation in operating equipment
- Manufacturability and formability
- Low magnetostriction

Key Figures of Merit (Cost)

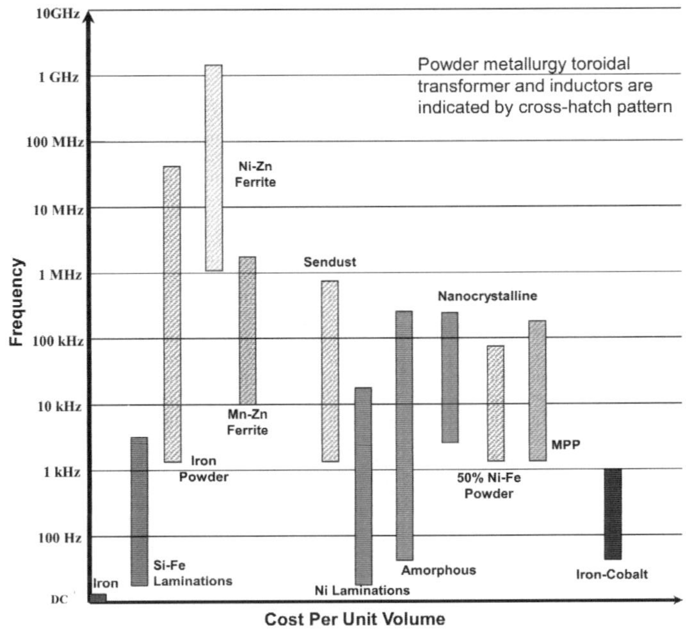

Material Cost

For example, frequency of rotating motor (sinusoidal excitation):

$$f = \frac{\text{rpm x poles}}{60}$$

(10,000 **x** 8)/60= 1,333 Hz

Cost of Operation

	Hours/day	Days/week	Weeks/year	Hours / year
Cost reduction through efficiency improvement	24	7	52	8736
Motors for comparison purposes are single phase	1 HP =	745.7 watts		

Motor Horsepower (HP)	**0.5**	**10**	**100**	**500**	**1000**	**1000**
Watts	373	7,457	74,570	372,850	745,700	745,700
Motor % Load	100%	100%	100%	100%	100%	100%
Energy Cost, cents per kWh	$ 0.10	$ 0.10	$ 0.10	$ 0.10	$ 0.10	$ 0.16
Base motor efficiency, %	70%	91%	91%	91%	91%	91%
Cost of operation per hour	$ 0.05	$ 0.82	$ 8.19	$ 40.97	$ 81.95	$ 131.11
Cost of operation per year	$ 465	$ 7,159	$ 71,587	$ 357,936	$ 715,872	$ 1,145,395
High efficiency motor, %	85%	94%	94%	94%	94%	94%
Cost of operation per hour	$ 0.04	$ 0.79	$ 7.93	$ 39.66	$ 79.33	$ 126.93
Cost of operation per year	$ 383	$ 6,930	$ 69,303	$ 346,513	$ 693,025	$ 1,108,840
Cost savings per year, $	**$ 82.11**	**$ 228.47**	**$ 2,284.70**	**$ 11,423.49**	**$ 22,846.98**	**$ 36,555.17**

Permeability and Saturation

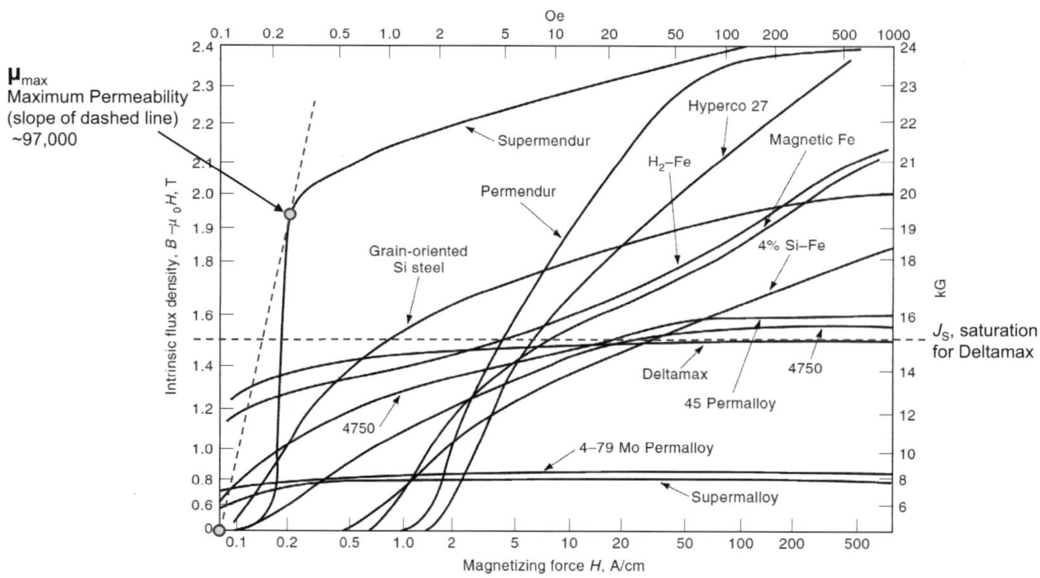

Source: Kirk-Othmer Encyclopedia of Chemical Technology; Magnetic Materials, Bulk; Jack Wernick, Bell Telephone Laboratories, Inc.

Hysteresis Energy

Difference between permanent and soft magnetic materials

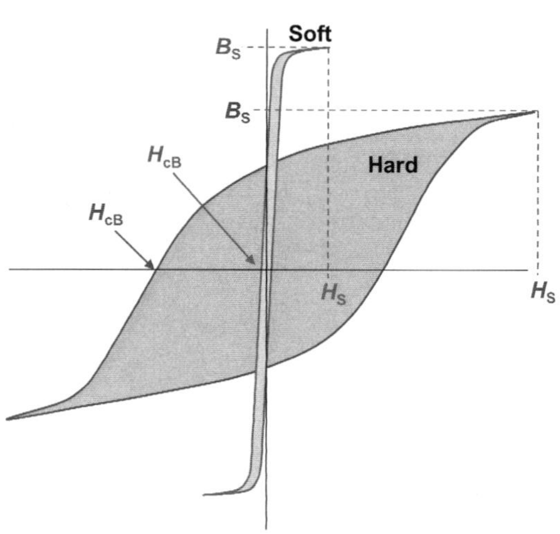

- A narrow hysteresis loop implies a small amount of dissipated energy. This is desirable to minimize hysteresis energy loss in transformers and rotating machinery (motors).
- The energy expended in driving the material through its hysteresis loop is represented by the area within the loop (the shaded area).
- A narrow loop with low hysteresis energy is typical of soft magnetic materials.

These are "Normal" or "B" curves, not the B-H Intrinsic curves.

Hysteresis Loss - Frequency Effects

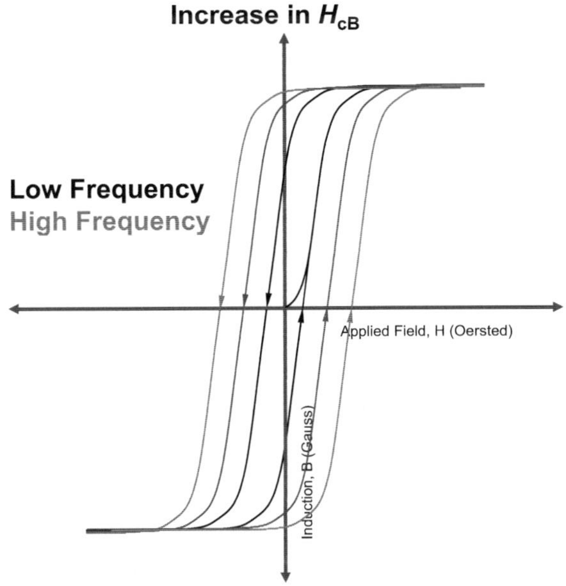

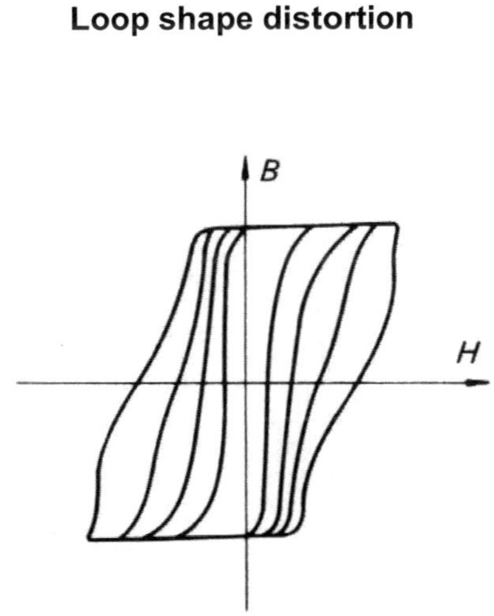

Slide 9 | © Magnetics & Materials LLC

Magnetics 2019

Core Loss

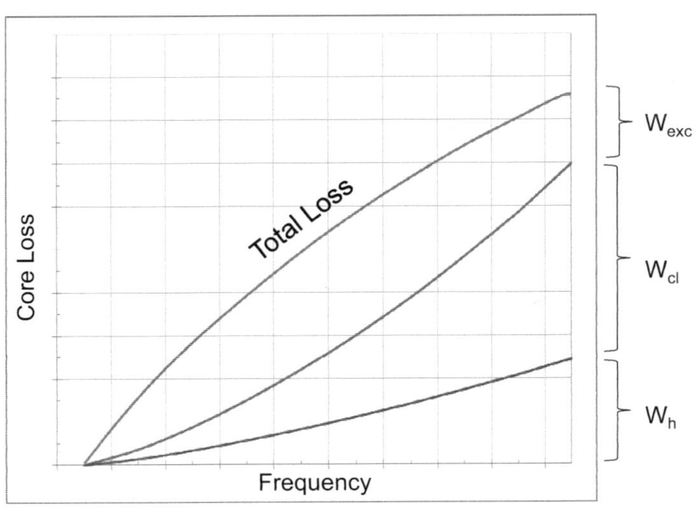

$$W = W_h + W_{cl} + W_{exc}$$

Total core loss = Hysteresis Loss + Classical (eddy current) loss + Excess or Anomalous Loss

Slide 10 | © Magnetics & Materials LLC

Magnetics 2019

Loss Variables by Categories

1: Hysteresis
2: Eddy Current
3: Laminations
4: Magnetostriction
5: Material & Resistivity

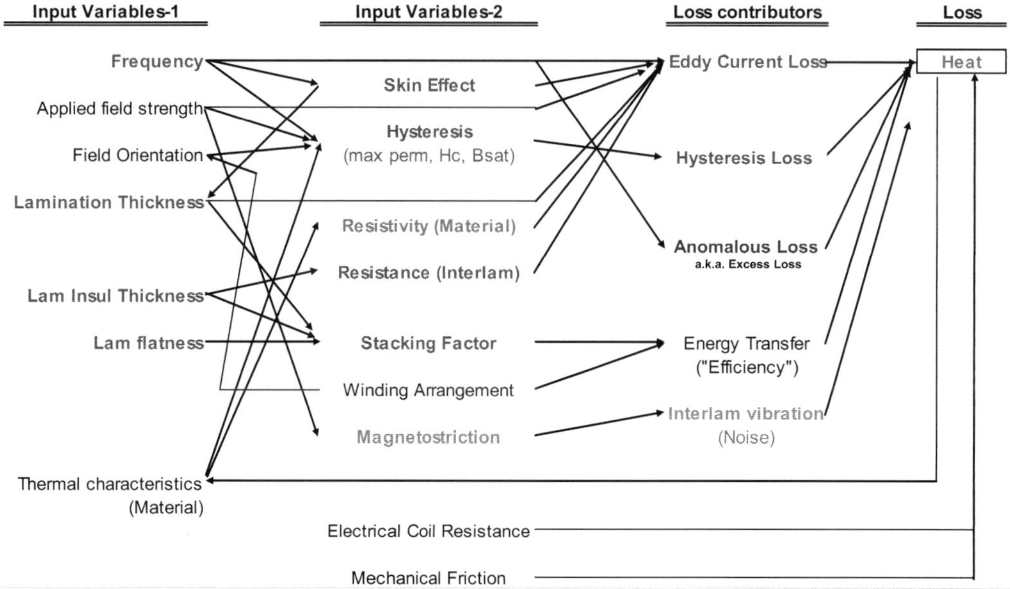

Slide 11 | © Magnetics & Materials LLC

Magnetics 2019

Core Loss Measurements

0.011 Silectron 53 (AISI M4) Core Loss

Test: Epstein; SRA; Parallel; A343

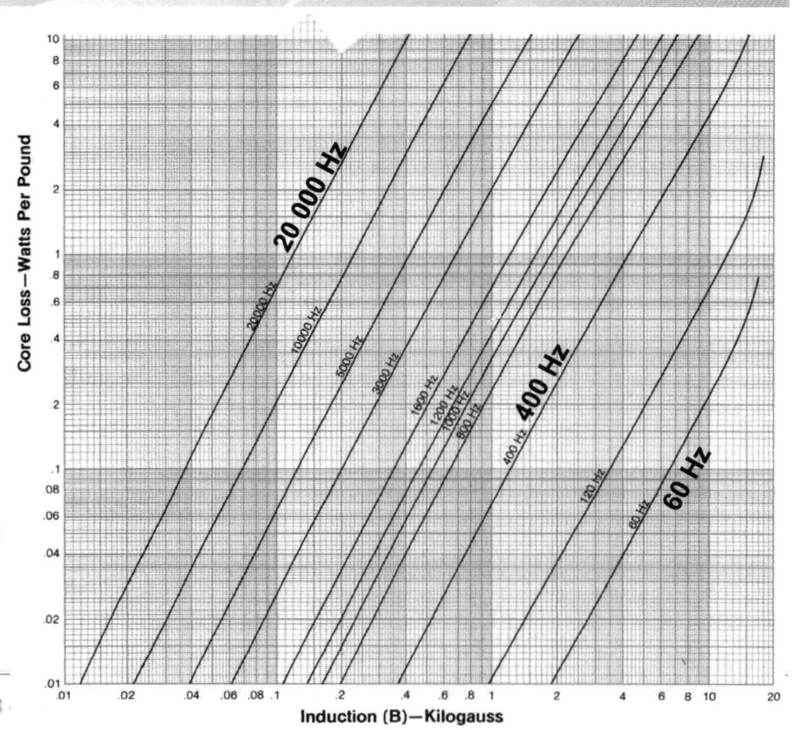

Slide 12 | © Magnetics

Soft Magnetic Material Forms

- Bulk Materials
- Sheet or Strip Products
- Powders

Converted to composite or fully dense bulk material, e.g. SMCs

IEC Classifications for Soft Magnetic Materials

Source: IEC International Standard 60404-1 ed3.0 (2016-10)

- A. Irons
- B. Low carbon mild steels
- C. Silicon Steels
  - C1. Solid material
  - C2. Flat material
    - C21. Isotropic steels
    - C22. Anisotropic steels
    - C23. Thin silicon steels
- D. Other steels
  - D1. Solid material
  - D2. Flat material
- E. Nickel-Iron alloys
  - E1. 72-83 Ni
  - E2. 54-68 Ni
  - E3. 45-50 Ni
    - isotropic
    - anisotropic
  - E4. 35-40 Ni
  - E5. Approx 30 Ni (temp. compensation)
- F. Iron-Cobalt alloys
  - F1. 47-50 Co
    - isotropic
    - Non-isotropic
  - F2. 35 Co
  - F3. 23-27 Co
- G. Other Alloys
  - G1.Al-Fe alloys
  - G2. Al-Si-Fe alloys
- H. Soft Magnetic Ceramics
  - H1. Soft ferrite
- I. Amorphous
  - Amorphous metallic glass
- J. Nano-crystalline
  - Nano-crystalline

Slater-Pauling Curve

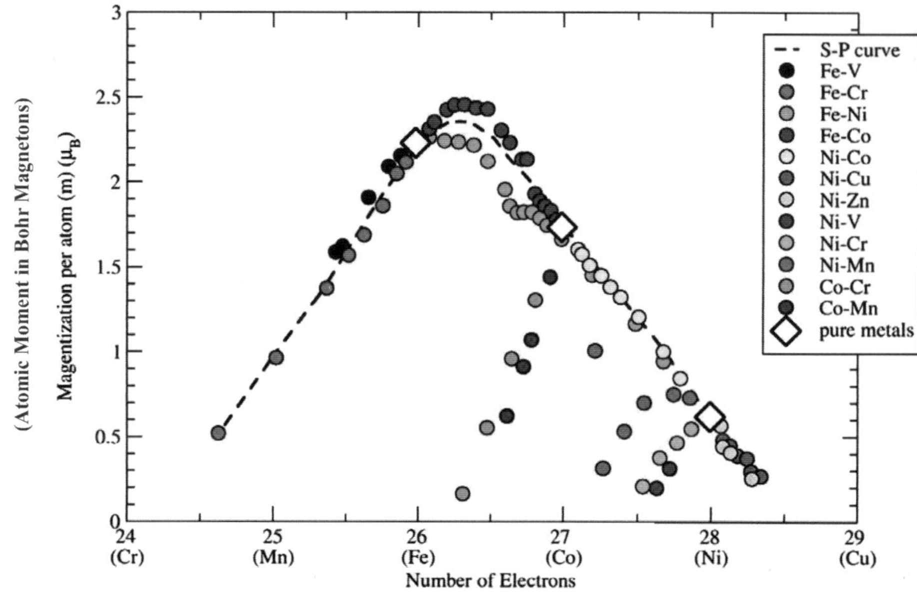

John C. Slater

Linus Pauling

R.M. Bozorth, Ferromagnetism, IEEE, 1993, p.438-441

Color-edited by Dr. Bill McCallum

Soft Magnetic Materials: Compositions and Properties

	Material	Co	Cr	Ni	Mo	V	Cu	Other	J_S G	H_{cB} Oe	μ_{init}	μ_{max}	Resist. μ-ohm•cm
Soft Magnetic Materials	Low carbon steel (M-19)								19,000	0.2-0.5	300	10,000	47
	Iron-Silicon (Si-Fe)							3 - 6	19,700	0.6	350	50,000	50
	Deltamax			50					16,000	0.04-0.16	500	100,000	45
	Alloy 4750			48					15,500	0.02-0.10	7,000	100,000	45
	Mu Metal		2	77			5		7,500	0.01-0.03	20,000	~100,000	60
	Supermalloy			79	5				7,800	~0.005	60,000	800,000	65
	Perminvar (7-70)	7		70					12,500	0.6	850	4,000	16
	Kovar	17		29					12,000			3,000	49
	Perminvar (45-25)	25		45					15,500	1.2	400	2,000	19
	Hiperco 27	27	0.6	0.6					24,200	1.0	650	10,000	
	Hiperco 35	35	0.5						24,200	1.0	650	10,000	20
	2V-Permendur	49				2			24,000	2.0	800	4,900	26
	Supermendur	49				2			24,000	0.2		92,500	
	Hiperco 50A	49				2			24,000	< 1		15,000	40
	Permendur	50							24,500	2.0	800	5,000	7
	Metglas 2705M	79		3.5	3.8			9.2	7,700	0.4		600,000	136
	Metglas 2714A	85		3				8	5,700			1,000,000	142

Composition (%), Fe bal.: Co, Cr, Ni, Mo, V, Cu, Other

Comparing Magnetic Properties

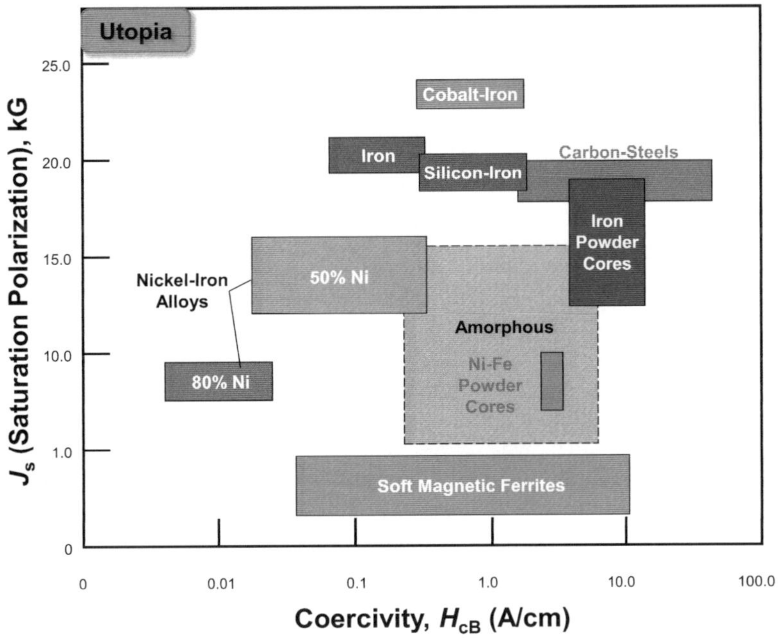

Saturation vs. Permeability Comparisons

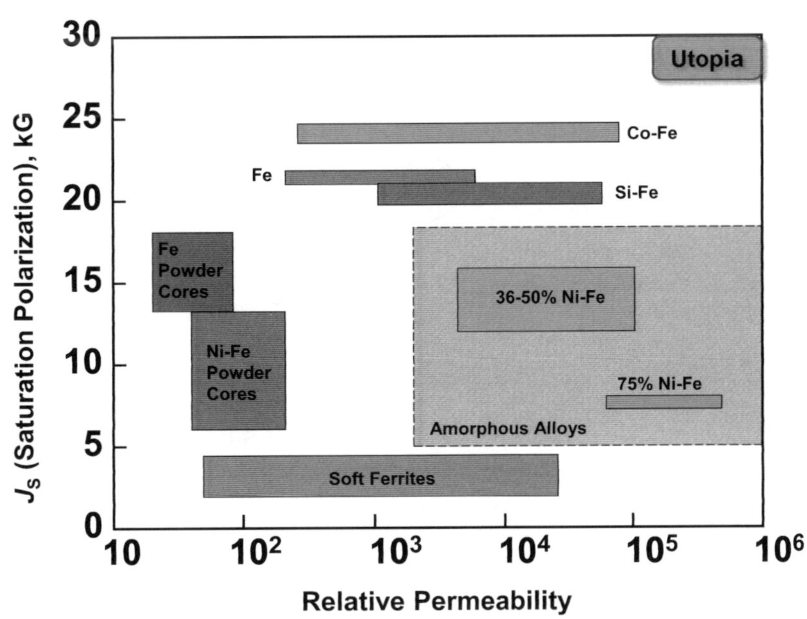

Resistivity of Silicon-Iron (Si-Fe)

Composition change to increase resistivity also...

- Decreases saturation polarization
- Increases yield strength (brittleness)

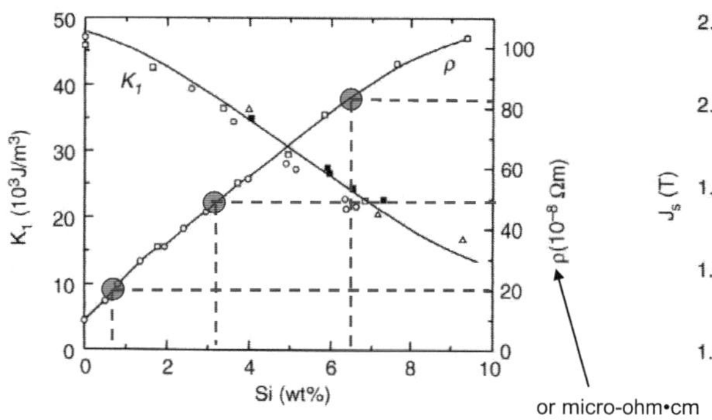

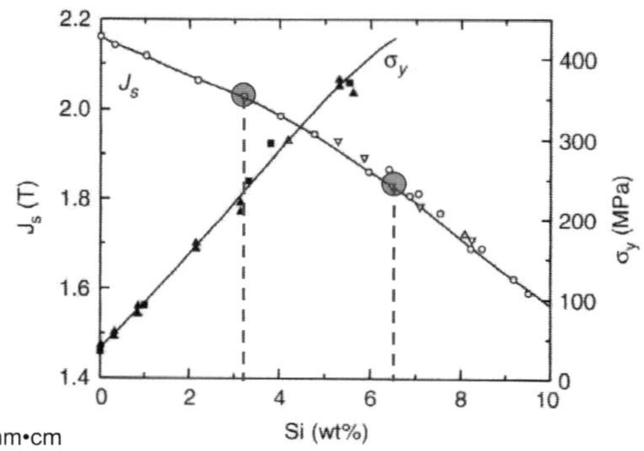

K_1 = Magnetocrystalline Anisotropy constant

ρ (Rho) = Electrical Resistivity

J_S = Saturation Polarization

Sigma = Yield Stress

Magnetostriction of Si-Fe

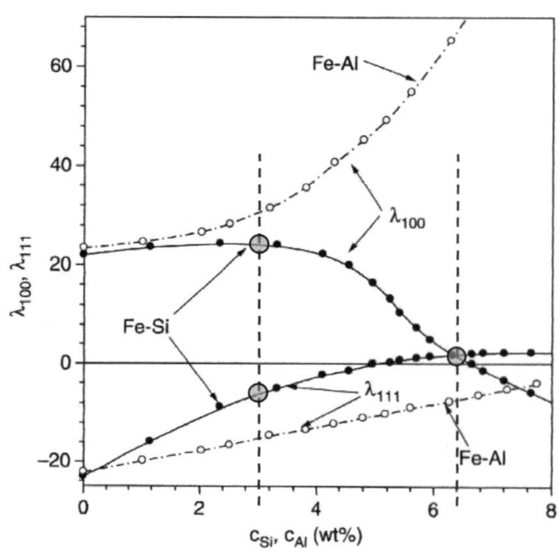

Measurement and Characterization of Magnetic Materials, Fausto Fiorillo, p.49

6%+ Si-Fe... Other materials

- Ames Laboratory
  - Researchers developing new steel for better electric motors
    A research team led by Cui is working to meet the demand for better materials and performance in electric motors. To support their work, they've just won a three-year, $3.8 million grant from the DOE's Vehicle Technologies Program.
  - https://www.news.iastate.edu/news/2016/09/27/electricalsteel
- AK Steel
  - AK Steel Receives New $1.2 Million Award from U.S. Department of Energy to Explore the Development of New Steels for Lightweighting for Automotive Applications
    The three-year project will be conducted in collaboration with DOE, Oak Ridge National Laboratory Materials Science and Technology Division, and the Advanced Steel Processing and Products Research Center in the Department of Metallurgical & Materials Engineering at the Colorado School of Mines.
  - https://ir.aksteel.com/news-releases/news-release-details/ak-steel-receives-new-12-million-award-us-department-energy

Metglas®

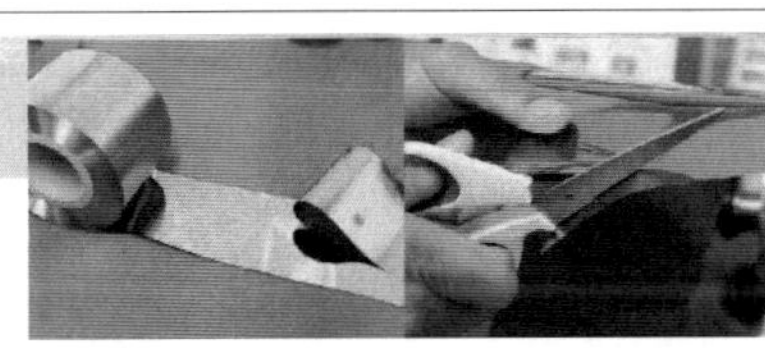

Key Products:

Metglas®
Amorphous Metals
Glassy Metals
Transformer Core Alloys
Metglas Brazing Filler Metal
Distribution Transformer Core Ribbon
Industrial Transformer Core Ribbon
Pulse Power Cores

Key End Applications:

Electrical Distribution Transformers
Industrial Power Distribution Transformers
Material for Anti -Theft tags
High Efficiency Inverters and Inductors
Solar Inverters, Wind Inverters
Harmonic Filters
Pulse Power Cores for Lasers
High Power Magnetic Forms for Medical Use
High Purity Brazing Filler Metals

		2605SA1	2605HB1M	2605SA3	2714A	2826MB
Characteristic	Unit	Iron-based	Iron-based	Iron-based	Cobalt-based	Nickel-based
Bsat	Tesla	1.56	1.63	1.41	0.57	0.88
Max. Permeability, μ_{max}	n/a	300,000	300,000	35,000	1,000,000	800,000
Electrical Resistivity	$\mu\Omega\cdot$cm	130	120	138	142	138
Magnetostriction	$\%\bullet10^{-6}$	27	27	20	<0.5	12
Curie Temperature	°C	395	364	358	225	353

http://www.metglas.com/metglas_company_history/overview/

Amorphous Metal for Motors

- Developing a Higher-Efficiency Motor Technology Using Amorphous Metals
  - Hitachi news release, October 24, 2018
  - Hitachi Metals, Ltd. ("Hitachi Metals") has successfully developed a motor core structure whereby amorphous metals known as Metglas® are used for part of the motor core to achieve a higher rate of efficiency. We will promote R&D with an eye to applying this technology to motors for driving EV*2 and propose new applications of materials for motors along with verification data.
- Development of Motor with Amorphous Metal
  - Hitachi publication: November 8, 2018
  - http://www.hitachi.com/rd/portal/contents/story/amorphous/index.html

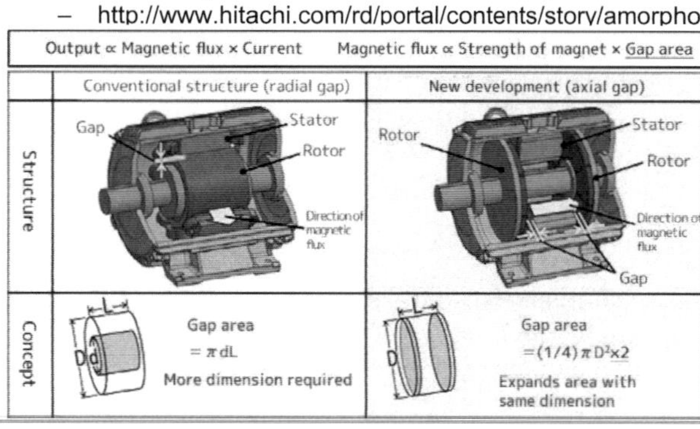

3-D Printing

- CAMAL Uses #-D-Printing to Create Metallic Glass Alloys in Bulk
  - Press release, March 26, 2018
  - Researchers from the Center for Additive Manufacturing and Logistics (CAMAL) housed in the ISE Department [of NC State University] have now demonstrated the ability to create amorphous metal, or metallic glass, alloys using 3D-printing technology...
  - https://www.ise.ncsu.edu/blog/2018/03/26/camal-uses-3d-printing-to-create-metallic-glass-alloys-in-bulk/

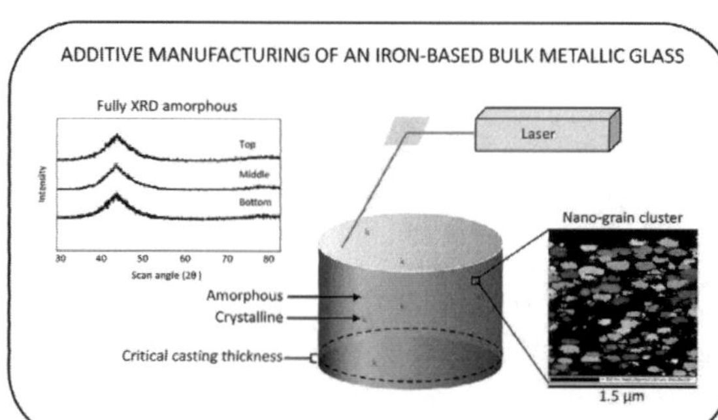

3D Printing

- 3D printing of large, complex metallic glass structures
  - Yiyu Shen, Yingqi Li, Chen Chen, Hai-LungTsai
  - https://doi.org/10.1016/j.matdes.2016.12.087
- Research on additive manufacturing of metallic glass alloy
  - Yiyu Shen, PhD Thesis, spring 2018
  - http://scholarsmine.mst.edu/cgi/viewcontent.cgi?article=3693&context=doctoral_dissertations

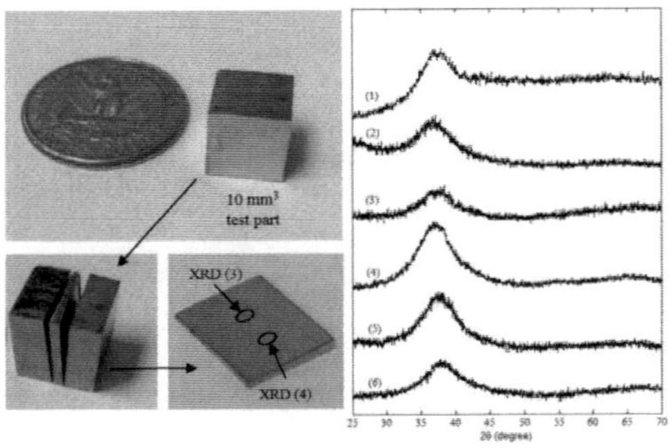

Figure 4. XRD test of printed sample. Left: photo of the 3D test sample; right:

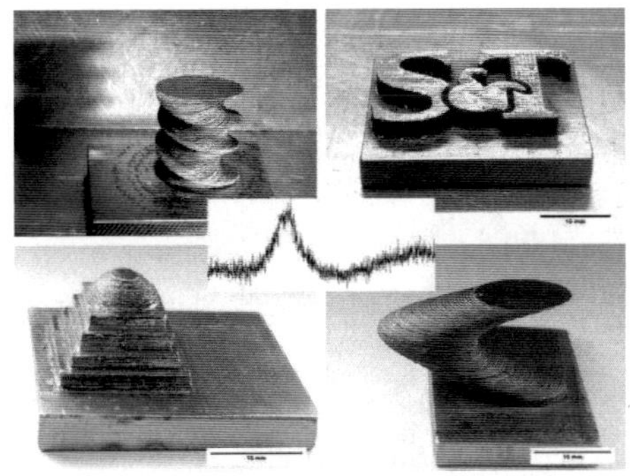

Nano-crystalline

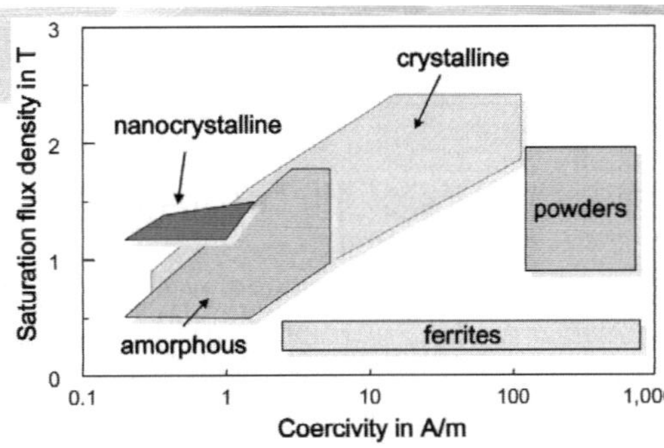

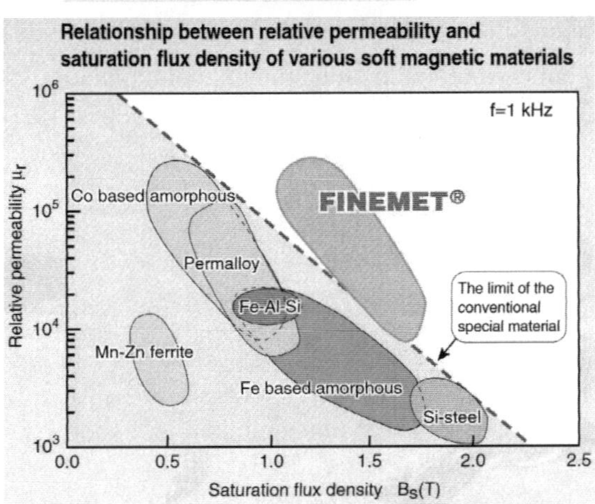

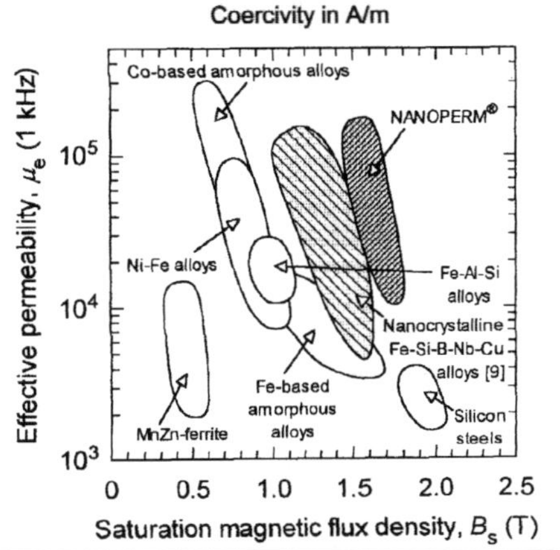

Summary Data

TABLE 1. Typical values of grain size D, saturation magnetization J_s, saturation magnetostriction λ_s, coercivity H_c, initial permeability μ_i, electrical resistivity ρ, core losses P_{Fe} at 0.2 T, 100 kHz and ribbon thickness t for nanocrystalline, amorphous and crystalline soft magnetic ribbons.

Alloy	D (nm)	J_s (T)	λ_s (10^{-6})	H_c (A/m)	μ_i (1 kHz)	ρ (μΩcm)	P_{Fe}(W/kg)	t (μm)	Ref.
$Fe_{73.5}Cu_1Nb_3Si_{13.5}B_9$	13	1.24	2.1	0.5	100 000	118	38	18	(a)
$Fe_{73.5}Cu_1Nb_3Si_{15.5}B_7$	14	1.23	~0	0.4	110 000	115	35	21	(b)
$Fe_{84}Nb_7B_9$	9	1.49	0.1	8	22 000	58	76	22	(c)
$Fe_{86}Cu_1Zr_7B_6$	10	1.52	~0	3.2	48 000	56	116	20	(c)
$Fe_{91}Zr_7B_3$	17	1.63	-1.1	5.6	22 000	44	80	18	(c)
$Co_{68}Fe_4(MoSiB)_{28}$	amorphous	0.55	~0	0.3	150 000	135	35	23	(b)
$Co_{72}(FeMn)_5(MoSiB)_{23}$	amorphous	0.8	~0	0.5	3 000	130	40	23	(b)
$Fe_{76}(SiB)_{24}$	amorphous	1.45	32	3	8 000	135	50	23	(b)
80%Ni-Fe (permalloys)	~100 000	0.75	<1	0.5	100 000 (d)	55	>90 (e)	50	(b)
50%-60%Ni-Fe	~100 000	1.55	25	5	40 000 (d)	45	>200 (e)	70	(b)

(a) after ref. [3]
(b) typical commercial grades for low remanence hysteresis loops [10, 11]
(c) after ref. [12]
(d) 50 Hz- values
(e) lower bounds due to eddy currents

Amorphous and Nanocrystalline Soft Magnets; G. Herzer, Vacuumschmelze GmbH & Co KG
Published in Proceedings of the NATO Advanced Study Institute on Magnetic Hysteresis in Novel Materials, Mykonos, Greece, 1-12 July 1996, ed. George C. Hadjipanayis; NATO ASI Series (Series E:Applied Sciences Vol. 338), Kluwer Academic Publishers, (Dordrecht/Boston/London) 1997, (ISBN 0-7923-4604-1)

References

- *Advanced Materials for Motor Laminations: Past, Present and Future*
  - John Petro, Petro and Associates
  - https://metglas.com/wp-content/uploads/2016/12/Advanced-Materials-for-Motor-Laminations.pdf
- *Modern soft magnets: Amorphous and nanocrystalline materials*
  - G. Herzer, Vacuumschmelze GmbH & Co KG, 2013
  - http://faculty.neu.edu.cn/atm/lis/mag/ModernSoftMagnets.pdf
- *Soft Magnetic Material Status and Trends in Electric Machines*
  - A. Krings, A. Boglietti, A. Cavagnino, S. Sprague; IEEE Transactions on Industrial Electronics, Vol.64, No.3, March 2017
  - https://ieeexplore.ieee.org/document/7577727
- *Understanding Electric Motors and Loss Mechanisms*
  - B. Sarlioglu, University of Wisconsin, Madison (WEMPEC), 2016
  - https://www.irc.wisc.edu/export.php?ID=421

Steve Constantinides
Magnetics & Materials LLC
4785 County Road 33
Honeoye, NY 14471
E-mail: steve@magmatllc.com
www.magmatllc.com

Honeoye Lake in the Finger Lakes region of western New York

Magnetic Answers for Market Driven Needs

Jeffrey Whalen, PhD

Research Faculty I, The National High Magnetic Field Lab
STEM Entrepreneur in Residence, The Jim Moran School of Entrepreneurship at Florida State University
Founder and Director, MagCorp

JIM MORAN SCHOOL
OF ENTREPRENEURSHIP

Jim Moran School of Entrepreneurship

FLORIDA STATE UNIVERSITY

Background

- Entrepreneurship major and minor in the College of Business since 2008
- The gift of $100 million from Mrs. Jan Moran and the Jim Moran Foundation enables the development of a School of Entrepreneurship outside of the College of Business.

FLORIDA STATE UNIVERSITY

Before | **After**

FLORIDA STATE UNIVERSITY

What Makes JMS Different

- First public university entrepreneurship school in the country outside colleges of businesses.
- First interdisciplinary entrepreneurship school in the country with entrepreneurs as faculty from every college at FSU.
- Entrepreneurship education will be experiential with task oriented classes to provide the tools students need to be innovative.
- Mission to work with the community to enhance the students' academic experience.
- Opportunity pipelines for graduating students through the STEM education and research resources of the National High Magnetic Field Lab

NATIONAL HIGH
MAGNETIC FIELD LABORATORY

NATIONAL HIGH
MAGNETIC FIELD LABORATORY

- The **only facility of its kind** in the United States and the **largest** and **highest-powered magnet laboratory in the world.**
- Home to magnets up to 2 million times stronger than the earth's magnetic field.

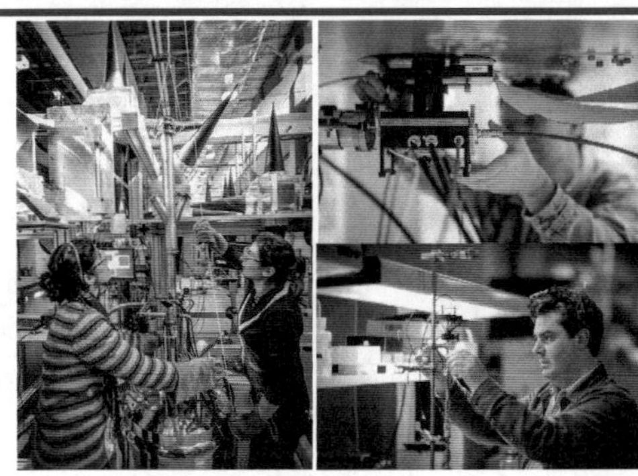

- A Federal – State funding partnership between the National Science Foundation, U.S. Dept. of Energy and the State of Florida
- Campuses located at Florida State University, the University of Florida, and Los Alamos National Laboratory.

High Magnetic Fields Lead to Big Discoveries in:

Many of the world's materials, energy and life challenges are bigger than one scientific discipline can solve.

The MagLab's interdisciplinary research environment brings together scientists across the spectrum from PHYSICS to CHEMISTRY to BIOLOGY to ENGINEERING who explore fundamental questions about **MATERIALS, ENERGY and LIFE** with the help of the world's highest magnetic fields.

World Record Magnets

High magnetic field laboratories are located in China, France, Germany, Japan, The Netherlands and the United States.

The National MagLab is home to 17 world record magnet systems:

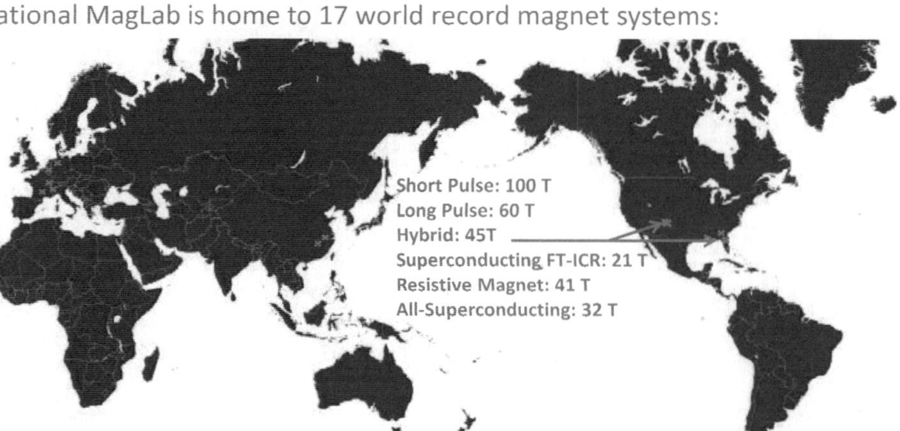

The MagLab attracts Researchers from Around The World

In 2016, the MagLab hosted experiments by 1,778 users from 321 institutions throughout the world.

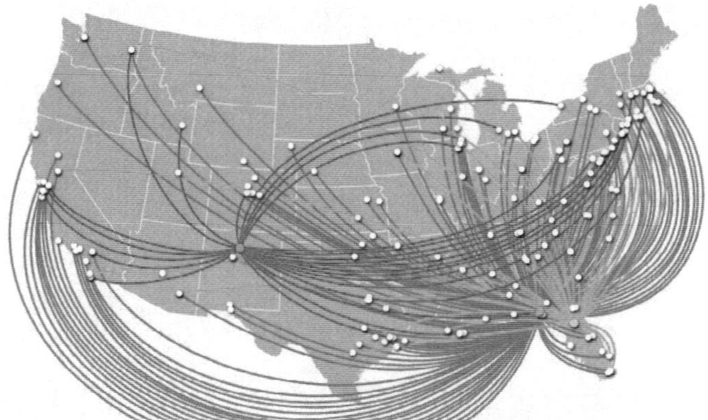

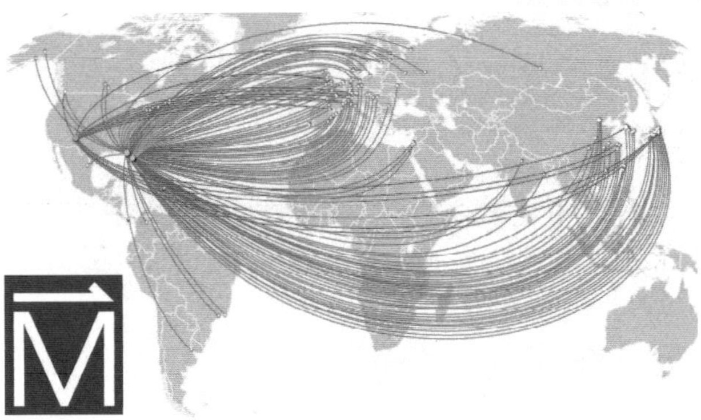

DOMESTIC INSTITUTIONS

- 145 UNIVERSITIES
- 19 GOVERNMENT LABS
- 10 INDUSTRY

INTERNATIONAL INSTITUTIONS

- 107 UNIVERSITIES
- 31 GOVERNMENT LABS
- 9 INDUSTRY

2016 LAB STATS

Users	1,778	Percentage of Users who were new	24	Awards & Honors	14
MagLab World Records	14	Articles Published in Peer-reviewed Journals	420	Patents & Other Products	5
Number of Principal Investigators	653	Books, Chapters, Reviews & other One-time Publications	3	Ph.D. Dissertations & Master Theses	68

Leveraging the MagLab for Enterprise Applied Magnetism Development

- Largest group of magnet science experts worldwide under one roof
- Greatest diversity of unique magnetic test and measurement instrumentation
- Modernized engagement models for more effective partnerships
- Expansive network of key players in the global magnet science ecosystem

---

The Problem Solving Gap

THE MAGLAB EXISTS TO SOLVE PROBLEMS OF THE **FUTURE**

WHO CAN SOLVE THE PROBLEMS OF **TODAY?**

MagLab core operations must prioritize the mission set forth by the NSF, so enterprise projects take a backseat.

An incredible opportunity exists that is not being fully capitalized.

So much more is possible.

The whole world knows the MagLab is the crown jewel of magnet science. Industry needs a way to tap into this expertise to answer real problems.

Magnetic Answers for Market-Driven Needs

MAG CORP

We didn't make this up. You (industry) has spoken.

1) The dreaded IP negotiation process

2) Relatively slow communication & agreement execution timelines

3) Nobody speaks the industry language

   No advocate exists for facilitating communication.

The Pain & Confusion

Consulting
- Finding an expert
- Negotiation
- Pay expert?

Sponsored Research
- New contact at Sponsored Research
- Negotiations (again!)
- Pay Sponsored Research?

Product Development
- New contract again – Licensing manager
- Negotiate with licensing manager (again!)
- Pay who?

The MagCorp Solution

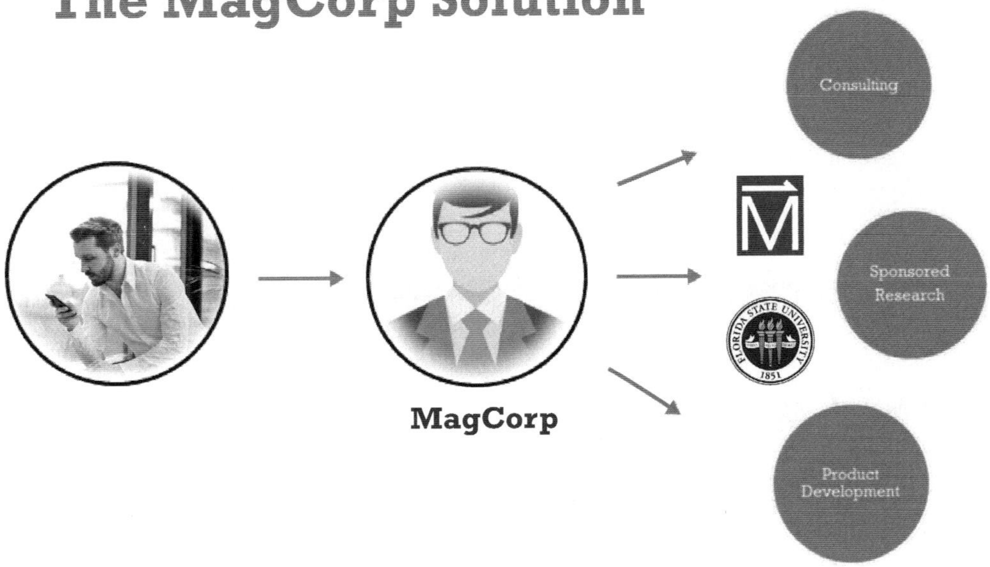

MAG CORP

MagCorp is the most rapid & agile magnet science innovation foundry & commercialization accelerator ever created.

Perfect alignment of the key assets of the MagLab.

MagCorp serves as a vessel for industry & federal sponsored research that leverages a standalone business model offering new engagement models better suited for industry-based sponsored R&D.

With support from The National Science Foundation, MagCorp is positioned to be the first commercial arm of The National High Magnetic Field Lab that is specifically created to address development needs in commercial magnetism applications.

The MagCorp Stepwise Engagement Model

Breaking it down to manageable steps toward the end goal.

MagCorp does business with a transparent & clearly pre-defined partnering process.

- Lowers the risk to all parties
- Allows for "time to get to know each other"
- Increases risk and commitments as projects mature
- Swift executing agreements and quickly responsive to sponsors needs
- We speak the same language
- Complete operational control & flexibility
- Platform for tech transfer of SBIR/STTR phase 3 projects

How to Leverage MagCorp

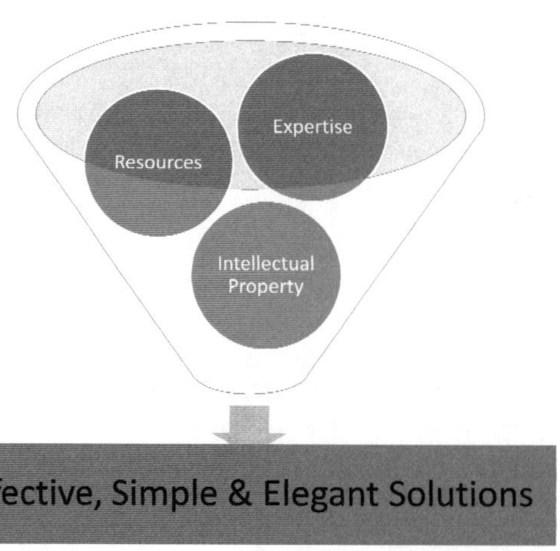

MagCorp leverages everything awesome about the National High Magnetic Field Lab for commercial applications that were previously not addressable.

What kinds of projects can MagCorp take on?

Just some examples:

- Consumer Products
- Electronics
- Robotics
- Medical
- Transportation
- Construction
- Mining & Separations
- Shipping
- Composites & Bonded Magnets
- Petroleum
- Prospecting & Drilling
- Textiles & Smart Fabrics

Connect with Us on What Matters to You

Technical

Jeffrey Whalen
jeffrey@maglabcorp.com

Operational

Lezlee Richerson
lezlee@maglabcorp.com

Legal

Abby Queale
abby@maglabcorp.com

Rare Earth Magnets: Yesterday, Today And Tomorrow

John Ormerod
Senior Technology Advisor
Magnet Applications, Inc.

MAGNETICS 2019
January 23-24 • Orlando, FL

MAGNET APPLICATIONS
A Bunting® Magnetics Company

Outline

- Introduction To Magnet Applications, Inc.
- Markets And Applications.
- History Of RE Magnets.
- Current Materials And Technologies.
- Future Trends And Developments.
- Final Thoughts.

MAGNET APPLICATIONS
A Bunting® Magnetics Company

The AC Induction Motor (and BLDC)

"I would not give my rotating field discovery for a thousand inventions, however valuable. A thousand years hence, the telephone and the motion picture camera may be obsolete, but the principle of the rotating magnetic field will remain a vital, living thing for all time to come."

Nikola Tesla 1856-1943

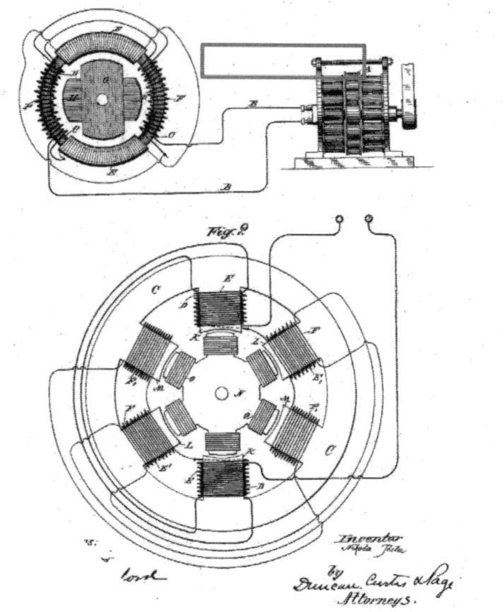

MAGNET APPLICATIONS

A Bunting Magnetics Company

Introduction To Magnet Applications, Inc.

MAGNET APPLICATIONS

A Bunting Magnetics Company

Introduction: Magnet Applications, Inc.

- Visit the latest website at: http://magnetapplications.com.
- A Bunting Magnetics Company: https://buntingmagnetics.com/.
- Only North American manufacturer of compression bonded NdFeB and injection molded ferrite, NdFeB and hybrid magnets.
- Supply full range of engineered magnets and magnetic assemblies.
- Located in DuBois, PA – Originally established in UK over 50 years ago – sister company located in Berkhamsted, UK.
- Primary applications are BLDC motors and sensors in the automotive, medical, defense and industrial markets.

MAGNET APPLICATIONS
A Bunting Magnetics Company

Introduction: Magnet Applications, Inc.

- Pre-production magnetic design services including 3D magnetic modeling.
- State of the art manufacturing capabilities including in-house coating and complete magnetic testing suite.
- Investing in R & D for next generation of magnetic materials e.g. high Br compression bonded, 3D printed magnets.
- The backing of strong family ownership – in business for 60 years.
- ITAR / DFARS registered for Defense Industry.
- ISO-9001 Certified Quality System with a strong continuous improvement culture.
- Very strong international supply chain for the complete range of permanent magnet materials.

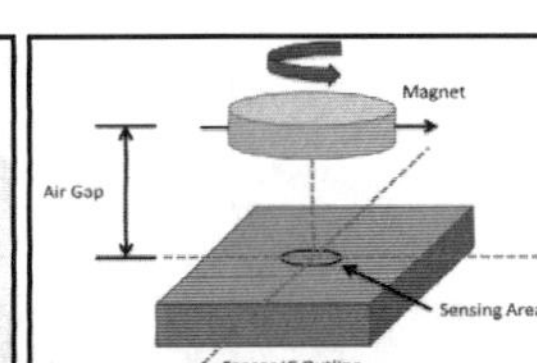

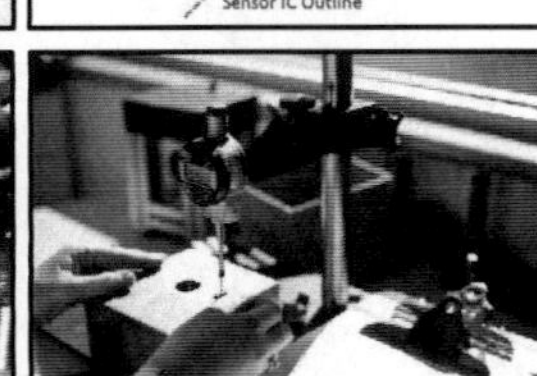

MAGNET APPLICATIONS
A Bunting Magnetics Company

Markets and Applications

MAGNET APPLICATIONS
A Bunting Magnetics Company

History of Permanent Magnet Development Is It Time For A New Breakthrough?

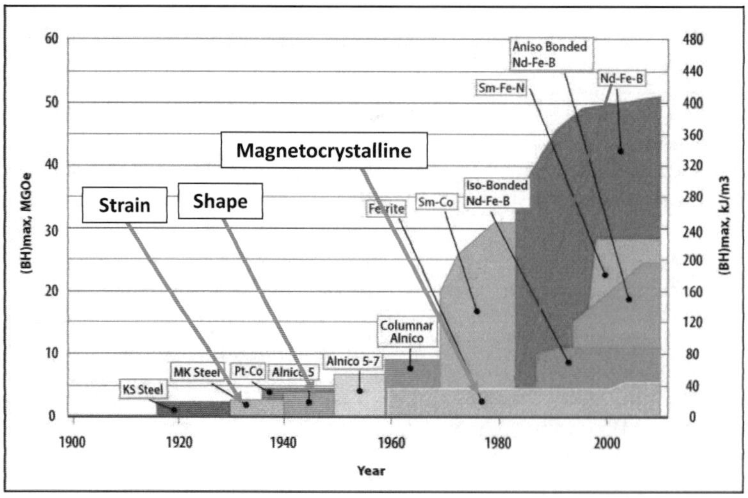

MAGNET APPLICATIONS
A Bunting Magnetics Company

The 5 Commercially Important Classes Of Permanent Magnets

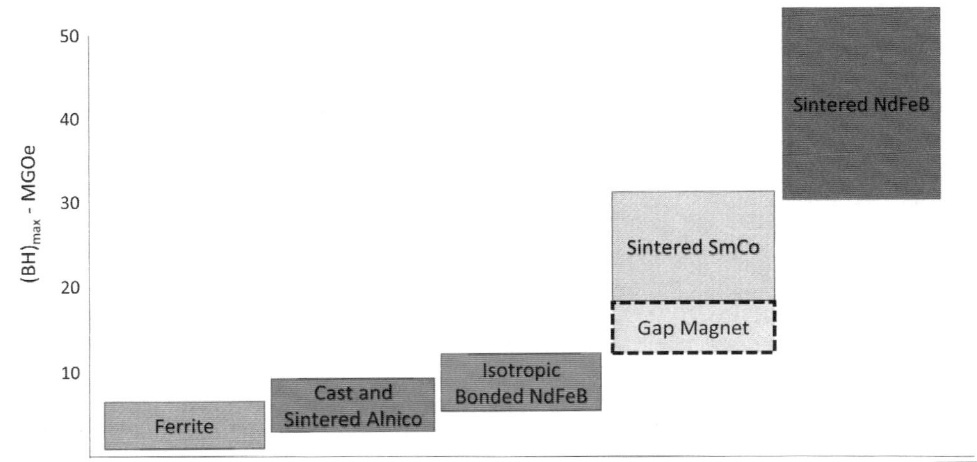

MAGNET APPLICATIONS
A Bunting. Magnetics Company

Permanent Magnet Market Size

It's Whatever You Want It To Be!

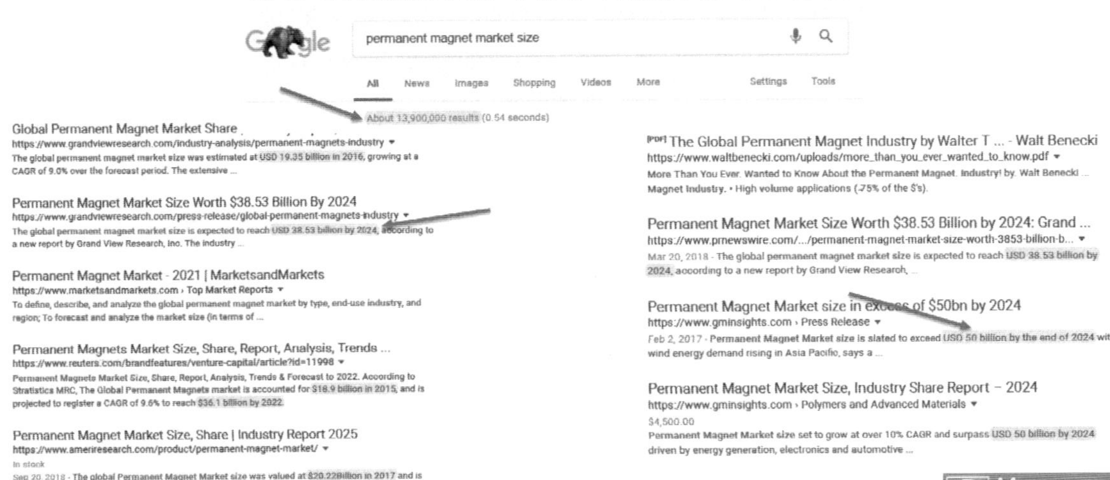

MAGNET APPLICATIONS
A Bunting. Magnetics Company

Estimated Permanent Magnet Market - 2018

Material	Weight (000's kg)	Value ($ Millions)
NdFeB	160,000	11,200
Ferrite	830,000	5,800
Bonded NdFeB	11,000	1000
SmCo	4,200	400
Alnico	6,300	350
Other	2000	150
	Total	Approximately $19 B

Source: Magnetics and Materials LLC, WTBenecki LLC, numerous industry sources

MAGNET APPLICATIONS
A Bunting® Magnetics Company

Market ($) Is Dominated By NdFeB And Ferrite

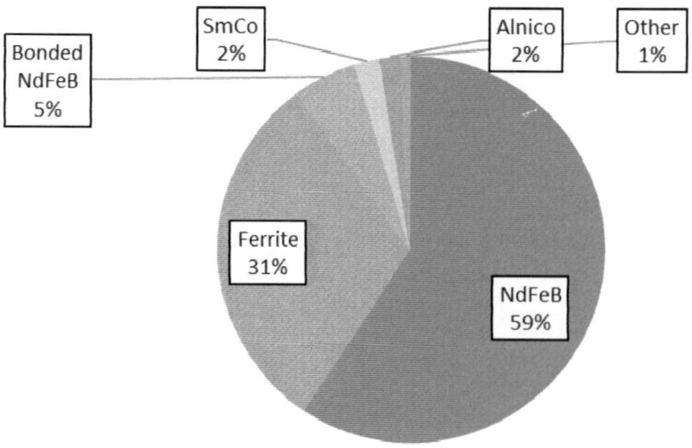

MAGNET APPLICATIONS
A Bunting® Magnetics Company

Production (Tons) Is Dominated By Ferrite

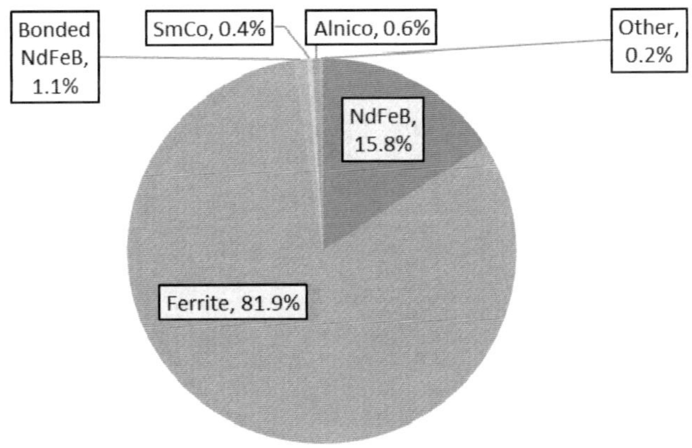

MAGNET APPLICATIONS
A Bunting Magnetics Company

Major Functions Of A Magnet

Application Category	Physical Law	System Function is Proportional to	Application Examples
Electrical to Mechanical (with solid conductor)	Lorentz Force law	B	Loudspeakers, PM motors, HDD/ODD VCM
Mechanical to Electrical	Faraday's Law of Induced voltage	B	Generators, Alternator, Tachometer, Magneto, Microphone, Eddy current devices, sensors
Magnetostatic Field Energy to Mechanical Work	Coulomb Force Principles	B^2	Magnetic Chucks, Conveyors, Magnetic Separators, Reed Switches, Synchronous Torque Couplings
Electrical to Mechanical (with free charged particles)	Lorentz Force law	B	Travelling Wave Tubes, Magnetrons, Klystrons, MRI

MAGNET APPLICATIONS
A Bunting Magnetics Company

Market By Major Application Type

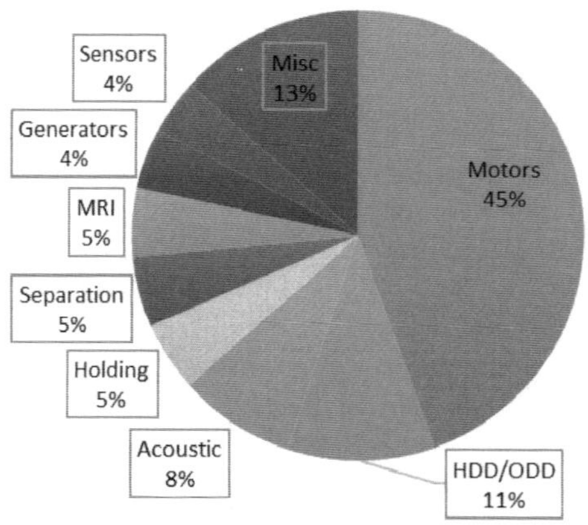

MAGNET APPLICATIONS
A Bunting® Magnetics Company

Automotive Applications – NdFeB Is Gaining Ground!

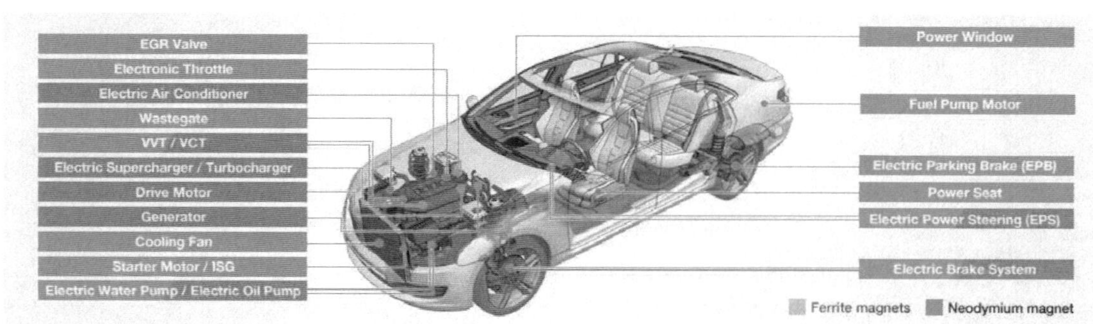

Source: TDK: https://product.tdk.com/info/en/products/magnet/technote/ap_automotive.html

MAGNET APPLICATIONS
A Bunting® Magnetics Company

Current And Future Major Applications

- **Hybrid and electric cars & trucks are in a rapid growth phase:**
  - **22,000 tons of RE magnets in 2020.**
  - **Forecast to be largest consumer of RE magnets by 2030.**
- **Electric bicycles is another large and growing application.**
  - **estimated 17,000 tons in 2020**
- **HDD (servers, cloud storage):**
  - **RE magnet estimated in 2018 is 8,000 tons.**
  - **Future demand flat to declining.**

Source: Magnetics and Materials LLC, WTBenecki LLC, numerous industry sources

MAGNET APPLICATIONS
A Bunting Magnetics Company

Electrified Vehicle Forecasts

7 million (2020)

52 million (2030)

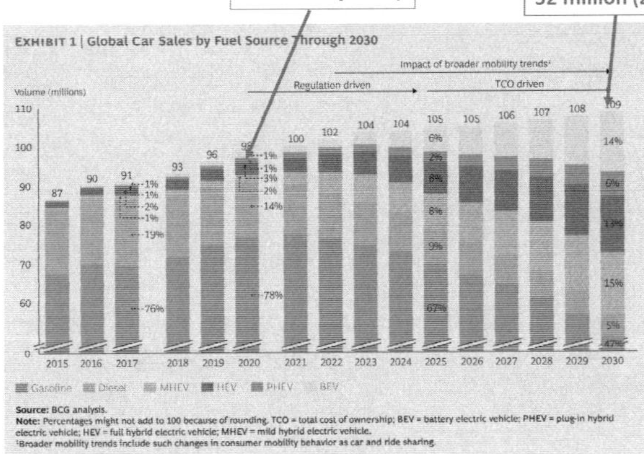

Source: https://www.greencarcongress.com/2017/11/20171103-bcg.html

11 Million (2020)

64 Million (2030)

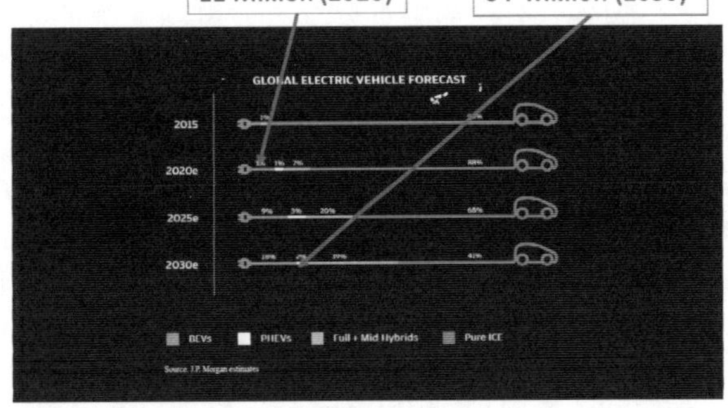

Source: https://www.jpmorgan.com/global/research/electric-vehicles

MAGNET APPLICATIONS
A Bunting Magnetics Company

Some (Total EV)Forecasts Are Even More Bullish

HEV and EVs will be only vehicles capable of meetings increasingly stringent emissions legislation

- Annual NEV sales reaching >98M units by 2028, increasing from 12.3M units in 2018
- HEV and EV model sales are forecast to exceed 58M units in 2028
- Huge demand increase for raw materials, not only in battery applications, but also in motor and electronics/wiring
- Rare earths are part of the story, though there is competition

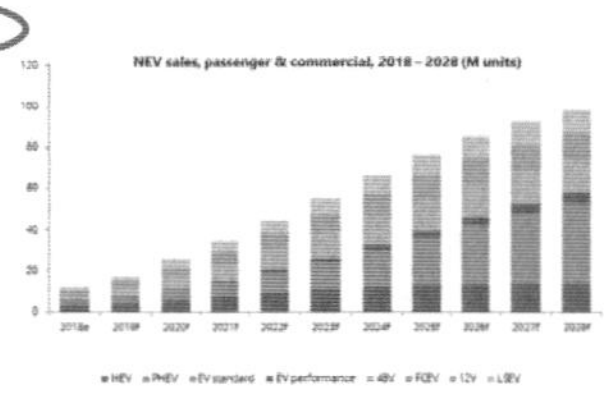

Roskill

Source: Roskill

NdFeB permanent magnets part of this generation of NEVs

- Drivetrain motors require higher quality and larger permanent magnets compared to traditional applications
- Pure battery EVs and LSEVs use more permanent magnets per motor than HEVs (Toyota Prius: 1.5kg NdFeB)

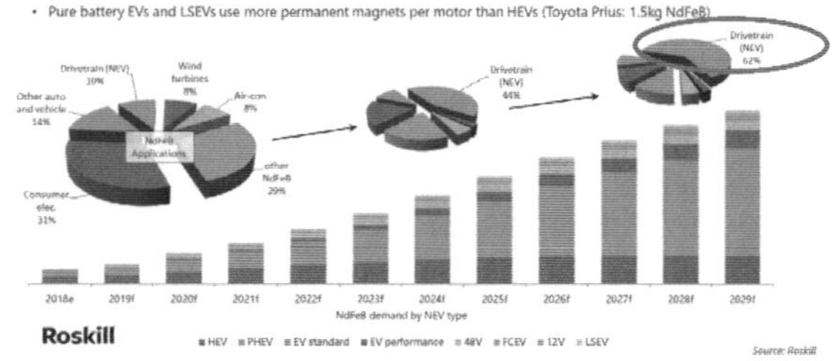

Roskill

Source: Roskill

Source: Roskill Information Services, Metal Events RE Conference, November 2018

MAGNET APPLICATIONS
A Bunting® Magnetics Company

EV/HEV's Everywhere – Impact On Raw Materials

Initial adoption driven by legislation

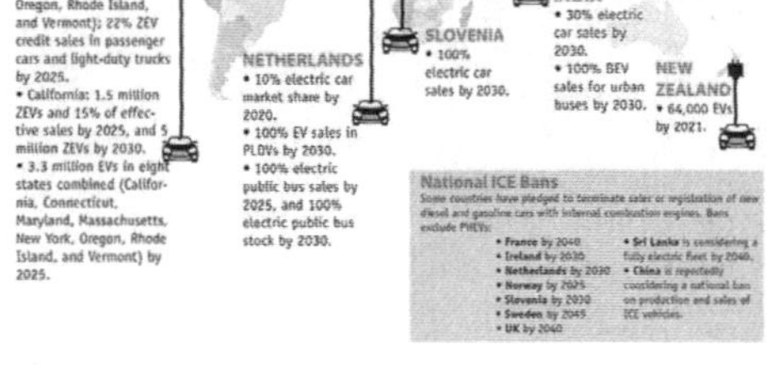

Source: https://www.powermag.com/the-big-picture-the-electric-vehicle-push/

..........EVs use between 1kg and 3kg of neodymium-iron-boron **(NdFeB) magnets in standard drivetrain motors. https://roskill.com/news/rare-earths-bmws-fifth-generation-ree-free-electric-drivetrain/#.XDMIKGlo9gV.linkedin**

64 million vehicles in 2030 X 2 kg NdFeB magnets = 128,000 tons

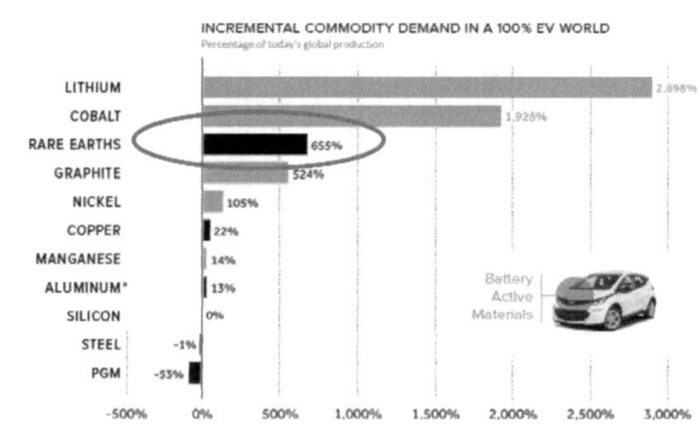

Source: http://www.visualcapitalist.com/massive-impact-evs-commodities/

MAGNET APPLICATIONS
A Bunting® Magnetics Company

Don't Just Take My Word

HML FY 2018 Management Plan

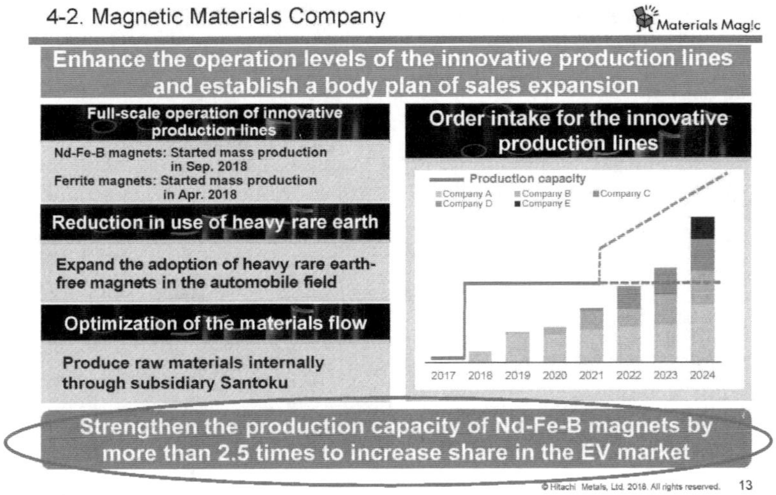

Source: https://www.hitachi-metals.co.jp/e/ir/pdf/pre/20181025en.pdf

MAGNET APPLICATIONS
A Bunting® Magnetics Company

Current And Future Major Applications

- Hybrid and electric cars & trucks are in a rapid growth phase:
  - 22,000 tons of RE magnets in 2020.
  - Forecast to be largest consumer of RE magnets by 2030.
- Electric bicycles is another large and growing application.
  - estimated 17,000 tons in 2020
- HDD (servers, cloud storage):
  - RE magnet estimated in 2018 is 8,000 tons.
  - Future demand flat to declining.

Source: Magnetics and Materials LLC, WTBenecki LLC, numerous industry sources

MAGNET APPLICATIONS
A Bunting® Magnetics Company

Current And Future Major Applications

- Hybrid and electric cars & trucks are in a rapid growth phase:
  - 22,000 tons of RE magnets in 2020.
  - Forecast to be largest consumer of RE magnets by 2030.
- Electric bicycles is another large and growing application.
  - estimated 17,000 tons in 2020
- HDD (servers, cloud storage):
  - RE magnet estimated in 2018 is 8,000 tons.
  - Future demand flat to declining.

Source: Magnetics and Materials LLC, WTBenecki LLC, numerous industry sources

MAGNET APPLICATIONS
A Bunting Magnetics Company

Current And Future Major Applications

- Direct Drive wind turbines:
  - RE magnet weight forecast in 2020 is 38,000 tons.
- Automotive (ICE):
  - Over 100 PM devices in a typical car.
  - Estimated 12,000 tons usage in 2020.
- General industrial and commercial motors for robotics, appliances, HVAC etc.
  - Estimated 15,000 tons in 2020
- Acoustic transducers.
  - Micro magnets (> 5 billion magnets)
  - Estimated 5,000 tons in 2020
- Magneto calorific cooling for refrigeration and HVAC is a potential major application.

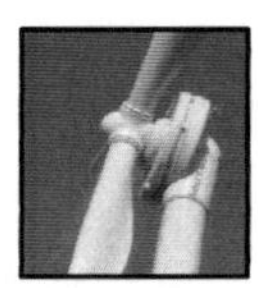

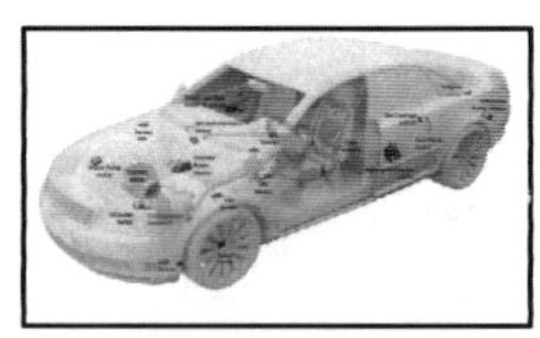

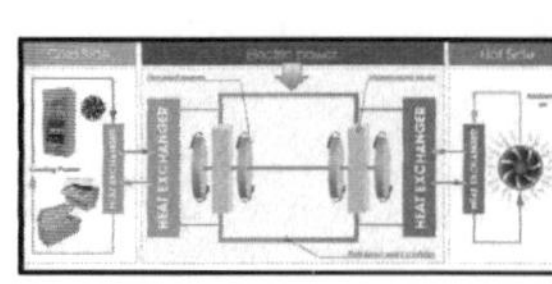

Source: Magnetics and Materials LLC, WTBenecki LLC, numerous industry sources

MAGNET APPLICATIONS
A Bunting Magnetics Company

Current And Future Major Applications

- **Direct Drive wind turbines:**
  - RE magnet weight forecast in 2020 is 38,000 tons.
- **Automotive (ICE):**
  - Over 100 PM devices in a typical car.
  - Estimated 12,000 tons usage in 2020.
- **General industrial and commercial motors for robotics, appliances, HVAC etc.**
  - Estimated 15,000 tons in 2020
- **Acoustic transducers.**
  - Micro magnets (> 5 billion magnets)
  - Estimated 5,000 tons in 2020
- **Magneto calorific cooling for refrigeration and HVAC is a potential major application.**

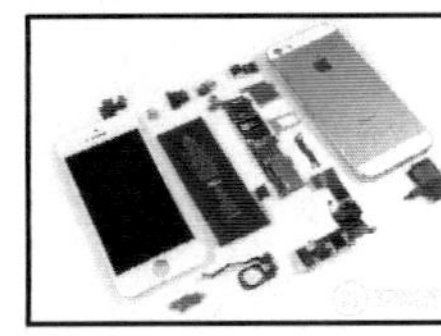
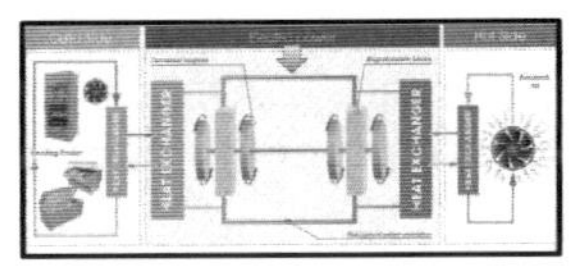

Source: Magnetics and Materials LLC, WTBenecki LLC, numerous industry sources

MAGNET APPLICATIONS
A Bunting Magnetics Company

Current And Future Major Applications

- **Direct Drive wind turbines:**
  - RE magnet weight forecast in 2020 is 38,000 tons.
- **Automotive (ICE):**
  - Over 100 PM devices in a typical car.
  - Estimated 12,000 tons usage in 2020.
- **General industrial and commercial motors for robotics, appliances, HVAC etc.**
  - Estimated 15,000 tons in 2020
- **Acoustic transducers.**
  - Micro magnets (> 5 billion magnets)
  - Estimated 5,000 tons in 2020
- **Magneto calorific cooling for refrigeration and HVAC is a potential major application.**

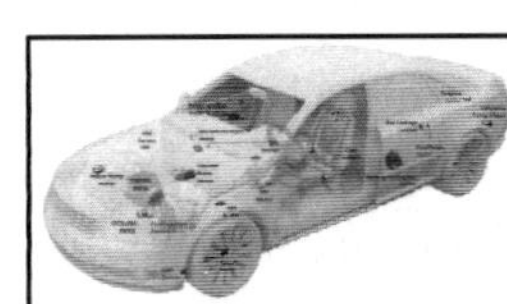

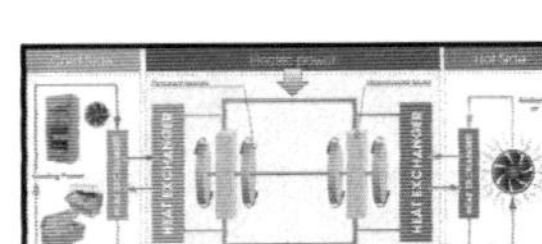

Source: Magnetics and Materials LLC, WTBenecki LLC, numerous industry sources

MAGNET APPLICATIONS
A Bunting Magnetics Company

Current And Future Major Applications

- **Direct Drive wind turbines:**
  - RE magnet weight forecast in 2020 is 38,000 tons.
- **Automotive (ICE):**
  - Over 100 PM devices in a typical car.
  - Estimated 12,000 tons usage in 2020.
- **General industrial and commercial motors for robotics, appliances, HVAC etc.**
  - Estimated 15,000 tons in 2020
- **Acoustic transducers.**
  - Micro magnets (> 5 billion magnets)
  - Estimated 5,000 tons in 2020
- **Magneto calorific cooling for refrigeration and HVAC is a potential major application.**

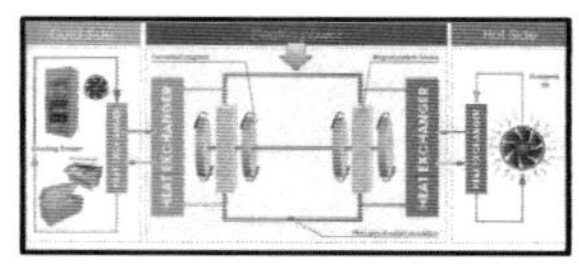

Source: Magnetics and Materials LLC, WTBenecki LLC, numerous industry sources

MAGNET APPLICATIONS
A Bunting® Magnetics Company

Current And Future Major Applications

- **Direct Drive wind turbines:**
  - RE magnet weight forecast in 2020 is 38,000 tons.
- **Automotive (ICE):**
  - Over 100 PM devices in a typical car.
  - Estimated 12,000 tons usage in 2020.
- **General industrial and commercial motors for robotics, appliances, HVAC etc.**
  - Estimated 15,000 tons in 2020
- **Acoustic transducers.**
  - Micro magnets (> 5 billion magnets)
  - Estimated 5,000 tons in 2020
- **Magneto calorific cooling for refrigeration and HVAC is a potential major application.**

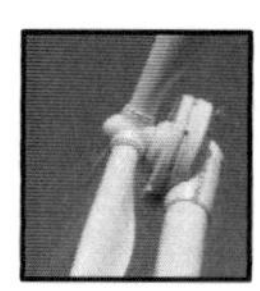

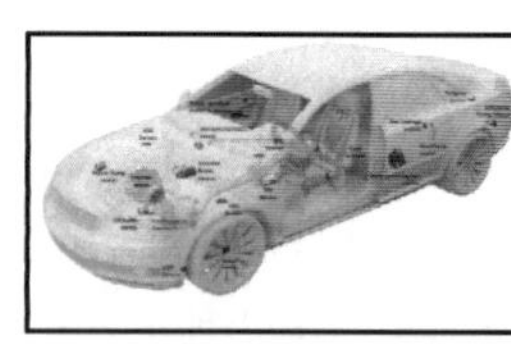

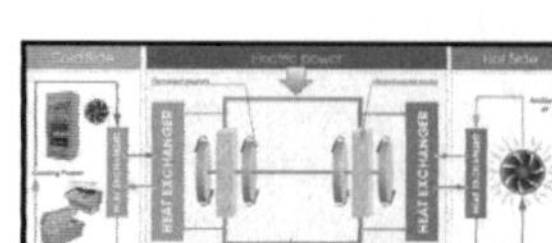

Source: Magnetics and Materials LLC, WTBenecki LLC, numerous industry sources

MAGNET APPLICATIONS
A Bunting® Magnetics Company

History Of RE Magnets

MAGNET APPLICATIONS®
A Bunting® Magnetics Company

New Era Of Permanent Magnets

- Following the successful development of Alnico magnets, with energy products up to 13 MGOe, future major advances in permanent magnet materials would require shifting emphasis from shape anisotropy to crystal anisotropy.
- This led, in the 1960s, to studies to identify anisotropic crystalline phases, preferably hexagonal or tetragonal, which combined high saturation magnetization with high magnetocrystalline anisotropy.

MAGNET APPLICATIONS®
A Bunting® Magnetics Company

New Era Of Permanent Magnets

- Several factors focused attention on rare earth intermetallic compounds.
  - First, several of the rare earth elements display magnetic ordering and large magnetic moments at low temperatures.
  - Second, it was known that, because of the large difference in atomic radii between the rare earth and Mn, Fe, Co and Ni atoms, there is a tendency to form several intermetallic compounds in the binary systems.
  - Third, previous work had shown that many of these intermetallic compounds exhibited magnetic ordering by the coupling of the rare earth magnetic moment with the 3d transition element moment.
  - This led to the breakthrough discovery by Strnat el al in 1966 that YCo_5 had a magnetocrystalline anisotropy field of over 140 kOe.

SmCo-Based Permanent Magnets

- In order to be possible candidates for permanent magnet materials, the compounds must combine the basic attributes of:
  - High saturation magnetization
  - Elevated Curie temperature and
  - Large magnetocrystalline anisotropy with a magnetically unique crystallographic axis.
- All these considerations were found to narrow the group of binary compounds from to RCo_5 and R2Co17 with R =Y, Ce, Pr, Nd or Sm.
- This led to the development of commercial Sm-Co magnets based on the binary SmCo5 (nucleation controlled) or multicomponent Sm2Co17 (domain wall pinning) systems.

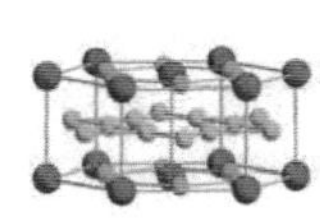

SmCo5 Crystal Structure

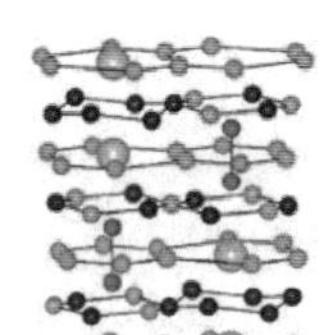

Sm2Co17 Crystal Structure

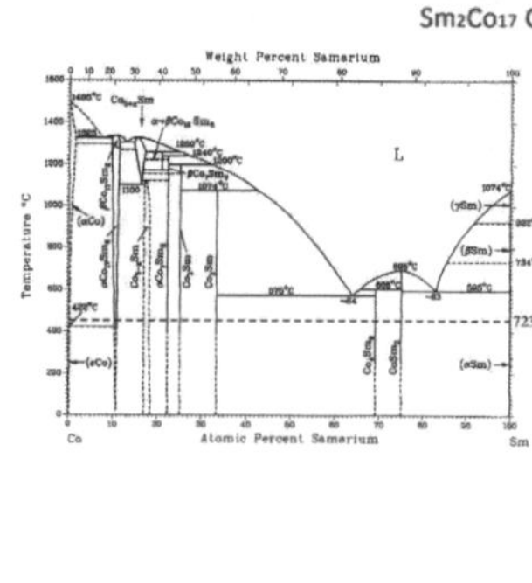

SmCo phase diagram

The NdFeB Era

A Search for a LREE Co-Free System

- **Historically, the development of RFe-based permanent magnets, by powder metallurgical processing, has been hindered for several reasons:**
  - **First, Fe forms much fewer intermetallic compounds with the rare earths than Co.**
  - **Second, stable compounds of the RFe_5 composition are absent.**
  - **Third, compounds which are stable, e.g. R_2Fe_{17}, have low Curie temperatures and planar preference anisotropy.**

The NdFeB Era

- **By a strange coincidence permanent magnets based on the Nd2Fe14B tetragonal compound were discovered, and the key inventive claims were filed, during 1982 by both General Motors Corporation (GMC) and Sumitomo Special Metals Corporation (SSMC). SSMC was later to form a JV with Hitachi and eventually merged as Hitachi Metals in 2007. GMC spun off the NdFeB magnet business as Magnequench; today part of Neo Materials.**
- **The Hitachi process is based on powder metallurgical processing whereas the Magnequench process is based on melt spinning or jet casting.**

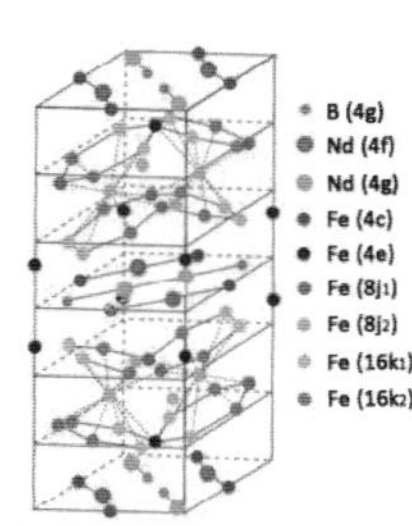

$Nd_2Fe_{14}B$ Crystal Structure

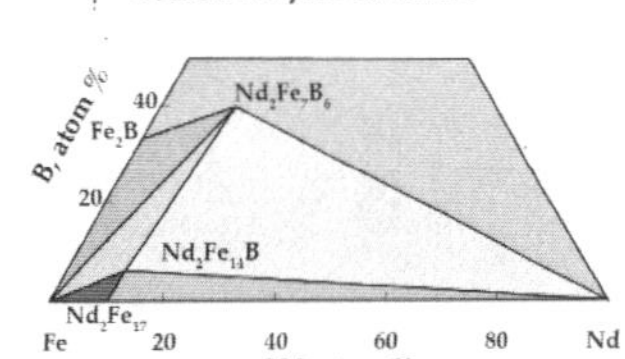

Current Materials And Processes

MAGNET APPLICATIONS
A Bunting Magnetics Company

Typical Powder Metallurgical Processing of NdFeB

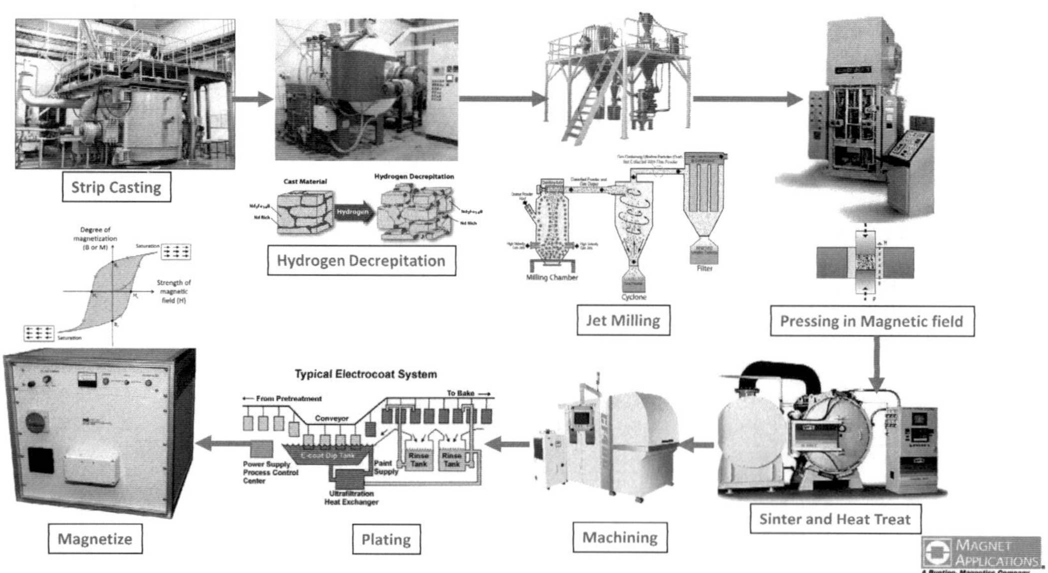

MAGNET APPLICATIONS
A Bunting Magnetics Company

Melt Spinning (Jet Casting) Of NdFeB

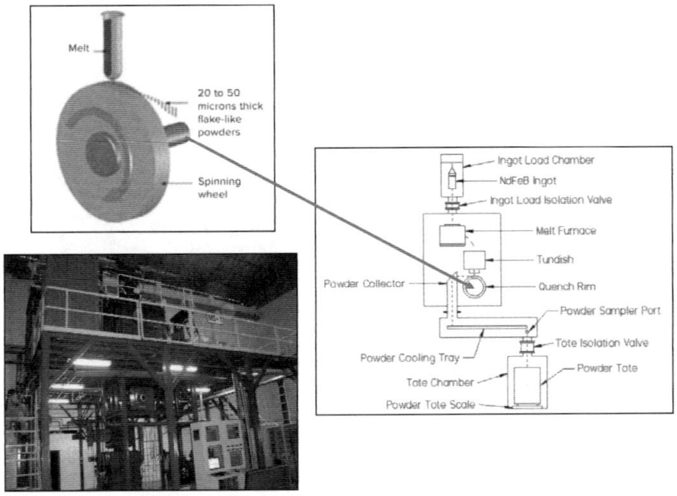

- This method of melt-spinning consists of melting the alloy or elements in a tube either under vacuum or inert gas. The melt, under argon pressure, is sprayed through an orifice in the tube onto a rotating, water-cooled copper wheel or disc. Cooling rates in excess of 10^6 K/s are achieved.
- GM commercialized this technology for the production of magnets, known as Magnequench.
- The isotropic powders are mainly used in bonded magnet production.

Source: J.J. Croat, Rapidly Solidified NdFeB PM's, Woodhead Publishing, 2018.

MAGNET APPLICATIONS®
A Bunting® Magnetics Company

Demagnetization Behavior At Temperature for NdFeB (N55M)

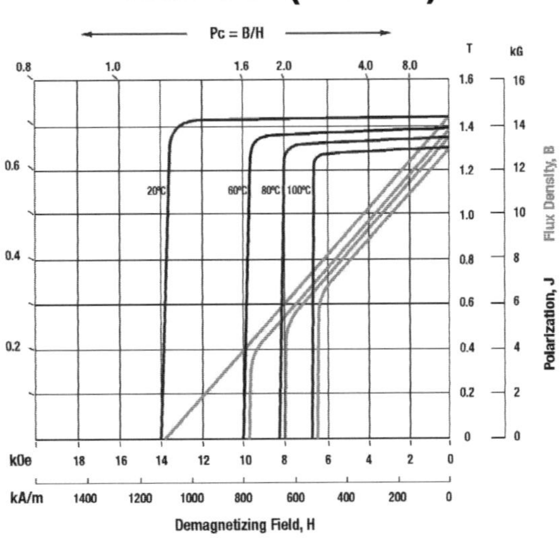

MAGNET APPLICATIONS®
A Bunting® Magnetics Company

Effect Of Dy On Coercivity

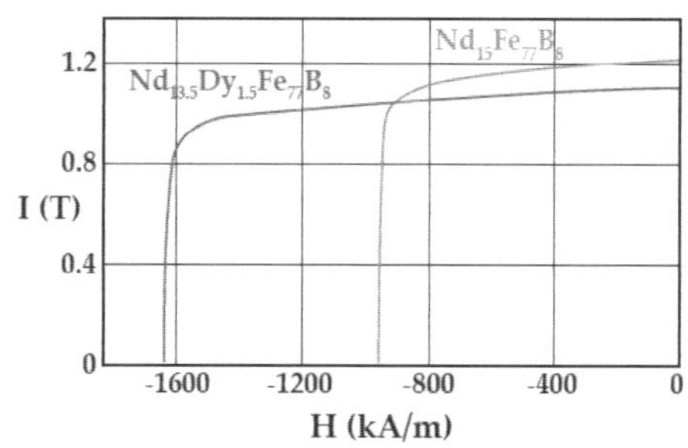

Reference: IEEE Transactions on Magnetics, Volume 20, Issue 5, September 1984, pp. 1584-1589

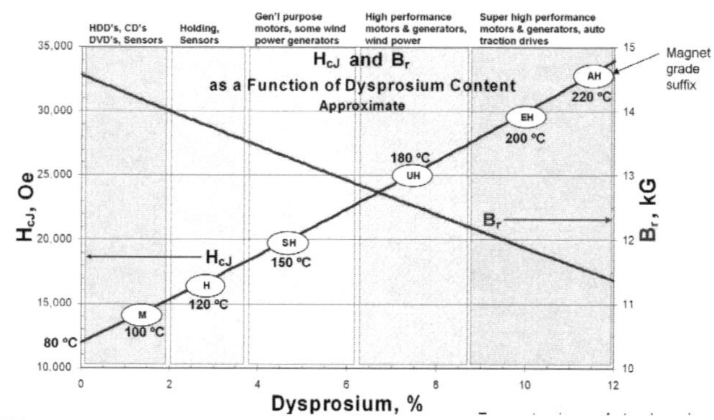

Source: Magnetics and Materials LLC, https://www.magmatllc.com/index.html

MAGNET APPLICATIONS
A Bunting® Magnetics Company

Rare Earth Price And Supply Disruption

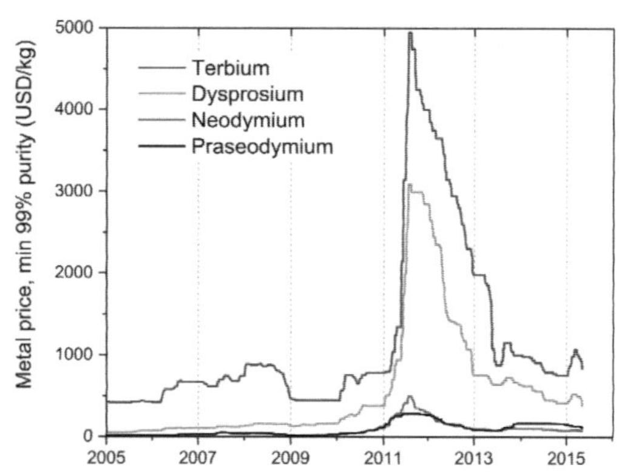

- Rare Earth prices spiked in 2011/2012 e.g. Dy2O3 price increased 50 fold.
- Major investment in search for RE-free substitution and application redesign.
- Drove efforts to reduce Dy content for higher temperature/coercivity grades

Reference: Ressources Policy, Volume 52, June 2017, Pages 349-357

MAGNET APPLICATIONS
A Bunting® Magnetics Company

Dy Diffusion At Grain Boundaries

Enhancement of coercivity with small degradation of remanence by diffusing HREE into grain boundary phases and surfaces of grains

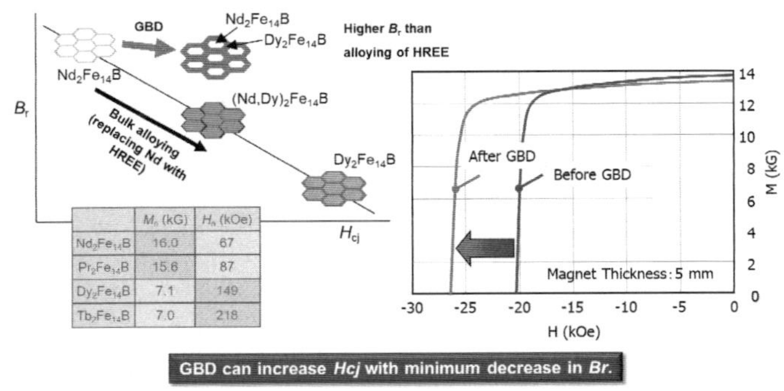

	M_s (kG)	H_A (kOe)
$Nd_2Fe_{14}B$	16.0	67
$Pr_2Fe_{14}B$	15.6	87
$Dy_2Fe_{14}B$	7.1	149
$Tb_2Fe_{14}B$	7.0	218

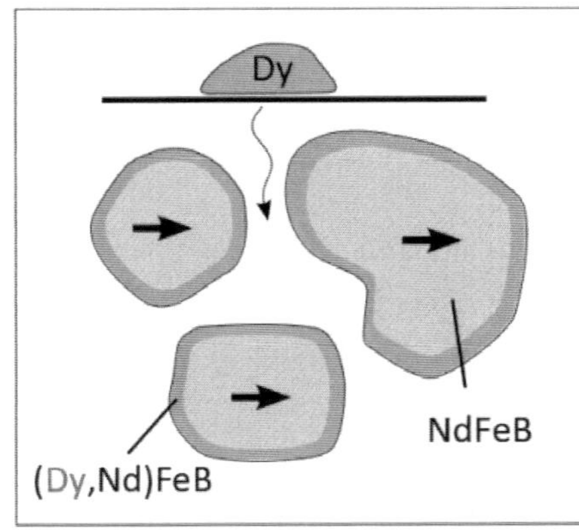

Reference: Yotaka Yoshida, Daido Steel, Magnetics 2016.

MAGNET APPLICATIONS
A Bunting Magnetics Company

Hot Deformed Oriented Fully Dense Magnets

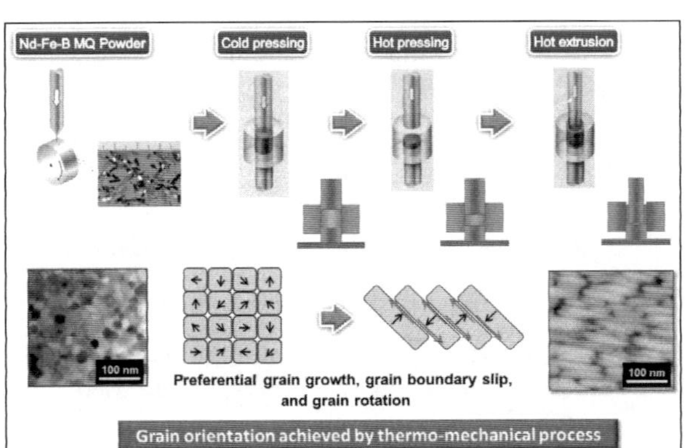

Daido Steel and Honda Adopt World's First Hybrid Vehicle Motor Magnet Free of Heavy Rare Earth Elements

– Honda Freed, on sale this fall, will be the first hybrid vehicle to adopt new magnet –

DAIDO STEEL HONDA
The Power of Dreams

Reference: Yotaka Yoshida, Daido Steel, Magnetics 2016.

https://world.honda.com/news/2016/4160712eng.html

MAGNET APPLICATIONS
A Bunting Magnetics Company

Dy Content versus Coercivity At 180 C

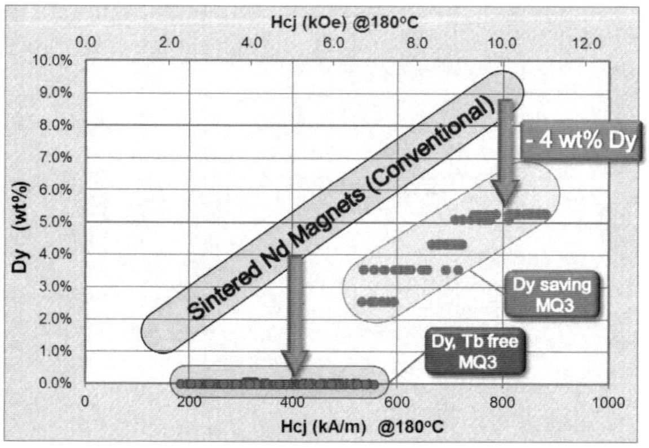

Approx. 4wt% less Dy is needed to achieve same Hcj as sintered Nd

Reference: Yotaka Yoshida, Daido Steel, Magnetics 2016.

MAGNET APPLICATIONS
A Bunting Magnetics Company

SmFeN Magnets

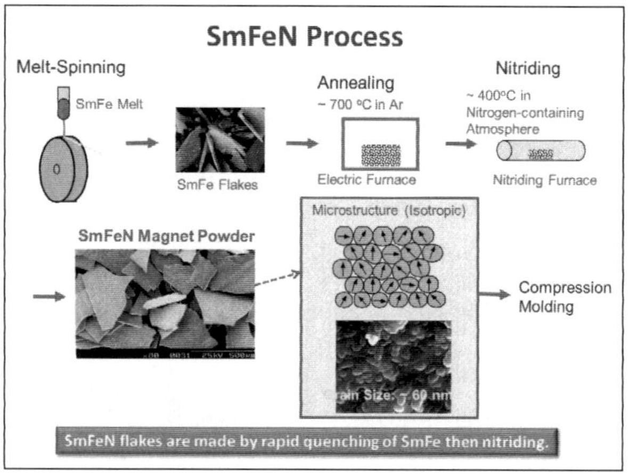

- SmFeN alloy is a promising candidate for high-performance permanent magnets.
- The $Sm_2Fe_{17}N_3$ intermetallic compound, which exhibits high saturation magnetization with a large anisotropy field and a high Curie temperature.
- $Sm_2Fe_{17}N_3$ intermetallic compound has been prepared by the production of Sm_2Fe_{17} alloy powder and subsequent nitrogenation of the powder by a gas-solid reaction. The resultant $Sm_2Fe_{17}N_3$ intermetallic compound has thus been produced in powder form for bonded magnets.

Reference: Yotaka Yoshida, Daido Steel, Magnetics 2016.

MAGNET APPLICATIONS
A Bunting Magnetics Company

La-Co Doped Hard Ferrite Magnets

- Ever since their discovery by Philips in the early 1950's, M-type ferrites have increasingly become widely used in many applications.
- Recently it has been discovered that both saturation magnetization as well as magnetocrystalline anisotropy of M-type ferrites can be modified by the substitution of rare earths into the crystal lattice.
- Approximately 40% improvement in (BH)max over conventional Sr-hexaferrite grades achieved.

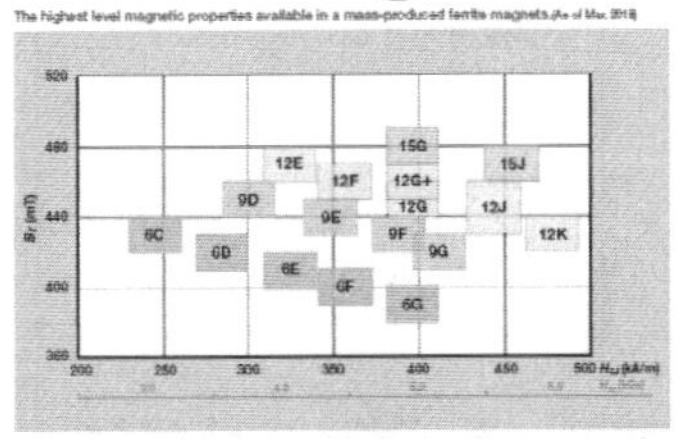

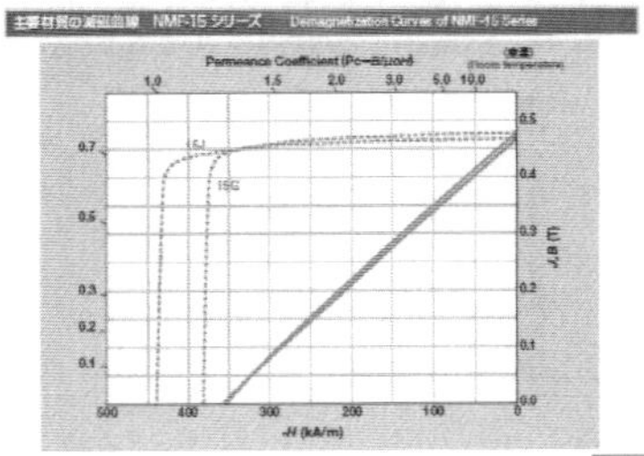

Source: Hitachi Metals, http://www.hitachi-metals.co.jp/e/products/auto/el/pdf/hg-a27-i.pdf

MAGNET APPLICATIONS
A Bunting. Magnetics Company

Anisotropic Bonded NdFeB – Two Processes

- HDDR (hydrogenation disproportionation desorption recombination) process:
  - HDDR is the thermal treatment of a NdFeB alloy under a H_2 atmosphere.
  - The alloy undergoes a series of solid state transformations.
  - The resultant powder consist of a fine grained textured $Nd_2Fe_{14}B$ phase that can be magnetically aligned during compression bonding or injection molding.

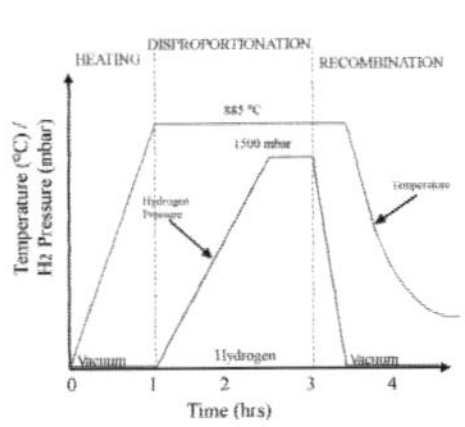

MQ3 powder
- Basically crushed hot-deformed MQ3 magnets

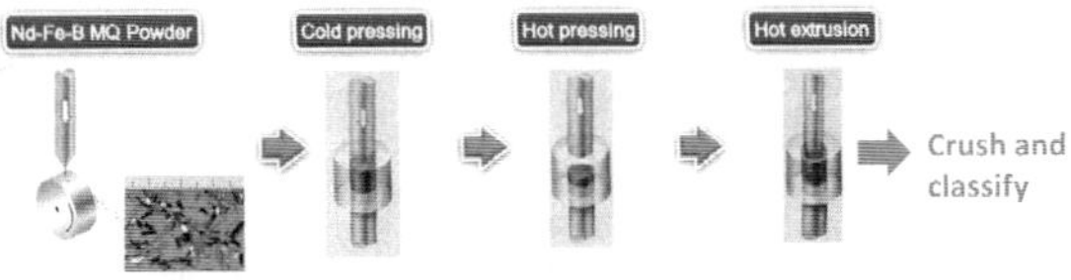

Estimated production of anisotropic NdFeB bonded magnets < 1000 tons.
Why? Possible reasons: 1. Magnetic orientation technology not common in the bonded magnet industry and, 2. The available data shows higher irreversible losses at elevated temperatures (compared to isotropic powders).

Source: R.S. Sheridan et al. / Journal of Magnetism and Magnetic Materials 401 (2016) 455–462

MAGNET APPLICATIONS
A Bunting. Magnetics Company

Future Trends and Developments

MAGNET APPLICATIONS
A Bunting® Magnetics Company

The Toyota Magnet Announcement

Toyota Develops New Magnet for Electric Motors Aiming to Reduce Use of Critical Rare-Earth Element by up to 50%

- **World's first neodymium-reduced, heat-resistant magnet developed by Toyota**
- **Key element of the foundation required to popularize electrified vehicles**

Toyota City, Japan, February 20, 2018—Toyota Motor Corporation (Toyota) announces that it has developed the world's first*1 neodymium-reduced, heat-resistant magnet. Neodymium magnets are used in various types of motors such as the high-output motors found in electrified vehicles, use of which is expected to increase rapidly in the future. The new magnet uses significantly less neodymium, a rare-earth element*2 ("rare earth"), and can be used in high-temperature conditions.

The newly developed magnet uses no terbium (Tb) or dysprosium (Dy), which are rare earths that are also categorized as critical materials*3 necessary for highly heat-resistant neodymium magnets. A portion of the neodymium has been replaced with lanthanum (La) and cerium (Ce), which are low-cost rare earths, reducing the amount of neodymium used in the magnet.

Source: https://newsroom.toyota.co.jp/en/corporate/21139684.html

MAGNET APPLICATIONS
A Bunting® Magnetics Company

The Toyota Magnet Announcement

Or La and Ce Substituted No HREE EV Drive Magnet

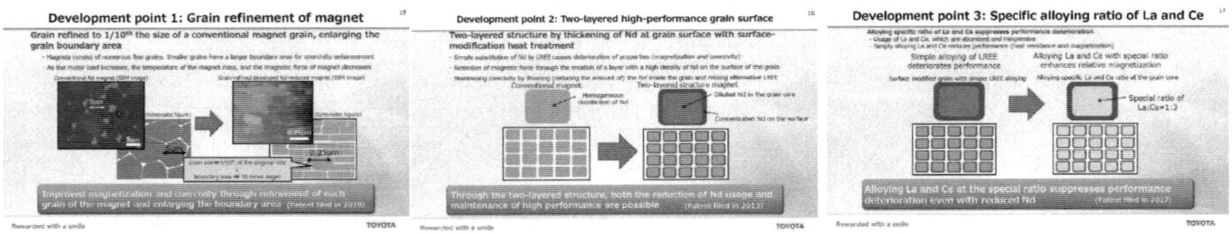

- Starting alloy fine grain size of 0.25μm is probably formed by melt spinning.
- Appears to be La/Ce substituted NdFeB alloy whose fine-grained microstructure enhances coercivity.
- Surface modification step increases Nd content at grain boundary surfaces.
- Similar to Dy-diffusion processing?

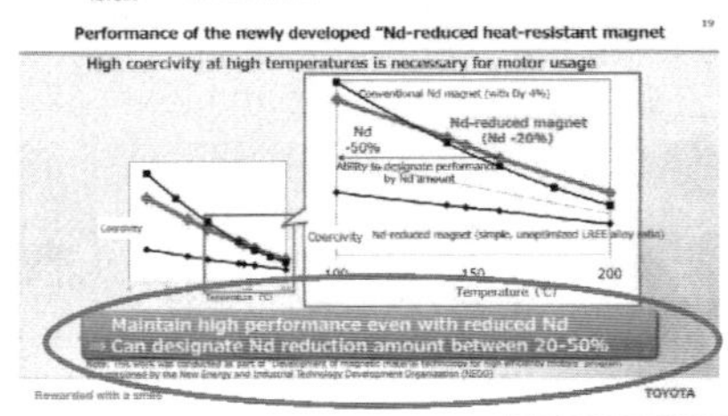

Source: https://newsroom.toyota.co.jp/en/corporate/21139684.html

MAGNET APPLICATIONS
A Bunting. Magnetics Company

New Permanent Magnet Materials

It's A Challenge To Hit The Sweet Spot

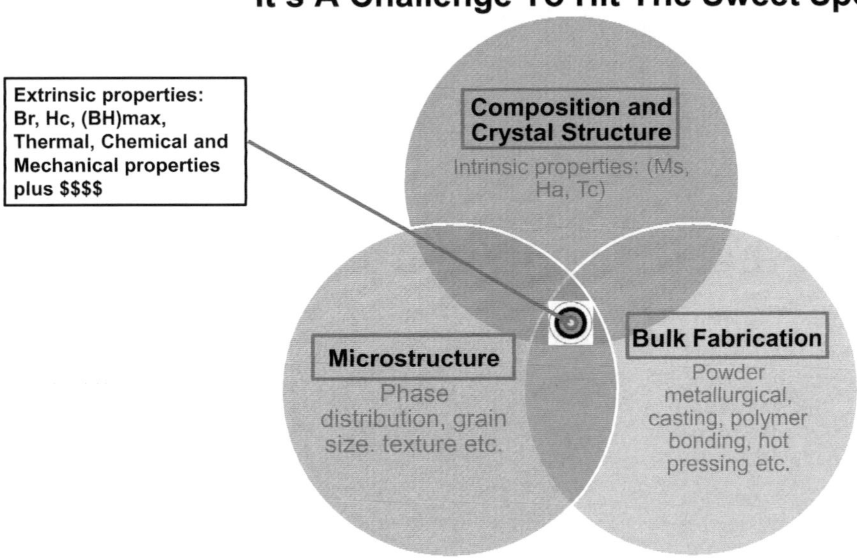

MAGNET APPLICATIONS
A Bunting. Magnetics Company

Some New Material Developments

Exchange Spring/ Nanocomposite

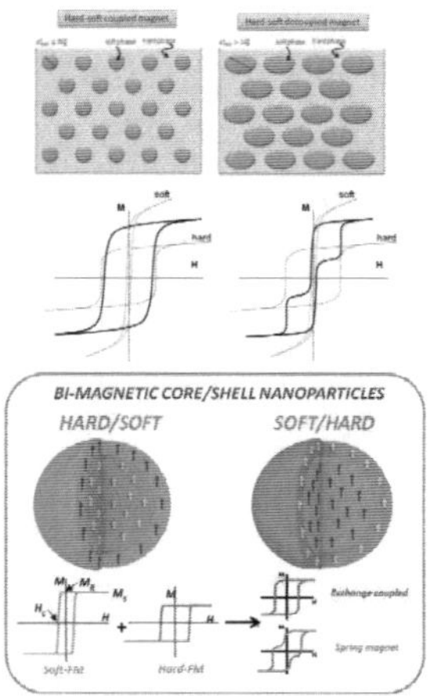

Fe16N2

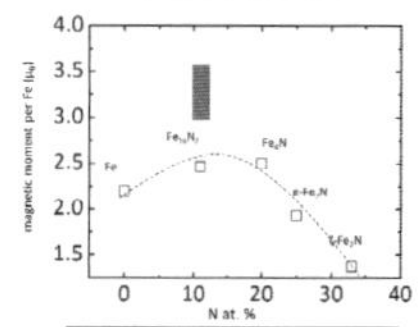

Co Nanowires

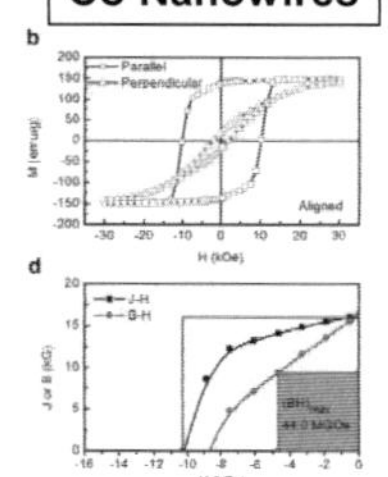

Is Nd2Fe14B Just Too Good?

Numerous Other Compositions

TABLE 7.3
Extrinsic parameters of some representative permanent magnetic materials

Material	B_R (T)	$\mu_0 H_C$ (T)	$(BH)_{max}$ (x10^3 J/m^3)
Alnico (isotropic)	0.6-1.0	0.1-0.2	10-30
Alnico (anisotropic)	1.3-1.4	0.3-0.4	40-80
$AFe_{12}O_{19}$ (sintered)	0.39	0.3	28
$SrFe_{12}O_{19}$	0.2-0.4	0.13-0.37	10-40
$SmCo_5$ (metal-bonded)	0.92	1.88	175
$SmCo_5$ (polymer-bonded)	0.58	1.00	60
$Sm_2Co_{17}/SmCo_5$ (sintered)	1.08	1.0	225
$Nd_2Fe_{14}B$ (sintered)	1.0-1.4	1-2.5	200-440
$Nd_2Fe_{14}B$ (polymer bonded)	0.6-0.7	0.75-1.5	50-100
$Nd_2Fe_{14}B/\alpha$-FeCo (nanocomposite)	1.4-1.6	1.0-1.8	320-480
$L1_0$-MnAl (alloy)	0.5-0.6	0.2-0.4	40-70
$L1_0$-MnAl (nanoparticles)	0.25-0.5	0.36-0.56	38
MnBi (nanostructured powder)	0.25	1.9-2.1	14
MnBi (bonded)	0.50	1.1 (300 K) 2.5 (540 K)	60
Zr_2Co_{11} (isotropic ribbons)	0.6	0.2	42
Zr_2Co_{11} (aligned nanoparticles)	0.84	0.44	132
$HfCo_7$ (isotropic ribbons)	0.7	0.2	35
$HfCo_7$ (aligned nanoparticles)	0.9	0.45	100

Sources: L. H. Lewis and F. Jiménez-Villacorta, "Perspectives on Permanent Magnetic Materials for Energy Conversion and Power Generation" (Invited Review), *Metall. Mater. Trans. A* 44, 2 (2013)

Gandha, K., Elkins, K., Poudyal, N., Liu, X.B. & Liu, J.P. High Energy Product Developed from Cobalt Nanowires. Sci. Rep. 4, 5345; DOI:10.1038/ srep05345 (2014).

MAGNET APPLICATIONS
A Bunting® Magnetics Company

Final (Crazy) Thoughts

MAGNET APPLICATIONS
A Bunting® Magnetics Company

Is There An Optimum Price-Performance Metric (2016)? Niche And Mass Market Materials

Material	Average $(BH)_{max}$ (MGOe)	Average price ($/kg)	Price/Performance ($/kg per MGOe)	Market %
NdFeB	40	75	1.9	60
Ferrite	3.8	7.1	1.9	31
Bonded NdFeB	8	90	11.3	5
SmCo	25	100	4.0	2
Alnico	7	58	8.3	2

MAGNET APPLICATIONS
A Bunting® Magnetics Company

It's Magnet Volume Not Weight!

- By experience we specify magnets by dimensions and geometry not weight.
- We buy and use a volume of magnet material.

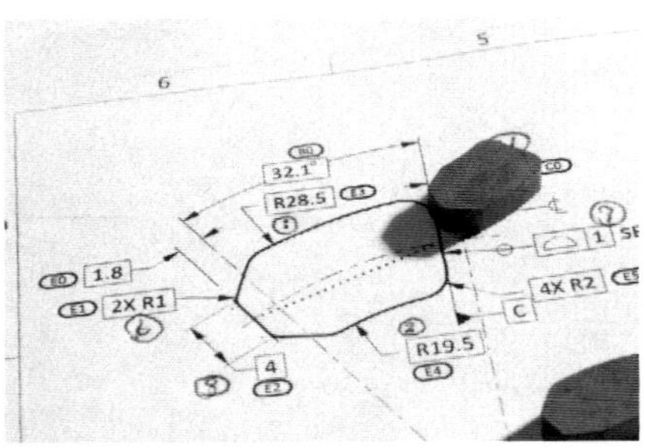

$$H_g^2 = (B_m H_m) V_m / V_g$$

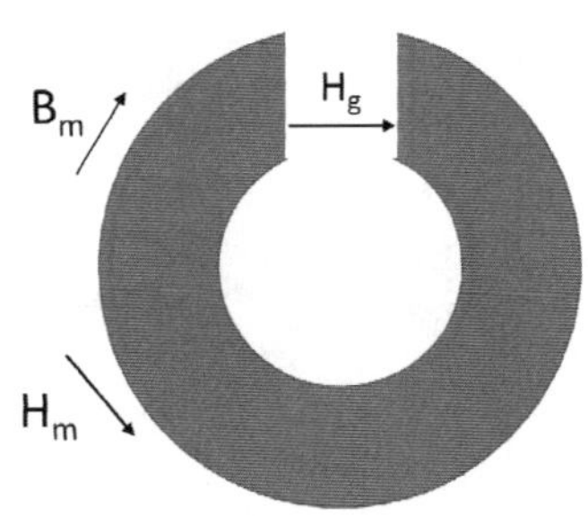

MAGNET APPLICATIONS
A Bunting® Magnetics Company

Is There An Optimum Price-Performance Metric (2018)? Based On Magnet Volume

Material	Average $(BH)_{max}$ (MGOe)	Average Price ($/kg)	Density (g/cm³)	Average Price ($/m³ x 10³)	Price/Performance ($/m³ per MGOe x 10³)
NdFeB	45	70	7.5	525	12
Ferrite	3.5	6.4	5.0	32	9
Bonded NdFeB	8	91	5.1	464	58
SmCo	25	95	8.4	798	32
Alnico	7	56	7.3	409	58

MAGNET APPLICATIONS
A Bunting Magnetics Company

Niche And Mass Market Materials

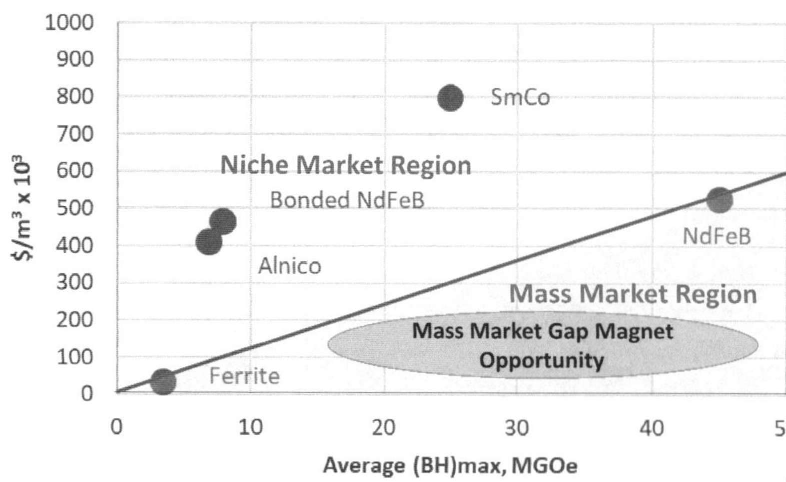

MAGNET APPLICATIONS
A Bunting Magnetics Company

Fe Is Really A Good Magnetic Element

Price/Performance Metric For Elements!

Element	Crystal Structure	Atomic Magnet Moment (μ_B)	Curie Temperature (°C)	Price per Atomic Moment ($/$\mu_B$ x10^{-26})
Fe	BCC	2.22	770	6
Co	HCP, FCC	1.72	1115	319
Ni	FCC	0.61	354	188
Gd	HCP	7.62	19	69
Dy	HCP	10.2	-185	623

MAGNET APPLICATIONS
A Bunting. Magnetics Company

Market Share Versus Fe Content

Fully Dense Magnet Materials

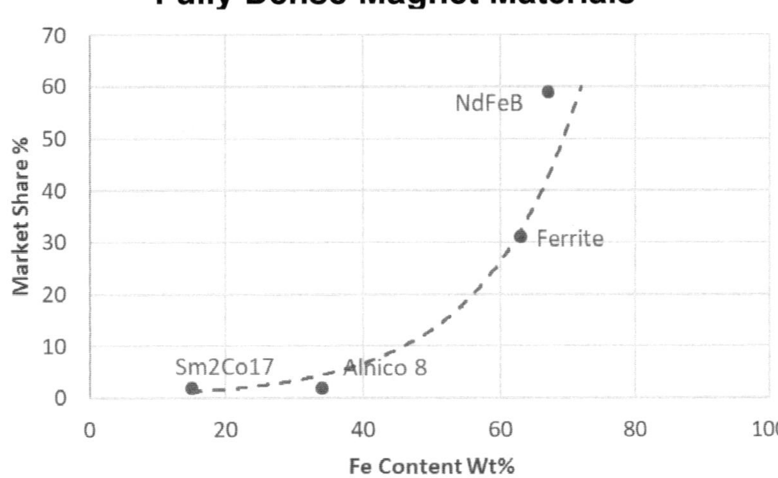

MAGNET APPLICATIONS
A Bunting. Magnetics Company

Next Mass Market PM Material Composition

My Prediction

- **Composition:**
  - $Fe_{(1-n)}(A,B,C,D........Z)_n$
  - Includes at least one other known element A,B,C,D.......Z
  - Where n = weight fraction
  - n << 0.4
  - In other words lots of Fe

MAGNET APPLICATIONS®
A Bunting® Magnetics Company

Thank you for your attention
Any Questions?

MAGNET APPLICATIONS®
A Bunting® Magnetics Company

Dr. John Ormerod
Senior Technology Advisor
Magnet Applications, Inc.
DuBois, Pennsylvania, USA
http://www.magnetapplications.com/
https://www.linkedin.com/in/jormerod/
+1 414 899 2859
John_ormerod@magnetus.com
John@jocllc.com

Rare Earth Magnets Alternates ?

Sim Narasimhan
P2PTechnologies
Moorestown; NJ
Sim.narasimhan@outlook.com

P2PTech

- ***P2P Technologies is LLC, registered in NJ, USA.***
- ***Intellectual Property strategies; Business Strategies***
- ***Guidance in material selection and processing of metal powders***
- ***Sales of Neo , rare earth, and Ferrite permanent magnets***
- ***Global Sales Marketing including India, China, Korea and USA***
- ***Seminars on Powder Metallurgy, Permanent magnets for beginners and advanced level***

P2PTech

BH_{max}; energy product defines the magnet volume in an application (Vol α 1/BHmax)

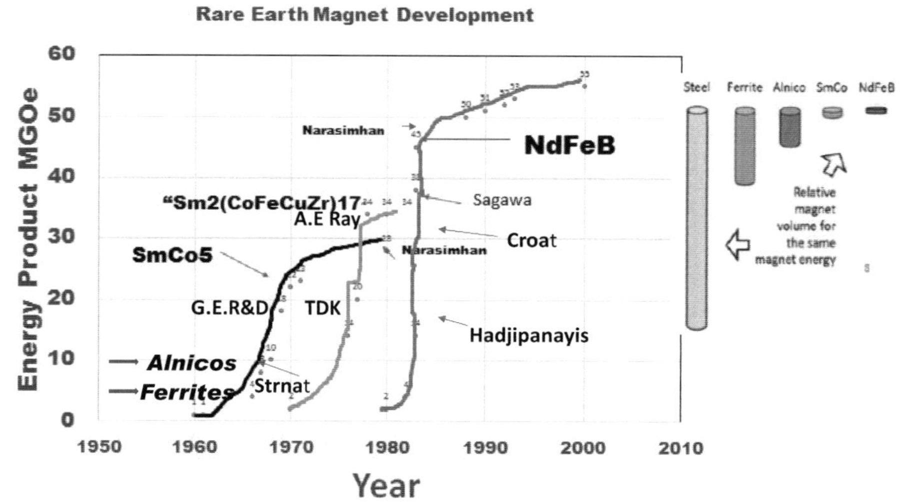

P2PTech

The Choice of NdFeB

- ***NdFeB magnets were introduced in 1984 to the market mainly focusing on Disk drive markets and other motors operating below 100C.***
- ***Nd was considered available in plenty compared to Sm and Cobalt price escalation were incentives for introducing NdFeB magnets***
- ***The need for Dy was recognized to increase the coercive for motors operating at 150C.***
- ***The low curie temperature of NdFeB was short coming then and now.***

Need for Alternates

- ***Resource concentration***
- China produces :
- 97%rare earth ores,
- 97% rare earth oxides
- 89%rare earth alloys,
- 75% of neodymium iron boron magnets

60% of samarium cobalt magnets.

Need for Alternates

- ***Heavy rare earths Dy, Tb are in short supply and is not abundant in all rare earth ore bodies.***
- ***Environmental issues ,government imposed quotas***
- ***Nd is not the most abundant of the rare earths***
- ***Electric vehicles and clean energy demands are increasing***

Options to reduce stress on material supply

- *Use more abundant rare earths*
- *New sources-Mine tailings*
- *Recycling*
- *Substitute materials*

Table 1. Overview of global clean technologies demand at 2016/20/25/30.

Year	Wind Power (MW)	Lighting			Electric Vehicles		Batteries	Catalytic Converter
		LFL	CFL	LED	Electric Cars	Electric Bicycles	NiMH Batteries	
		(Million Cps)			(Car)		(Battery)	(Million Cars)
2016	63,350	2142	2903	2675	750,000	35,000,000	580,125	95
2020	79,005	1604	1491	4828	2,140,0000	35,500,000	1,251,900	100
2025	76,810	1116	662	5874	7,953,375	36,200,000	715,803	111
2030	107,488	776	294	7146	29,530,323	37,000,000	2,657,729	117

minerals MDPI

Review

Global Potential of Rare Earth Resources and Rare Earth Demand from Clean Technologies

Baolu Zhou, Zhongxue Li * and Congcong Chen

Rare Earths in Hybrid Vehicles

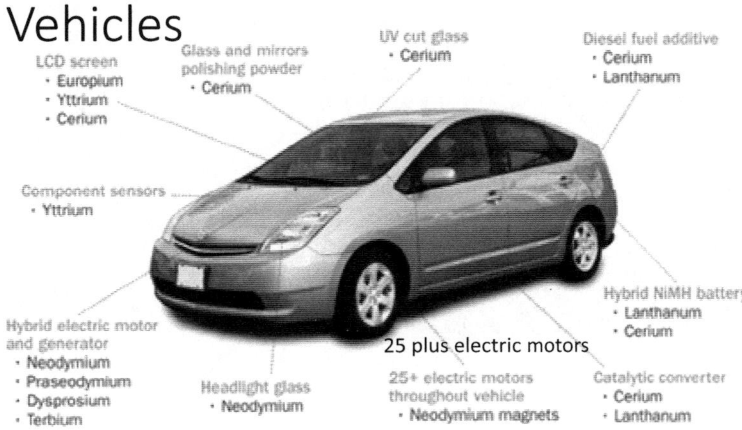

Science News 2011; Rare earths in Hybrid Vehicles

Average Volume of Rare earth for cleaner technologies

Table 2. The average volume of individual REE for clean technologies.

Application	La (kg)	Ce (kg)	Nd (kg)	Eu (kg)	Tb (kg)	Dy (kg)	Y (kg)
Wind turbines (/WM)			120			12	
Electric vehicles (/motor)			0.45			0.075	
Electric bicycles (/motor)			0.038			0.031	
NiMH battery (/battery)	0.61	0.86	0.255				
CFL (/bulb)	0.0000765	0.00018		0.0000405	0.000045		0.000558
LFL (/bulb)	0.000462	0.000137		0.0000945	0.000105		0.0013
LED (/bulb)				0.0000004			0.000005
Catalytic converter (/auto)		0.02					

Sources: US DOE [2], Ku et al. [38].

Rare Earth Global availability Extraction

Rare Earths

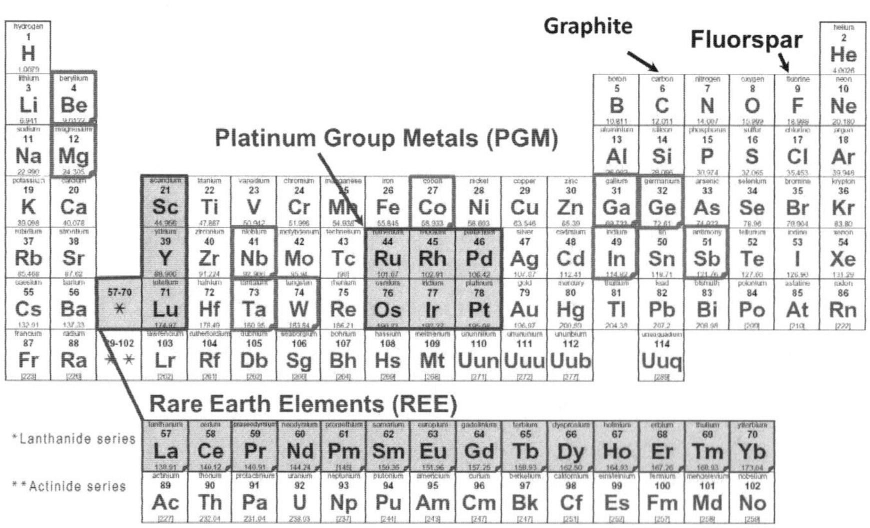

Global Distribution of Rare Earth Deposits

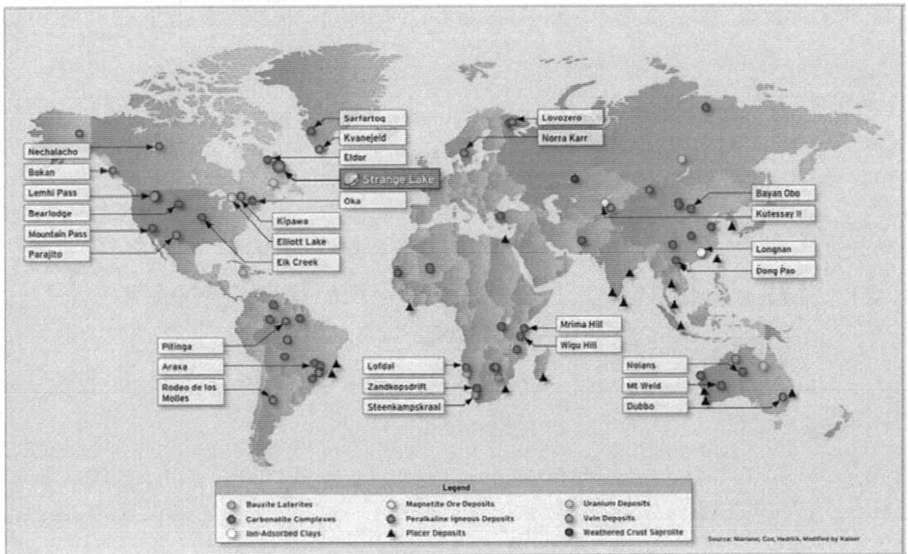

Global Rare Earth Deposits
175 deposits 59 are code complaint

Table S1. The global rare earth deposits.

Deposit	Country	Mineral	Ore (Mt)	REO (%)	REO (Mt)	References
Brockman	Australia	bertrandite, bastnaesite	41.4	0.21%	0.086	[1]
Browns Range	Australia	xenotime	8.98	0.63%	0.056	[2,3]
Charley Creek (JV)	Australia	monazite, xenotime	805.3	0.03%	0.235	[4]
Corkwood Yard	Australia	xenotime	0.359	0.00%	0.000	[5]
Crown	Australia	NA	37.7	1.16%	0.437	[6]
Cummins Range	Australia	monazite	4.9	1.74%	0.085	[7]
Dubbo	Australia	eudialyte, bastnasite	73.2	0.75%	0.549	[8]
John Galt	Australia	xenotime	0.051	0.35%	0.000	[5]
Korella	Australia	xenotime	13.72	0.07%	0.009	[5]
Mary Kathleen	Australia	apatite, titanite, garnet	5.5	6.40%	0.352	[5]
Milo	Australia	IOCG	176	0.06%	0.109	[9]
Mt Weld CLD	Australia	monazite, churchite	15	8.80%	1.319	[10]
Mt Weld Duncan	Australia	monazite, churchite	8.2	4.70%	0.385	[10]
Narraburra	Australia	monazite	73	0.03%	0.023	[11]
Nolans Bore	Australia	fluorapatite, allanite	56	2.60%	1.456	[12]
Olympic Dam	Australia	monasite, bastnasite	10400	0.42%	43.68	[13]
Swan	Australia	NA	13.7	1.51%	0.206	[14]
Yangibana	Australia	monazite	12.362	1.10%	0.135	[1]
Araxá	Brazil	monazite	28.28	4.22%	1.193	[15]
Catalão I	Brazil	monazite	119	5.50%	6.545	[16]
Catalão II	Brazil	REE-phosphates	25	0.98%	0.245	[17]
Poços de Caldas	Brazil	bastnaesite	7	2.89%	0.202	[17]
Serra Verde	Brazil	monazite, xenotime	911	0.00%	1.093	[18]
Morro dos Seis Lagos	Brazil	monazite	2900	1.50%	43.5	[19]
Tapira	Brazil	anatase, hydroxlapatite	150	0.03%	0.045	[20]
Barra do Itapirapuã	Brazil	bastnaesite	44.8	0.70%	0.313	[17]
Pitinga	Brazil	xenotime, gargarinite	164	0.00%	0.246	[19]
Guarapari	Brazil	monazite	0.00095	60.04%	0.001	[20]
Prado	Brazil	monazite	0.0045	19.98%	0.001	[20]
Gakara	Burundi	bastnaesite, monazite	0.2565	54.30%	0.139	[21]
Karonge	Burundi	bastnasite, monazite	0.06	1.59%	0.001	[20]
Kasagwe	Burundi	bastnasite	0.067	1.50%	0.001	[20]
Atlin-Ruffner	Canada	allanite	0.036	2.29%	0.001	[20]
Ashram Main	Canada	monazite, bastnaesite	249.07	1.89%	4.707	[22]
Ashram MHREO	Canada	monazite, bastnaesite	9.34	1.61%	0.150	[22]
Buckton	Canada	ionic clay	3433.5	0.03%	1.030	[23]
Buckton South	Canada	ionic clay	496.7	0.03%	0.149	[23]
Clay-Howells	Canada	monazite, aptite, silicate	8.477	0.73%	0.061	[24]
Eco Ridge	Canada	monazite	86.6	0.11%	0.098	[25]
Elliot Lake	Canada	brannerite, monzite	51.60	0.19%	0.098	[26]
Foxtrot	Canada	allanite, fergusonite	9.35	1.11%	0.103	[27]
Grande-Vallée	Canada	ionic clay	1040	0.06%	0.624	[28]
Hoidas Lake	Canada	allanite	4.823	1.64%	0.079	[29]

Extraction of rare earth

- *Geology*
- *Grade*
- *Tonnage available*
- *Processing Technologies*
- *Costs*
- *Environmental issues*

Challenges in Rare earth extraction from Ores

- *Rare earths are not concentrated in economic viable quantities*
- *Have similar Ionic radii making it to difficult to separate*
- *Occurs along with similar ionic radii Ca^{2+} ,Th^{4+} , U^{4+} creating a big environmental issues, mine tailings*
- *One ton of rare earth creates 12,000tons of waste water and 2,000 tons mine tailings*

Location	Mountain pass, CA China	Australia, Fl Brazil, China	China, Malyasia	China
Ore type	Bastnasite	Monazite	Xenotime	Laterite
La	23-33%	21-23%		1.82-43%
Ce	49-50%	43-45%		0.4-2.4%
Pr	4.3-6.2%	5-6%		0.7-9.0%
Nd	12-18%	17-18%		3.0-31.7%
Sm	0.8	3-4.9%		2.8-3.9%
Gd			3.5-5.0%	3.0-6.9%
Tb			0.9-1.2%	0-1.3%
Dy			8.3-9.1%	0-6.7%
Ho			2-2.6%	0-1.6%
Er			5.0-6.4%	0-4.9%
Tu			1-1.1%	0-0.7%
Yb			6-6.8%	0.3-2.5%

Light rare earths(La,Ce) are more abundant

Location	*Mountain pass, CA China*	*Australia, Fl Brazil, China*	*China, Malyasia*	*China*	*Saturation Induction of R2Fe14B phase T*	*Preferred Direction of Magnetization At RT*
Ore type	*Bastnasite*	*Monazite*	*Xenotime*	*Laterite*		
Y	*trace*	*1.4-2.4%*	*59-61%*	*8-65%*	*1.3222*	*C-axis*
La	*23-33%*	*21-23%*	*1.24%*	*1.82-43%*	*1.271*	-
Ce	*49-50%*	*43-45%*	*3.13%*	*0.4-2.4%*	*1.1438*	*C-axis*
Pr	*4.3-6.2%*	*5-6%*	*0.5%*	*0.7-9.0%*	*1.6*	*C-axis*
Nd	*12-18%*	*17-18%*	*1.6-3.5%*	*3.0-31.7%*	*1.61*	*C-axis**
Sm	*0.8*	*3-4.9%*	*1.1-2.2%*	*2.8-3.9%*	*1.4295*	*Plane*
Gd			*3.5-5.0%*	*3.0-6.9%*	*0.8037*	*C-axis*
Tb			*0.9-1.2%*	*0-1.3%*	*0.6359*	*C-axis*
Dy			*8.3-9.1%*	*0-6.7%*	*0.6381*	*C-axis*
Ho			*2-2.6%*	*0-1.6%*	*0.7532*	*C-axis**
Er			*5.0-6.4%*	*0-4.9%*	*0.8456*	*C-axis**
Tu			*1-1.1%*	*0-0.7%*	*1.0485*	*C-axis**
Yb			*6-6.8%*	*0.3-2.5%*	-	-
La+Ce	*72-83%*	*64-68%*				
Nd+Pr	*16-24%*	*22-24%*				
Dy			*8.3-9.1%*			

- At temperatures below -120C preferred direction changes away from C-axis

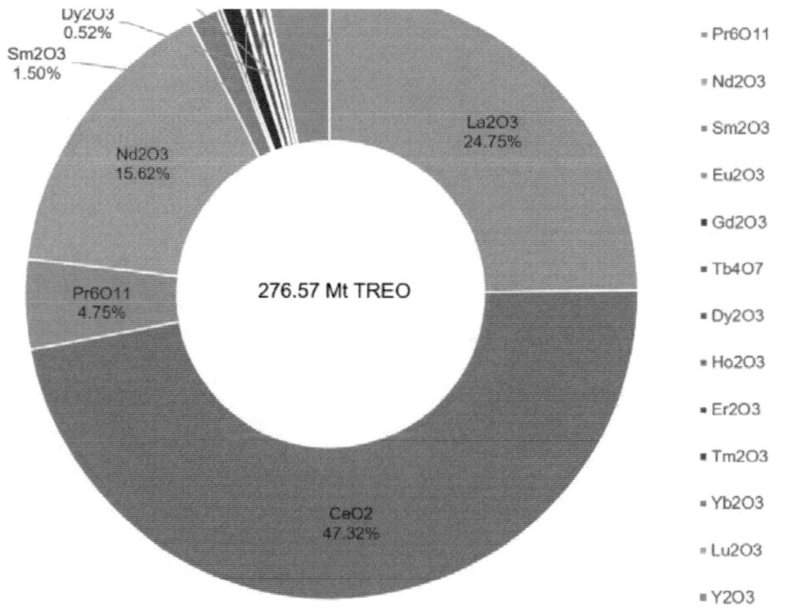

Figure 6. Code-compliant rare earth resources for 59 advanced-stage REE deposits (as of January 2017).

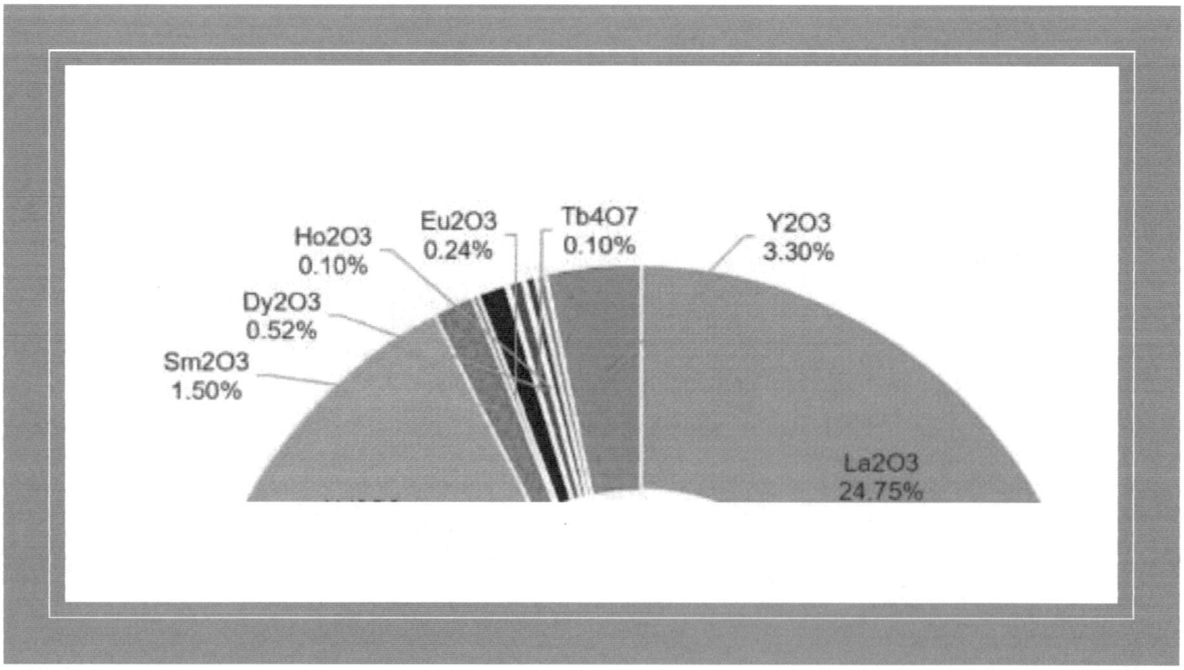

Global production is mainly in China(85%) and Australia(10%)

178 deposits widely distributed in the world totaling 478 megaton REO

58 of these deposits exceeded 0.1megaton of REO

By 2030 clean technologies would need 51.9 kilotons of ReO;Nd75%(15% of global deposits); Dy9%(0.52% of global deposits)

Using more abundant rare earths

Ce Containing Magnets

Magnet	Composition (wt%)	Approach	Hci(Koe)	Br(KG)	BHMax (MGOe)	Hk/ Hci %	P(g/cm3)
Ce=0	(PrNd)30.5FeBalM1.0B1.0	SMP	13.8	14.1	48.7	97.4	7.55
Ce=27	[(PrNd)0.73Ce0.27]30.5Fe balM1.0B1.0	SMP	10.4	12.8	39.0	94.3	7.56
Ce=27	[(PrNd)0.73Ce0.27]30.5Fe balM1.0B1.0	BMP	11.4	13.0	41.1	97.7	7.57
Ce=36	[(PrNd)0.64Ce0.36]30.5Fe balM1,0B1.0	BMP	10.3	12.7	38.8	96.4	7.57
Ce=45	[(PrNd)0.55Ce0.45]30.5Fe balM1.0B1.0	BMP	9.0	12.4	36.7	94.2	7.57

Yujing Zhang[a], Tianyu Ma[a,*], Jiaying Jin[a], Jiangtao Li[a], Chen Wu[a], Baogen Shen[b], Mi Yan[a,*]

Acta Materialia 128 (2017) 22–30

SMP and BMP magnets with Ce

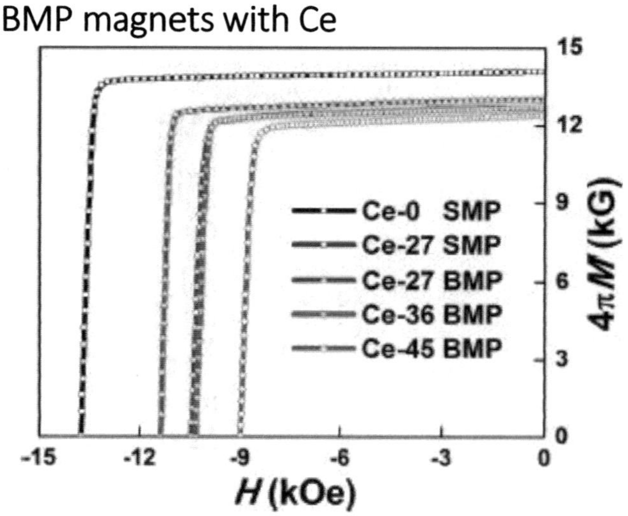

[(PrNd)0.5Ce0.5]30.5FeBal M1.0B1.0;blended with Ce=0...(PrNd)30.5FeBalM1.0B1.0 various proportions

Yujing Zhang[a], Tianyu Ma[a,*], Jiaying Jin[a], Jiangtao Li[a], Chen Wu[a], Baogen Shen[b] Mi Yan[a,*]

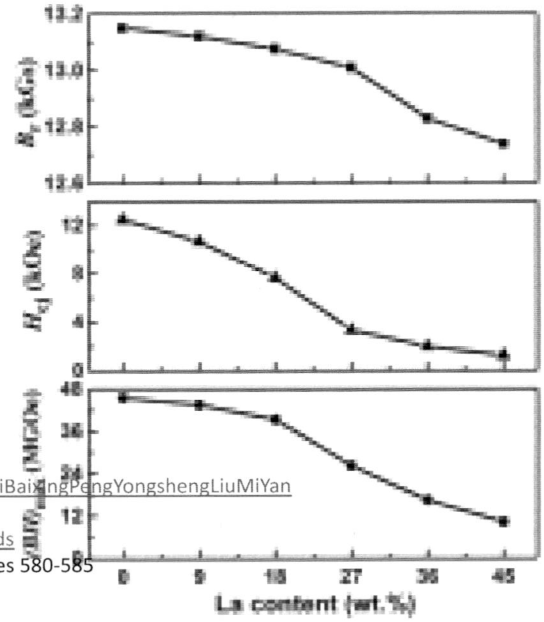

JiayingJinZhengWangGuohuaBaiBaixingPengYongshengLiuMiYan

Journal of Alloys and Compounds
Volume 749, 15 June 2018, Pages 580-585

Misch Metal:46-55wt%Ce,,20-30 w%tLa,13-20 wt% Nd,4-7wt% Pr, other rare earths 1to3 wt%

RongshunLai[ab]RenjieChen[ab]WenzongYin[ab]XuTang[ab]ZexuanWang[ab]ChaoxiangJin[a]DonLee[c]AruYan[ab]

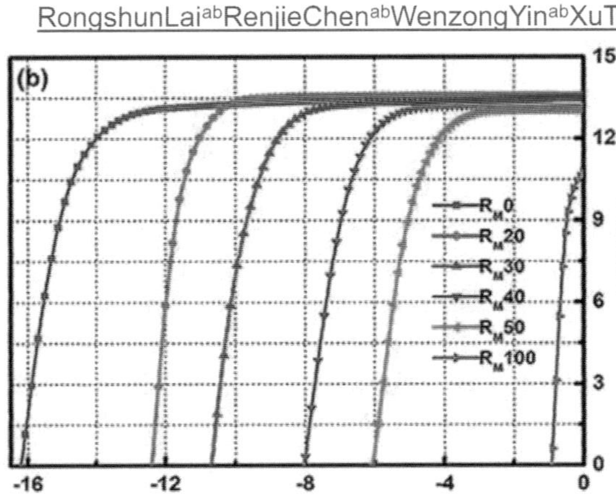

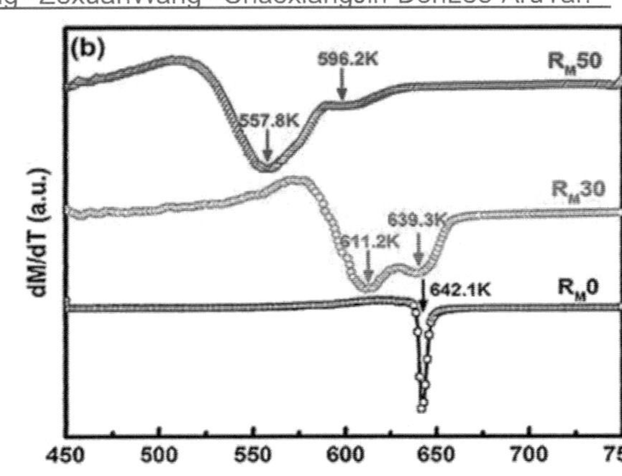

Remanence of 13.46 kGs and maximum energy product of 43.5 MGOe was achieved with 30 wt% misch-metal substitution.

Toyota Reduced Rare earth Technology

- Reduce Nd with more abundant La, Ce .
- Refine the grain size to compensate for coercive loss by the replacement ,finer grain higher coercive force.
- Replace iron with Cobalt ;compensate loss in coercive force with Al or other addition.

1. Grain refinement of magnet
2. Two-layered high-performance grain surface
3. Specific alloying ratio of lanthanum and cerium

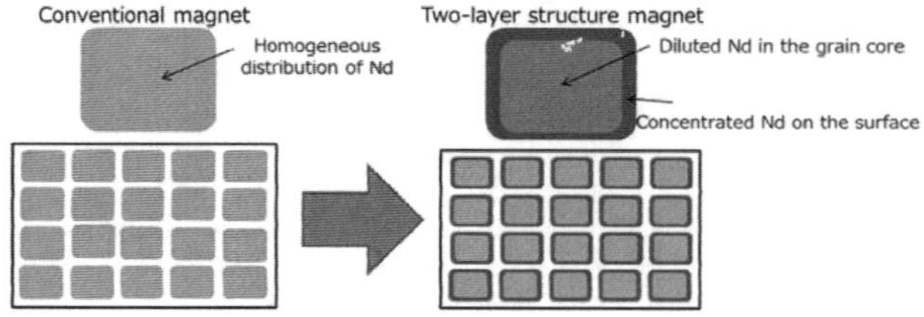

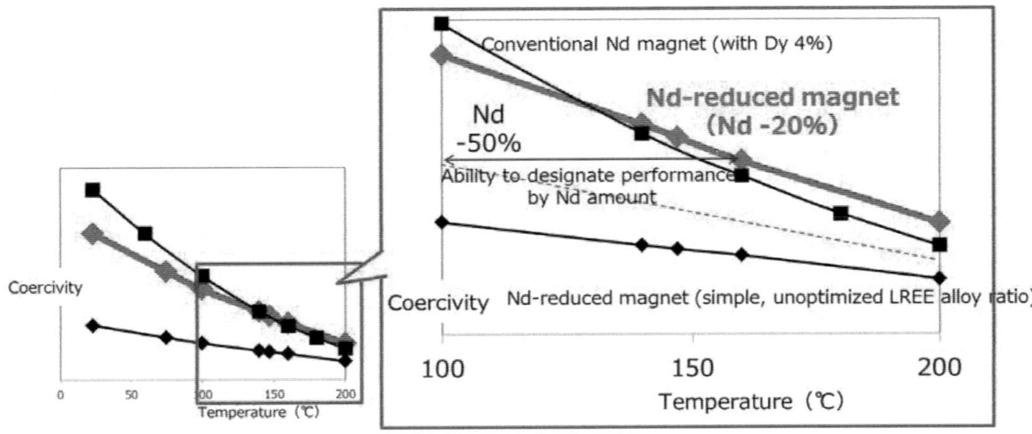

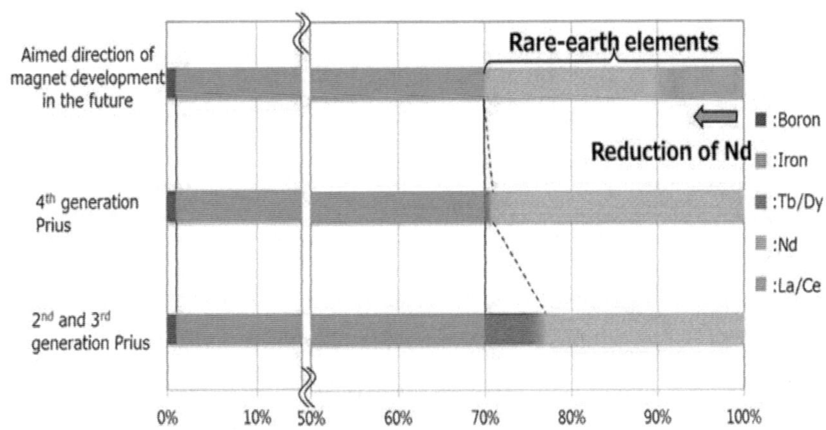

Toyota Develops New Magnet for Electric Motors Aiming to Reduce Use of Critical Rare-Earth Element by up to 50%

Heavy Rare Earth Dy issues

Anisotropy field for Dy2Fe14B is 15T, Nd2Fe14B is 6T

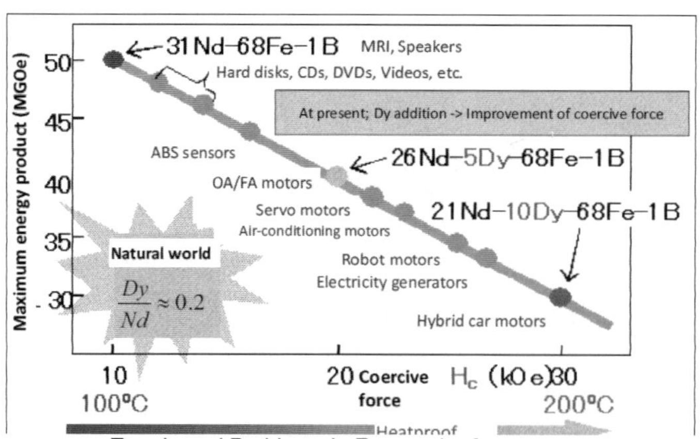

Sumio Kozawa.
Tohuku Univ

Trends and Problems in Research of
Permanent Magnets for Motors
– Addressing Scarcity Problem of Rare Earth Elements –

Neo Magnets containing Heavy rare earth temp.Dependence

Careful selection of magnet size to ensure B/H to be above 0.7is desired for temperature excursion up to 140C

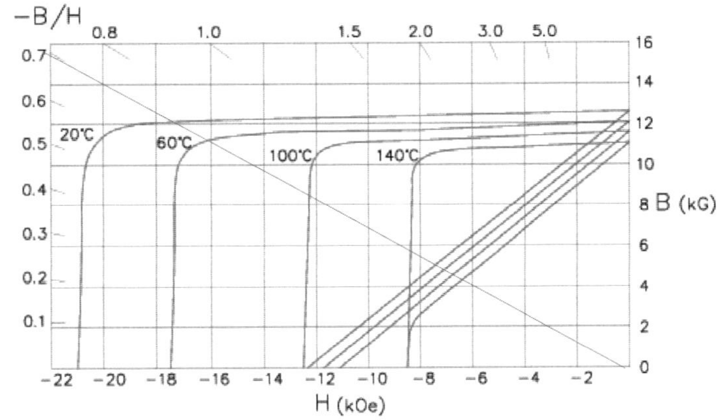

P2PTech

Reducing the Heavy Rare earth

- **Heavy rare earth such as Dy is expensive, typically $400/kg for dysprosium oxide compared to $25/kg for neodymium oxide**
- **Coercive force(magnetization reversal) in the neo magnets is by domain pinning in the grain boundary phase. If the grain boundary phase is enriched with Dy higher coercive force will be obtained.**
- **In the newly developed lower amount of heavy rare earth grades, after sintering a paste of Dy containing fluoride is applied on the magnets and heated to lower than sintering temperature to diffuse Dy in to the grain boundary phase .Dy does not diffuse into interior of the grain due to the lower temperature employed for diffusion process**
- **Diffusion process as above will use one third of Dy compared to prealloyed material with equivalent coercive force.**

Alloy design for Dyfree MAGFINE powder

Alloy design

ttype	compsotion(wt%)	(BH)max	iHc	Br
MF-15P	Nd27.5FeNbB+3%NdCuAl	43MGOe	15 kOe	13.8kG
MF-18P	Nd27.5FeNbB+6%NdCuAl	38MGOe	18 kOe	12.8kG

comparison of magnetic properties with various magnets

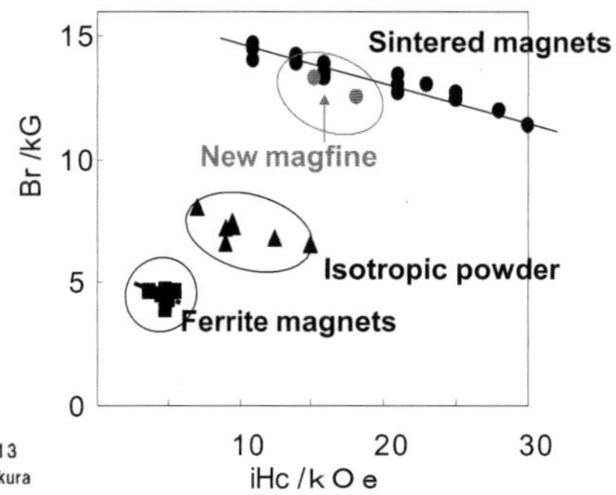

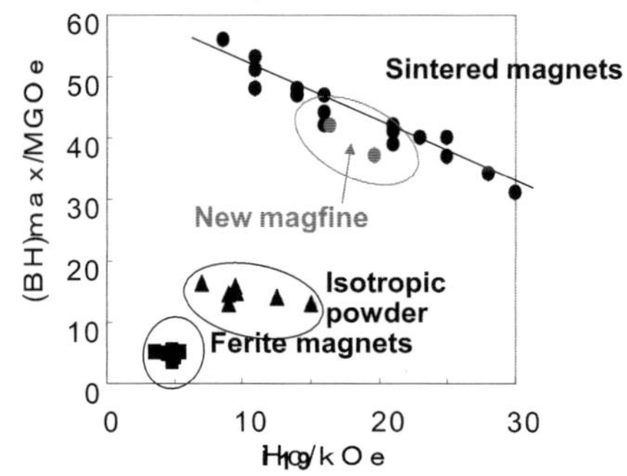

Dec. 6th . 2013
Yoshinobu Honkura
Adviser of Aichi Steel Corp.
Vice President of Magnetic Society of Japan

New Sources for Rare earths

- Coal Mine tailings- W. Virginia and others,45000tons of REE per year
- Bauxite Mines-- Jamaica working with Japan
- Cassiterite --Indonesia and others,10000 tons of minerals
- US Geological survey using enviornmentally friendly laser ablation technology to detect for rare earths.

New Sources for Rare earths

- ***The new owner of the Mountain Pass rare earths mine in California is MP Mine Operations LLC – an American-led consortium, with Chinese rare earths miner Leshan Shenghe Rare Earth Co. holding a non-voting minority interest.***
- ***Japanese companies are already mining rare-earth mineral deposits in Kazakhstan, India and Australia, as well as in Vietnam.***

New Sources for Rare earths

- ***researchers at the University of Tokyo reported at a conference in Tokyo in June that they have discovered seafloor sediments in Japanese waters that contain an estimated 6.8 million tonnes of rare-earth elements. And on 4 July, India's science minister Ashwani Kumar announced that the country planned to mine rare-earth minerals from the sea bed of the Central Indian Ocean Basin, using up to four specially commissioned ships.***
- ***The Alaska Industrial Development and Export Authority (AIDEA) has received legislative authority from the Alaska Legislature for a USD $145 million financing package for the future development of the Bokan Mine and Processing facilities. A significant portion of this proposed financing is intended for the development of a proximal rare earth element separation facility, and our recommendation will be for the construction of this component to be placed in Ketchikan, just 50 km Northeast of Bokan and accessible via marine transport."***
- ***Recycling***

Recycling rare earths

Table 2. The average volume of individual REE for clean technologies.

Application	La (kg)	Ce (kg)	Nd (kg)	Eu (kg)	Tb (kg)	Dy (kg)	Y (kg)
Wind turbines (/WM)			120			12	
Electric vehicles (/motor)			0.45			0.075	
Electric bicycles (/motor)			0.038			0.031	
NiMH battery (/battery)	0.61	0.86	0.255				
CFL (/bulb)	0.0000765	0.00018		0.0000405	0.000045		0.000558
LFL (/bulb)	0.000462	0.000137		0.0000945	0.000105		0.0013
LED (/bulb)				0.0000004			0.000005
Catalytic converter (/auto)		0.02					

Sources: US DOE [2], Ku et al. [38].

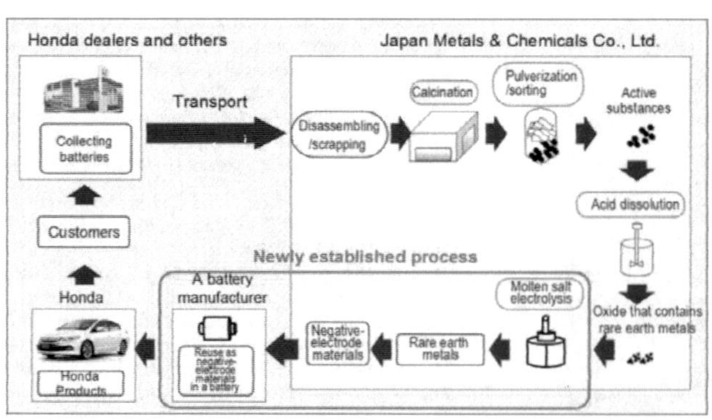

(Figure 4 (Honda Corporate, 2013))

Rare Earth Industry Supply Alternatives
ENVS 190A Thesis
Megan Emslander
MIT

Recycling

- University of Pennsylvania, Larry jones, H2TriNOX LRE separation
- Ames lab,Ryan Ott, Molten Mg to separate rare earths
- Ames lab water based solvent
- Preston Bryant, CEO of Momentum Technologies, Dallas, His company, working together with the Materials Science and Technology Division of the Oak Ridge National Laboratory (ORNL) in Tennessee, developed a way to recover 97 percent of the rare-earth materials from the magnets found in hard drives and cellphones.

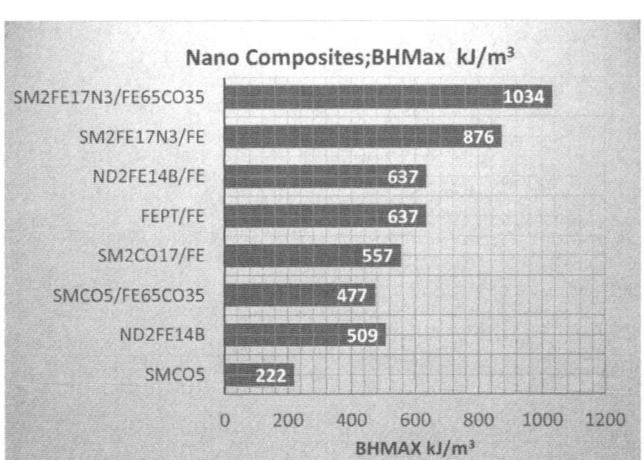

Nano Phase soft magnetic material in red

HAF=HighAnisotropy Ferromagnetic material

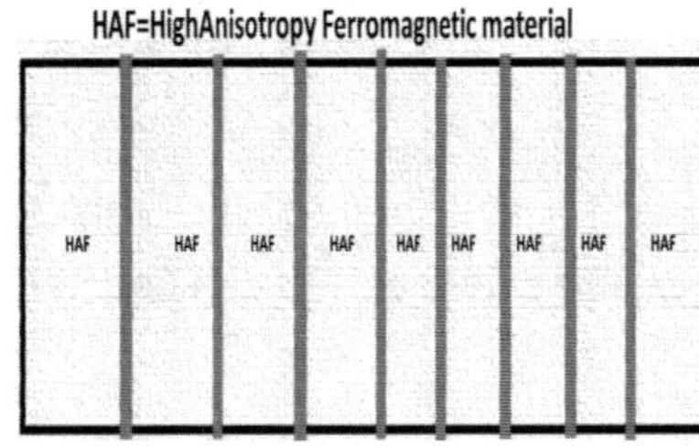

Ajay Misra 8th Annual CAFÉ Electric aircraft symposium; April 25-26, Santa Rosa, California,2014

Research Frontiers

Temp. Dependence of Neo type magnets

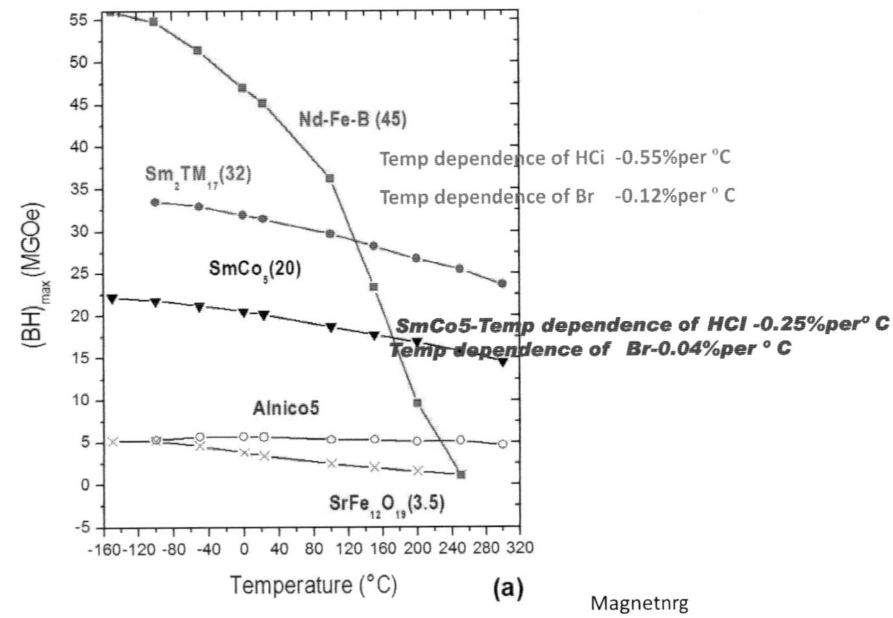

Magnetnrg

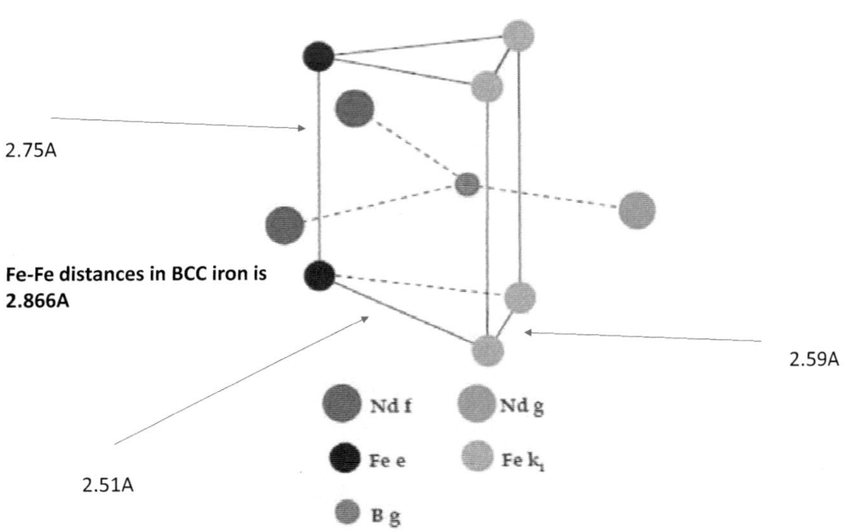

Figure 2 — Trigonal prism containing a boron atom in the $Nd_2Fe_{14}B$ structure. Distances between the B(*g*) atom and its nearest neighbors are B-Fe(k_1) = 2.09 Å, B-Fe(e) = 2.14 Å, B-Nd(*g*) = 2.86 Å, and B-Nd(*f*) = 3.34 Å. The vertical edge lengths are Fe(e) - Fe(e) = 2.75 Å, Fe(k_1) - Fe(k_1) = 3.12 Å. Distances in the triangular faces are Fe(e) - Fe(k_1) = 2.51 Å, Fe(k_1) - Fe(k_1) = 2.59 Å

Jan Herbst et.al

Bethe Slater curve

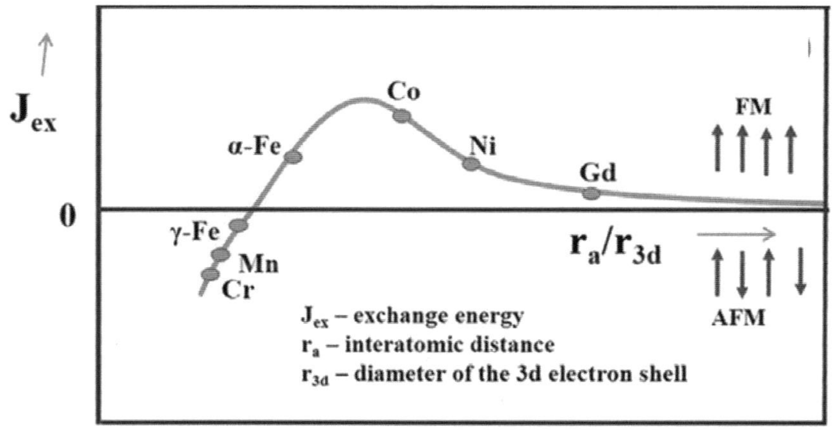

Improving temp. dependence of Br

Br temp dependence can be improved by adding Cobalt to increase the curie temperature ; Cobalt reduces the coercive force;

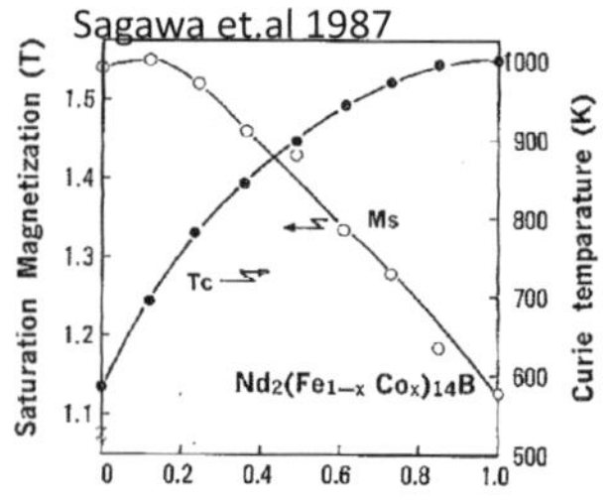

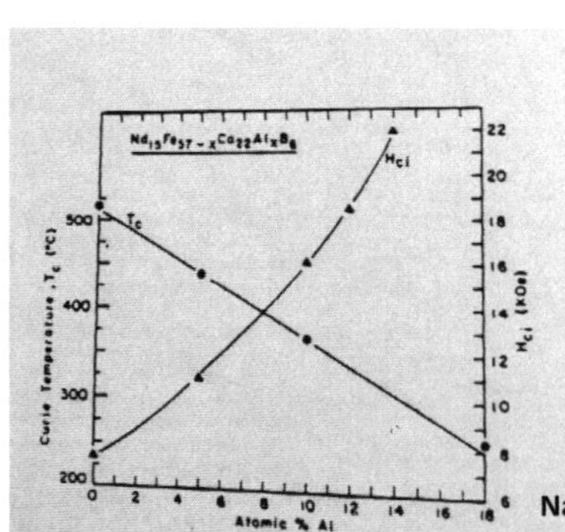

NdFeB temp Coeff -0.12%
30%Cobalt replacing Nd
Temp coeff -0.091%
Al=2;Temp coeff -0.097%
Al=6;Temp coeff -0.111%

Narasimhan and Ma;1986

Potential Permanent magnet Metals

Element	3d /4f electrons	Magnetic moment μB/atom
Mn	5(3d)	3.6
Fe	6(3d)	2.6
Co	7(3d)	1.6
Ni	8(3d)	0,6
La	0(4f)	0
Ce	1(4f)	2.54
Pr	2(4f)	3.58
Nd	3(4f)	3.62
Sm	5(4f)	0.85
Gd	7(4f)	7.94
Tb	8(4f)	9.72
Dy	9(4f)	10.65
Ho	10(4f)	10.6
Er	11(4f)	9.58
Tm	12(4f)	7.56
Yb	13(4f)	4.54

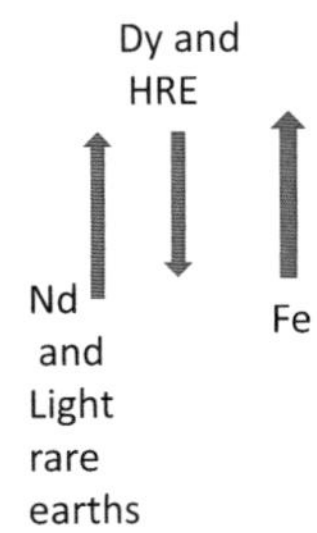

Heavy rare earths reduce the maximum induction achievable when alloyed with Fe,Co

2:14:1 Structure ;Nd2Fe14B

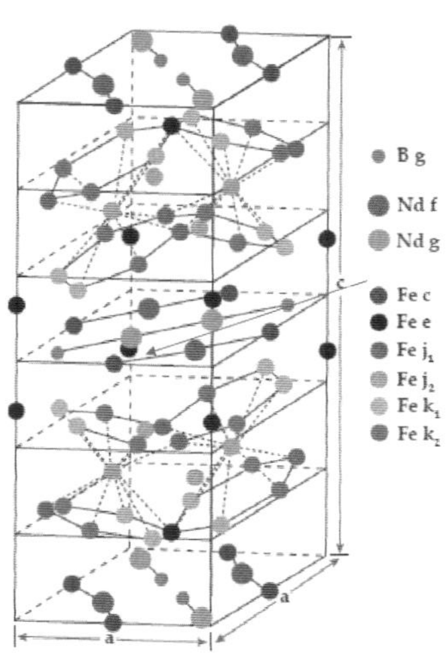

Figure 1 — Unit cell of $Nd_2Fe_{14}B$ ($P4_2/mnm$ space group). The c/a ratio in the figure is exaggerated to emphasize the puckering of the hexagonal iron nets.

Fe-Fe(j2)bond lengths range from 2.6 to2.8Å comparable to R2Fe17

Iron-Iron distances are smaller than in BCC iron leading to lower curie temperature

Also Iron sublattice has a strong anisotropy

Can Nd be replaced in this structure by non rare earth?

By Jan F. Herbst, John J. Croat, and Frederick E. Pinkerton, Physics Department, General Motors Research Laboratories, Warren, MI 48090-9055 and W.B. Yelon, University of Missouri Research Reactor, University of Missouri, Columbia, Missouri, 65201

Conclusions

- Number of ways are being explored to mitigate Rare earth supply
- Use of light rare earths like Ce La which are abundant in multiple ore bodies offer a great promise
- Toyota approach of reducing Neodymium using fine grain .Aichi by HDDR process and grain boundary diffusion of NdCuAl offer very good promise.
- Recycling of rare earth magnets will offer a longer term solution in about 10 years.

Conclusions

- Number of new are earth extraction plants globally offer a very good promise.
- Ideas are suggested for the exploration of newer magnets
- Current rare earth supply can sustain for all identified green technologies until 2030

Reducing the Rare-Earth Content of Strong Permanent Magnets

January 23, 2019

David Parker

Chevrolet Bolt EV (Permanent magnet motor)

OAK RIDGE NATIONAL LABORATORY
MANAGED BY UT-BATTELLE FOR THE DEPARTMENT OF ENERGY

Outline of Talk

- Technological and Economic Background
- Magnetic Materials Using **Abundant** Rare-Earths Ce and La ($LaCeCo_{16}Ti$, $CeCo_5$, $SmCeFe_{17}N_3$)
- Magnetic Materials Using **No** Rare Earths (Fe_3Sn, HfMnP, ZrMnP, L10 FeNi)
- Outlook and Summary

CMI | Critical Materials Institute

OAK RIDGE National Laboratory

What is the Critical Materials Institute?

A U.S. DOE-funded consortium of National Labs, universities, and Industry, founded in 2013 to "**assure supply chains** of materials critical to clean energy technologies, **enable innovation** in U.S. manufacturing and **enhance U.S. energy security**".

Specific interest here is to **develop substitutes** for rare-earth magnets such as $Nd_2Fe_{14}B$ and $SmCo_5$.

CMI | Critical Materials Institute

OAK RIDGE National Laboratory

Technological Background

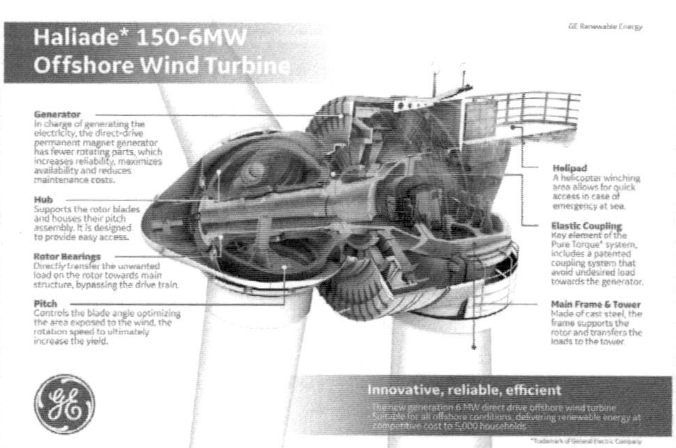

Direct-drive **permanent magnet** wind turbine generator (GE)

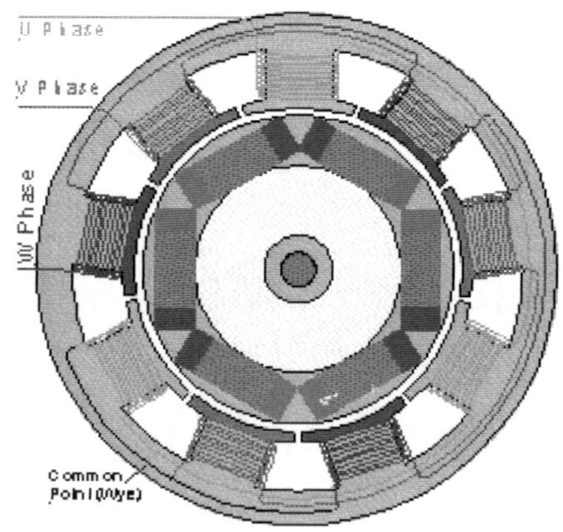

Early generation **Toyota Prius** permanent magnet motor

Many **clean energy technologies** (e.g. hybrid vehicle, wind turbines) employ **strong permanent magnets**, which presently require rare-earth materials (**Nd, Sm**) **whose supply remains uncertain**.

New High Performance Magnets

Objective for High Performance Magnets:

- Discover new, critical rare-earth poor ferromagnetic materials. Need following intrinsic properties:
  $M_{Saturation} > 1$ Tesla
  $T_{Curie} > 500$ K
  $H_{Anisotropy} > 3\ M_S$

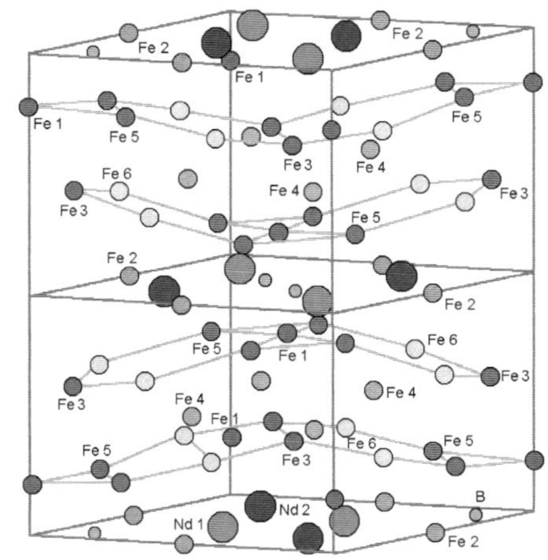

$Nd_2Fe_{14}B$ structure

These properties generally calculable from 1st principles. The anisotropy field is related to the magnetic anisotropy (MAE) – following slide.

1st Principles Calculation of Magnetic Anisotropy (MAE) and Anisotropy Field

- MAE is relativistic effect, so largest for heavy atoms ("v_{atomic}" ~ Zc/137). MAE is usually a strongly increasing function of atomic number and SO constant $\lambda \sim Z^4$.

Spin orbit λ values:

Element	λ (eV)
Fe	0.03
Mo	0.13
Nd	0.5
W	1
U	2

- MAE is quantified by anisotropy constant K_1 - the energy difference associated with the spin orientation changing.

The anisotropy field H_A is given as $\mu_0 H_A = 2\ \mu_0 K_1/M_s$. Typically after long hard experimental effort, one attains coercivities ~ 30% of H_A.

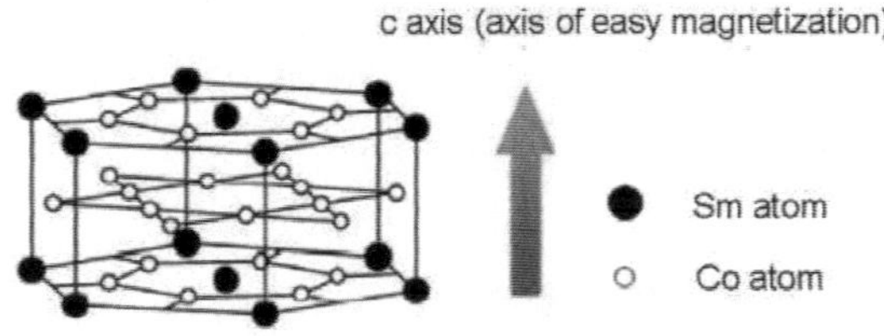

$SmCo_5$ crystal structure

Economic and Mineral Background

La and Ce generally **much less costly** (roughly factor of **10**) than "critical" RE elements such as Nd, Dy.

Technical question is:

Can magnets use **these elements**, rather than Nd, Sm, Dy, to generate magnetic anisotropy?

A tall order, given that Ce and La have **1 and 0 *4f*** electrons, respectively, while Nd and Sm have **4 and 6.**

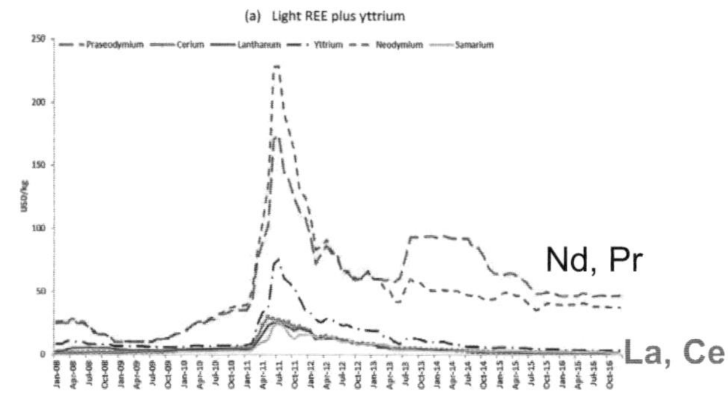

Rare Earth Prices, 2008 – 2016

Source: V. Fernandez, Energy Resources, 2017

Economic and Mineral Background

In trying to reduce the critical rare earths (Nd, Dy, "Sm") in magnets, **must note**:

Not all rare-earths are created equal.

In most RE mines, Mountain Pass especially, **La and Ce** are primary RE element content.

Would be highly beneficial to use these, rather than Nd/Dy/Sm, to generate magnetic anisotropy. **Will present several examples suggesting that we can.**

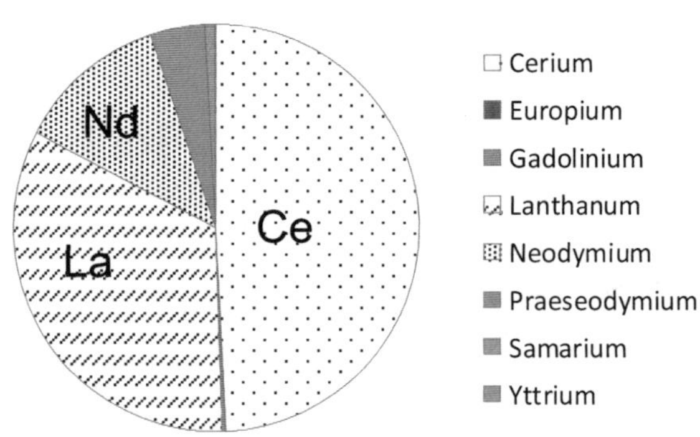

Mountain Pass (California) ore rare-earth element composition

N. Haque et al, Resources **3**, 614 (2014).

La – Ce Usage Example 1: $La_xCe_{2-x}Co_{16}Ti$

"2-17" phase Ce_2Co_{17} (cf. Sm_2Co_{17}) well-known with **M_s ~ 11 kG, T_c ~ 1000 K**, but too low magnetic anisotropy (**H_A ~ 10 kOe**).

2-17 phase **does not form** with pure La, but $La_2Co_{16}Ti$ phase **does.**

Have investigated effects of Cerium substitution on this alloy.

In general, **"the more the merrier"** with magnetic anisotropy – adding elements **often increases H_A**, and often helps with grain boundary phases (cf. **$Sm_2CuFeZrCo_{17}$** magnets).

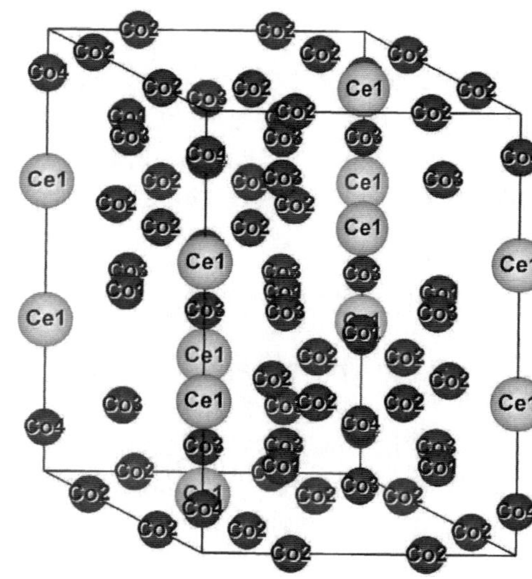

Ce_2Co_{17} structure

La – Ce Usage Example 1: $La_xCe_{2-x}Co_{16}Ti$

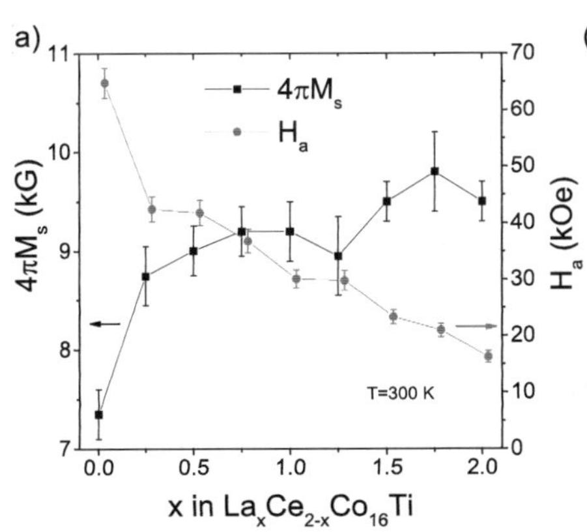

300 K Magnetization (black, left) and anisotropy field (red, right).

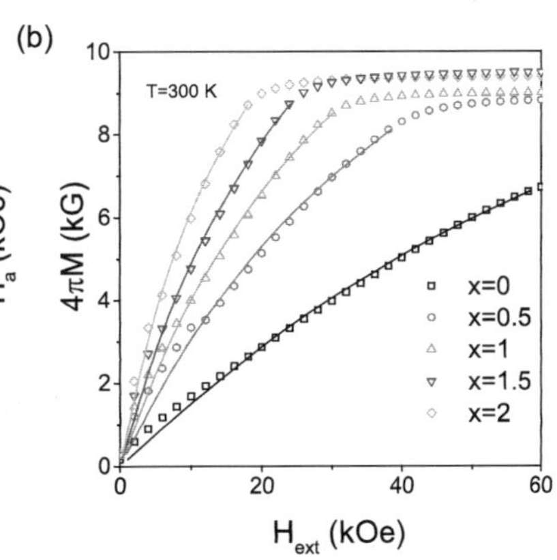

300 K field sweeps for several x

Experimental work (B.S. Conner et al, J. All. Comp. 2017) finds **high H_A = 65 kOe** for x=0, but **high M_s ~ 10 kG** for x near 2. "Rule of thumb" for possible high performance magnet is **H_A >= 3 M_s**, suggests range around x = 1 (**M_s = 9300 kG, H_A= 30 kOe**) is optimal in this alloy system. **BH_{max}** estimates on next slide.

La-Ce usage material 1: $La_xCe_{2-x}Co_{16}Ti$

- Achievement

$La_xCe_{2-x}Co_{16}Ti$ is potential high performance magnet (22 MG-Oe) with high magnetization (0.8 -1 Tesla @ 300 K), Curie temperatures above 650 K, and uniaxial anisotropy with anisotropy fields as high as 6 Tesla.

- Significance and Impact:

NO Critical RE. These materials could potentially fill in the ten-fold performance gap between RE magnets and non-RE magnets; also monetize production of Ce, La (excess products at Mountain Pass).

Current Co price: \$40/kilo (cf. Coey \$50/kilo price point for 200 kJ/m^3 magnet)

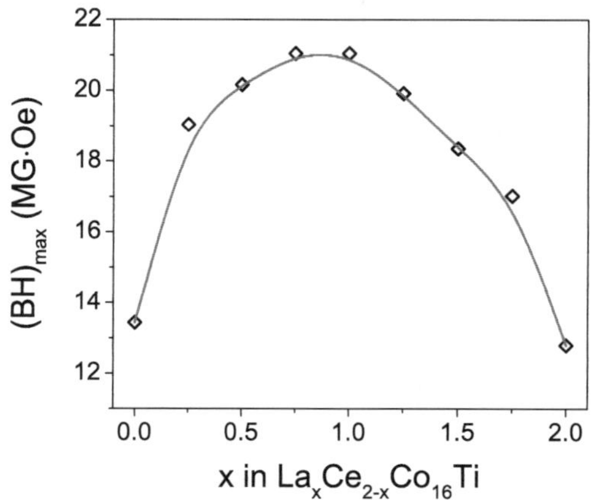

Curve of theoretical BH_{max} calculated from experimental data of B. Conner.

B. Conner et al, J. All. Comp. (2017)

CMI | Critical Materials Institute — THE Ames Lab — OAK RIDGE National Laboratory

Outlook: $La_xCe_{2-x}Co_{16}Ti$

Although potential BH_{max} of ~ 22 MG-Oe is a little low for mainly Co-based magnet, further optimization by adding Fe could easily push this higher (not yet studied by CMI) and reduce cost.

Two main technical questions to address in this light:

-competing phases in synthesis (5 component alloy)
-how would adding Fe affect magnetic anisotropy?

Finally, likely possible to bump up magnetic anisotropy by adding small amount of more critical RE such as Sm, Nd.

CMI | Critical Materials Institute — THE Ames Lab — OAK RIDGE National Laboratory

La – Ce Usage Example 2: Cu and Fe-alloyed $CeCo_5$

$CeCo_5$ (and $LaCo_5$) well-known as high-anisotropy (H_A ~ **200 kOe**) versions of Ce_2Co_{17} – similar story as $SmCo_5$ vs. Sm_2Co_{17}.

However, not yet used as basis for permanent magnet – somewhat lower T_c and M_s than $SmCo_5$. But in world **where RE elements such as Sm are supply-constrained**, makes sense to explore as **"gap magnet"** (Coey term).

'metallic phases of the type RCo_5 (R = Y, Ce,
vestigated, and it is concluded that these alloys
: magnets. They have extremely high uniaxial
y axis, high saturation (B_s = 8500 to 11 200 G)
›per limits for the possible energy product lie
forces of over 8000 Oe and $(BH)_{max}$ = 5.1 MGOe
t room temperature. Grinding of YCo_5 and
and 2700 Oe, respectively, followed by a de-

Field sweep of Ce-rich $MMCo_5$ (K. Strnat et al, J. Appl. Phys. **38**, 1001 (1967))

La-Ce Usage Example 2: $CeCo_5$-based "Gap Magnet" (Ames)

- **Achievement**

"COMPOSITE Ce/Fe/Co/Cu CRYSTAL" with $(BH)_{max.}$ = ~13 MGOe.

- **Significance and impact**

First magnet using Ce (not Nd/Sm/Dy) to reach 13 MGOe. Magnet based on $CeCo_5$ with Fe (improves M and T_c, lowers cost) and Cu (for coercivity) added.

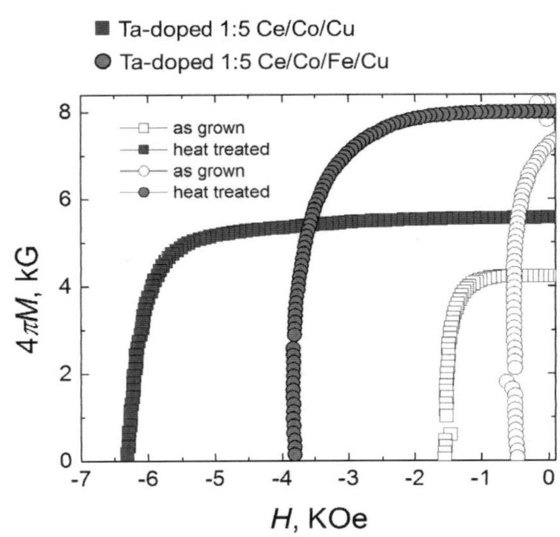

Demagnetization curves of the as-grown and heat-treated 1:5 Ce/Co/Cu and 1:5 Ce/Co/Fe/Cu magnets (A. Palasyuk)

CMI | Critical Materials Institute THE Ames Lab

La-Ce Usage Example 2: $CeCo_5$-based "Gap Magnet" (Ames)

Next steps

Want to increase performance further. Limit for **8 kG M_s** is **16 MG-Oe** – room for optimization.

"Obvious" strategy - to increase remanence by **adding Fe**, but one soon runs into solubility limits (cf. **instability of $CeFe_5$**).

But if we can get M_s to 10 kG, **BH_{max} limit becomes 25 MG-Oe – compete with $SmCo_5$.**

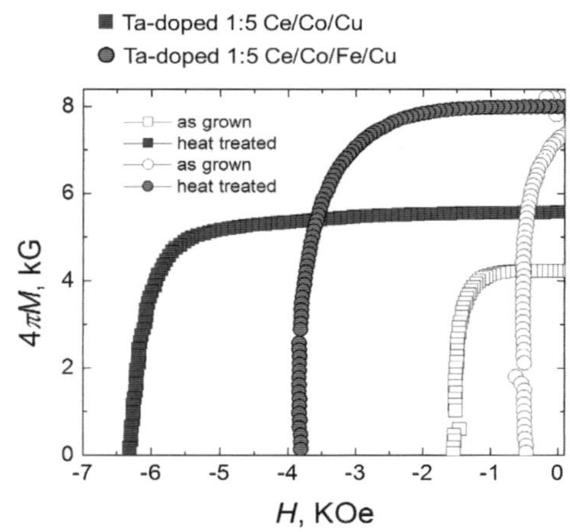

Demagnetization curves of the as-grown and heat-treated 1:5 Ce/Co/Cu and 1:5 Ce/Co/Fe/Cu magnets (A. Palasyuk)

MMM 2017 Abstract book, p. 632 and provisional patent application ISURF 4624/AL 676.

CMI Critical Materials Institute | The Ames Lab

La-Ce Usage Example 3: $Sm_2Fe_{17}N_3$-based alloys

$Sm_2Fe_{17}N_3$ well known as high-performance magnet, but problematic commercially due to **stability issues** – i.e. N stoichiometry. Similar issues with $Sm_2Fe_{17}C_3$ material.

N site is interstitial with not much near it – **not surprising** there is stability issue.

We may have found a way to address the stability issue (and **enhance** magnetic properties) – **see following.**

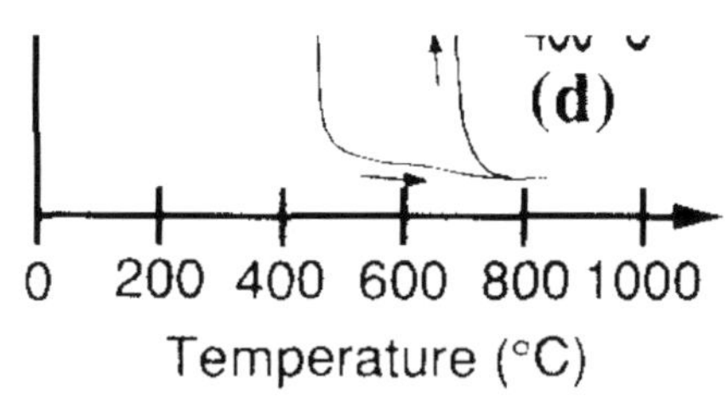

ig. 2. TMA traces of Sm_2Fe_{17} partic
75 °C, (b) 400 °C, (c) 425 °C, (d)
ıd (g) 600 °C. All samples were d

Thermogravimetric measurement (magnetization) on NH_3-flowed Sm_2Fe_{17} (Christodoulo 1995)

T. Pandey, M.-H. Du, and D. S. Parker. *Phys. Rev. Appl.* **9**, 034002 (2018).

CMI Critical Materials Institute | Oak Ridge National Laboratory

La-Ce Usage Example 3: substitution into 2-17-3 phases

Have considered La/Ce substitution into these phases. Initial motivation - **reduce Sm content** (would likely become critical if 2-17-3 phases were to be widely used).

Have computed N/C vacancy formation energy for all 6 phases. Periodic images at least 9 A apart. Calculations tricky for complex metallic rare-earth ferromagnet (**metastable states**).

As much as 70% increase in vacancy formation energy ΔE as result of alloying. Important because vacancy formation rate follows Arrhenius law - **~ $\exp(-\Delta E/k_b T)$**. At 900 K **rate is ~ 100 slower** if ΔE increases from 0.55 to 0.9 eV.

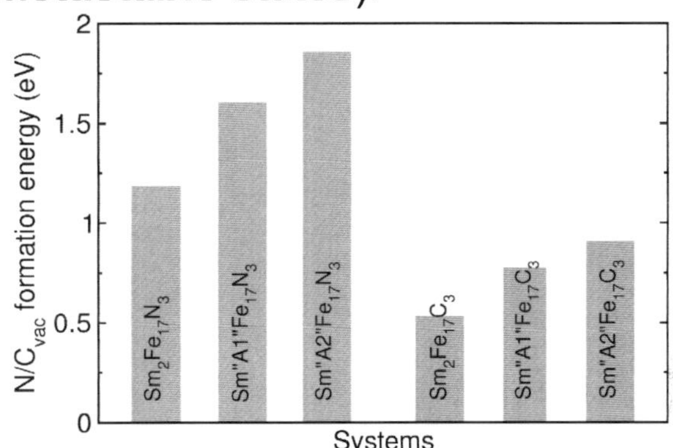

A1 = La, A2 = Ce

CMI Critical Materials Institute | The Ames Lab | Oak Ridge National Laboratory

La-Ce Usage Example 3: What is "enough" anisotropy?

Most high performance magnets have coercivity H_c at least as large as magnetization M_s. **Achievable H_c** is limited to about **1/3 of the anisotropy field H_A** so we need **$H_A > 3\ M_s$**.

System	Calculated K_1 (MJ/m^3)	H_A (T)	H_A/M_s
$SmLaFe_{17}C_3$	**1.2**	**2.2**	**1.6**
$SmCeFe_{17}C_3$	**1.7**	**3.0**	**2.2**
$SmLaFe_{17}N_3$	**4.1**	**6.8**	**4.5**
$SmCeFe_{17}N_3$	**7.2**	**12.0**	**8.0**

Both nitrides well exceed **$H_A > 3\ M_s$**. This is benefit of base 2-17-3 system – **magnetic anisotropies are so large** that reducing the Sm (which generates most of magnetic anisotropy) **still leaves one in usable range.**

CMI Critical Materials Institute | The Ames Lab | Oak Ridge National Laboratory

Entirely Non-RE Example 1: Fe_3Sn

Fe-based intermetallics **good place to look** for high-performance magnets: **Fe provides (ferro)magnetism** and other elements yield non-cubic structure (**good for anisotropy**).

Fe forms several binaries with Sn: FeSn, Fe_3Sn_2, Fe_5Sn_3, Fe_3Sn. We look at **most Iron-rich one Fe_3Sn.**

Fe_3Sn has large Curie point - **725 K** - and 300 K Magnetization – **14.8 kG.**

What about anisotropy?

B.C. Sales et al, Sci. Rep. **4**, 7024 (2014).

SCIENTIFIC REPORTS

OPEN Ferromagnetism of Fe_3Sn and Alloys

Brian C. Sales, Bayrammurad Saparov, Michael A. McGuire, David J. Singh & David S. Parker

SUBJECT AREAS: FERROMAGNETISM PHYSICS

Materials Science and Technology Division, Oak Ridge National Laboratory.

Entirely Non-RE Example 1: Fe_3Sn

Unfortunately, Fe_3Sn turns out to be **planar**, rather than **uniaxial.**

But H_A ~ 30 kG (3 Tesla). Yields K_1 of 1.8 MJ/m3 – good agreement with first-principles value of **1.59 MJ/m^3.**

Would be enough anisotropy to likely make **fairly high-performance, inexpensive** magnet (though not Neo-competitive), **if it had uniaxial anisotropy.**

Proof-of-principle for substantial magnetic anisotropy **without any RE content.**

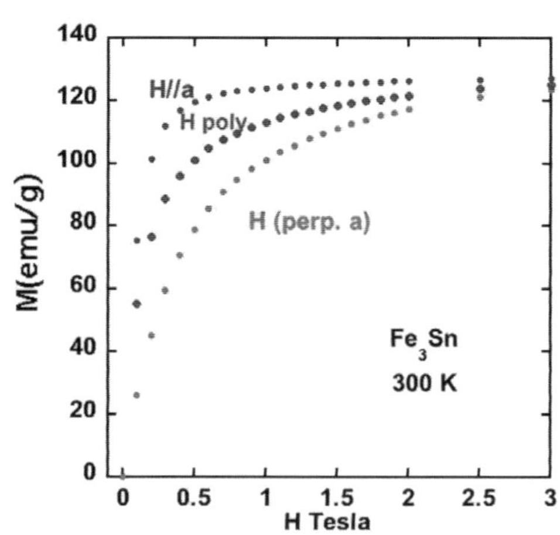

Oriented powder magnetization data on Fe_3Sn

Entirely Non-RE Example 2: ZrMnP and HfMnP

Manganese-based compounds known in permanent magnet community include MnAl and MnBi. MnBi unusual in having coercivity which increases with temperature – also **large anisotropy w/o RE elements**.

Recent CMI discovery of two Manganese-based ferromagnets – **ZrMnP and HfMnP** – with Curie points in 320 – 370 K range.

Form in orthorhombic structure. **Mn moment about $2\mu_B$** (similar to bcc Iron).

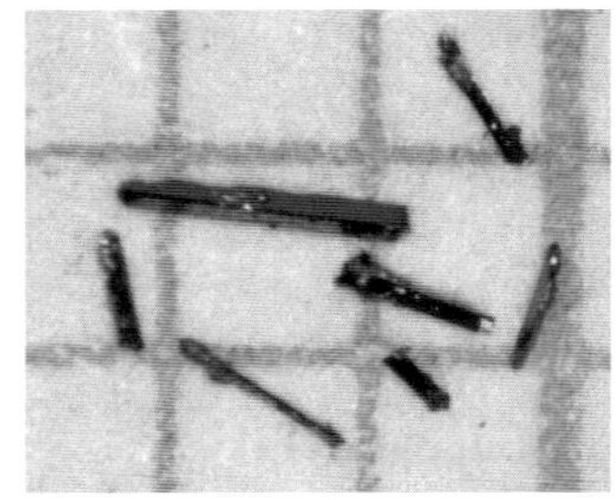

HfMnP crystals

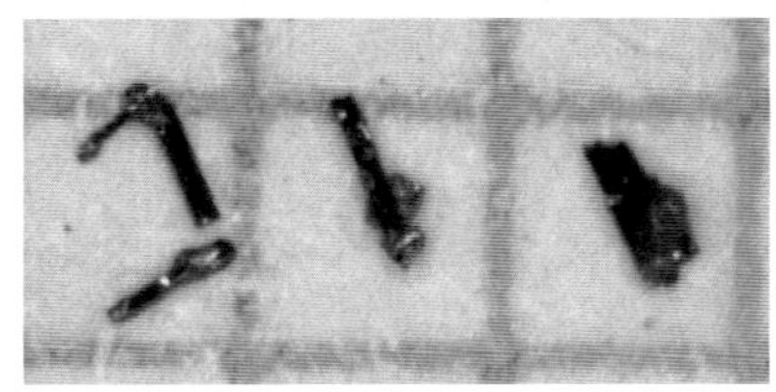

ZrMnP crystals

Entirely Non-RE Example 2: ZrMnP and HfMnP

Most surprising fact here is very large anisotropy fields H_A – **5 T for ZrMnP** and **10 T for HfMnP.**

One might think it due to the (relatively) low M_s ~ 0.5 T, since $H_A = 2K_1/M_s$, but that is not whole story.

Experimental "K_1" for HfMnP **about 2 MJ/m³ – half of Neo -** high for no rare-earth elements.

How is this possible? Does heavy Hf play a role?

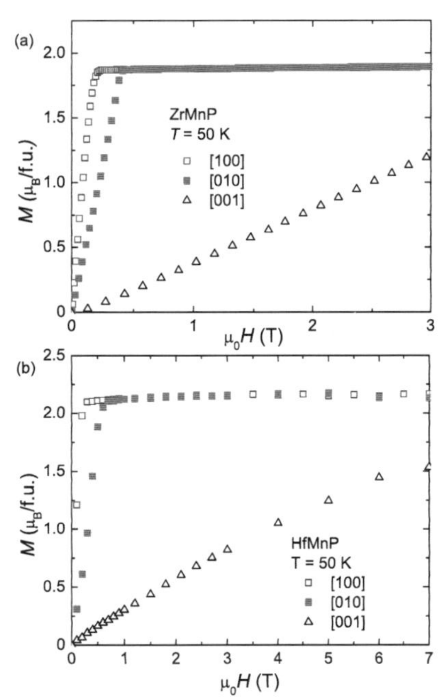

H- and axis-dependent magnetization ZrMnP - top, HfMnP -bottom

Entirely non-RE example 2: HfMnP and ZrMnP

Experiment and theory (DP) both find large anisotropy fields ~ 10 T in HfMnP* despite having no critical elements.

Theory finds 70% of anisotropy in HfMnP comes from Mn atoms. On a per-*3d* atom basis anisotropy energy is 8 times that of hcp Cobalt. Appears to arise from unusual electronic structure.

Should be possible to find Fe-based materials, with higher proportion of Fe, with similar behavior and larger M_{sat}, T_{Curie} (cf. "gap magnet".)

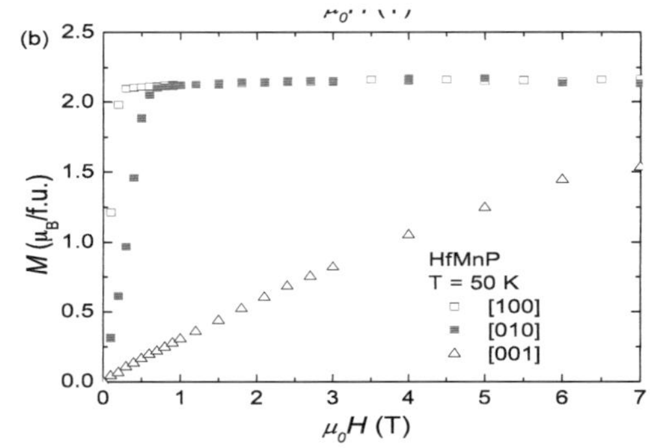

Magnetization curves of HfMnP at 50 K (T. Lamichhane)

*T. N. Lamichhane, V. Taufour, M. Masters, D.S. Parker, U. S. Kaluarachchi, S. Thimmaiah, S. L. Bud'ko and P. C. Canfield, Appl. Phys. Lett., **109**, 092402 (2016).

Entirely Non-RE Example 3: L10 FeNi (tetrataenite)

Iron-Nickel (i.e. disordered) alloys familiar from metallurgy, but known for several decades that in certain meteorites an ordered, non-cubic equiatomic composition FeNi is present.

Structure same as high-anisotropy materials FePt, CoPt.

L10 FeNi has rather promising permanent magnet properties (next slide).

Tetrataenite meteorite

Photo: Rob Lavinsky, irocks.com

Entirely Non-RE Example 3: L10 FeNi (tetrataenite)

L10 FeNi has 300 K M_s of 14.5 kG (nearly as much as Neo), H_A of ~ 20 kOe.

Magnetization would imply potential BH_{max} of 53 MG-Oe, though anisotropy field a little lower than ideal (only 1.4 x M_s).

But 25 or 30 MG-Oe should be possible, if synthesis issues can be mastered (next slide).

Already 1.2 kOe of coercivity in meteoritic sample, as high as 4 kOe in literature.

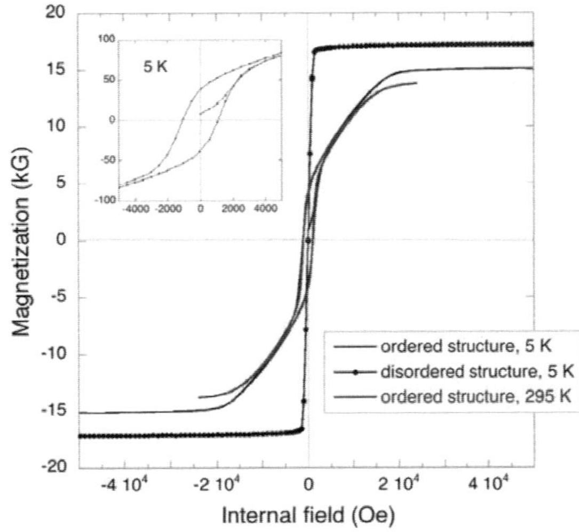

Magnetization curves of meteoritic L10 FeNi (from L.H. Lewis et al, J. Phys. Cond. Matt. **26**, 064213 (2014)).

Entirely Non-RE Example 3: L10 FeNi (tetrataenite)

Difficulty with L10 FeNi is reaction kinetics and associated order-disorder transition at ~ 300 C.

Forms in meteors at cooling rate Of 1 K/10^6 year, but clearly need better process for laboratory synthesis.

Active area of research within Critical Materials Institute (V. Pecharsky et al).

Challenging problem, but materials scientists very creative - recall that Aluminum once considered precious metal (prior to invention of Hall-Heroult process).

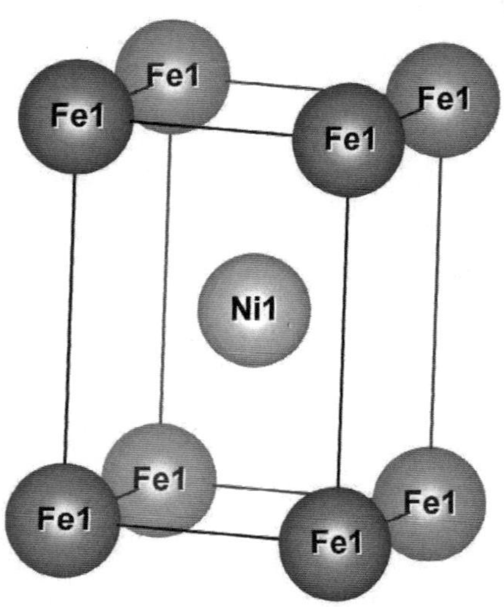

Tetragonal structure of L10 FeNi

Outlook - 1

- In general, BH_{max} has plateaued since the 1984 discovery, and subsequent development, of $Nd_2Fe_{14}B$.
- Will be difficult to greatly improve on RT performance, although exchange spring magnets remain possible.
- But it should be possible to come up with all manner of less "critical" magnets, address high-temperature issues without Dy, and fill in performance "gap" (Coey) between best RE-free (Alnico – 100 kJ/m^3) and 300 kJ/m^3 (HT Neo).

Magnet performance since 1940:
We indeed "Mind the Gap."

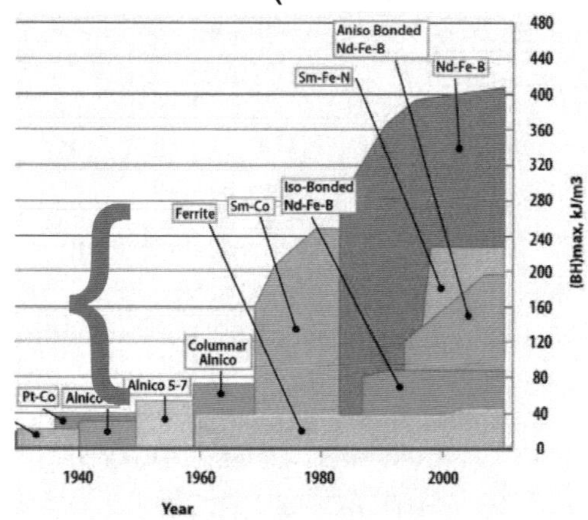

John Ormerod / Steve Constantinides

Outlook – 2 – "the next frontier"

Theory has role to play in magnet discovery. Can calculate many properties from first principles, including all-important magnetic anisotropy – only thing distinguishing Neo from Steel. Yet rare-earth elements such as Ce, Nd and Sm still present challenges to theory.

ORNL Supercomputer Summit

Rare-earth elements are now the main game in town for magnetic anisotropy, as our computations see. However, in certain materials (HfMnP [1], $Mn_3Si_2Te_6$ [2], L10 FeNi [3]), we see large anisotropy without rare-earths. Should be numerous others.

This is the "next frontier" for permanent magnet materials.

1. T.N. Lamichhane, V. Taufour, M.W. Masters, DP et al. Appl. Phys. Lett. **109**, 092402 (2016).
2. A.F. May, Y. Liu, S. Calder, DP et al, Phys. Rev. B **95**, 17440 (2017).
3. L.H. Lewis et al, J. Phys.: Cond. Matt. **26**, 064213 (2014).

Summary

We have described two recent CMI findings on permanent magnet materials:

- that in several materials ($LaCeCo_{16}Ti$, $CeCo_5$, and La/Ce-substituted $Sm_2Fe_{17}N_3$), **the non-critical rare-earths La and Ce can be used while maintaining good intrinsic properties** of permanent magnet materials; and, similarly

- in **numerous materials entirely lacking rare earths** (Fe_3Sn, HfMnP, ZrMnP, L10 FeNi), significant magnetic anisotropy can be attained, so that it should be possible to develop **RE-free "gap magnets".**

We look forward to **"gap"** and **high-performance** magnets emerging from these and similar systems.

CMI Critical Materials Institute | THE Ames Lab | OAK RIDGE National Laboratory

ELECTRON ENERGY CORPORATION

Magnet Expertise that Makes a World of Difference

Tunable Quadrupole Magnets for Next Generation Electron Ion Colliders

Jinfang Liu

Team:
Heeju Choi
Lori Haley
Melania Jasinski
Daniel Patches

Electron Energy Corporation
924 Links Avenue, Landisville, PA 17538, USA

Magnetics 2019, January 23-24, 2019, Orlando, Florida

ELECTRON ENERGY CORPORATION

Magnet Expertise that Makes a World of Difference

Outline

1. **Magnet Assemblies**
   a. **Halbach Dipole**
   b. **Halbach Quadrupole**
   c. **Linear Halbach Design**
2. **Quadrupole Magnet for Electron Ion Colliders**
   a. **DoE Program**
   b. **Quadruple magnet design**
   c. **Quadrupole Magnet Testing**

ELECTRON ENERGY CORPORATION

Magnet Expertise that Makes a World of Difference

Halbach Dipole

Halbach PM Dipole Cylinder:

$$B_g = B_r \ln(OD/ID)$$

There is no upper limit for magnetic flux density in Halbach dipole cylinders based on this equation.

ELECTRON ENERGY CORPORATION

Magnet Expertise that Makes a World of Difference

Halbach Dipole

Halbach PM Dipole Structures:

$$B_g = B_r \ln(OD/ID)$$

There is no upper limit for magnetic flux density in Halbach dipole cylinders based on this equation.

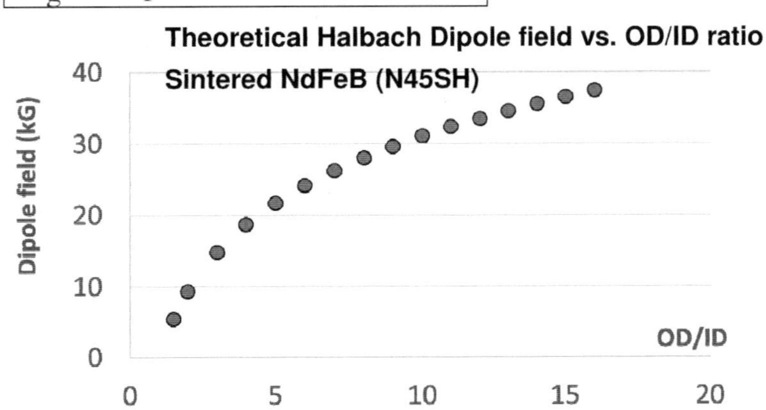

ELECTRON ENERGY CORPORATION

Magnet Expertise that Makes a World of Difference

Halbach Dipole

Halbach PM Dipole Structures:

$$B_g = B_r \ln(OD/ID)$$

There is no upper limit for magnetic flux density in Halbach dipole cylinders based on this equation.

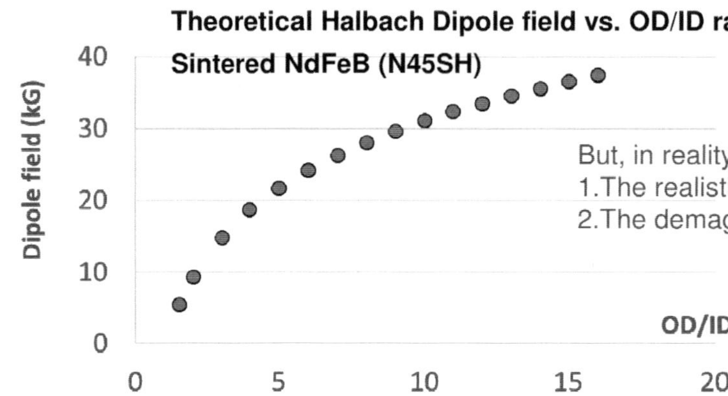

But, in reality it would be limited by:
1. The realistic size
2. The demagnetization effect

ELECTRON ENERGY CORPORATION

Magnet Expertise that Makes a World of Difference

High Field Halbach Cylinders

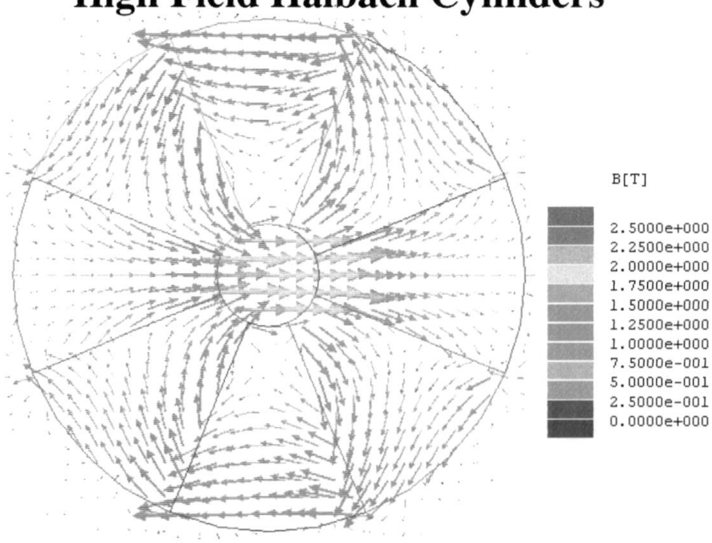

Both Sintered NdFeB and SmCo are good choices

Halbach Dipole Cylinder Examples

8-segment Design

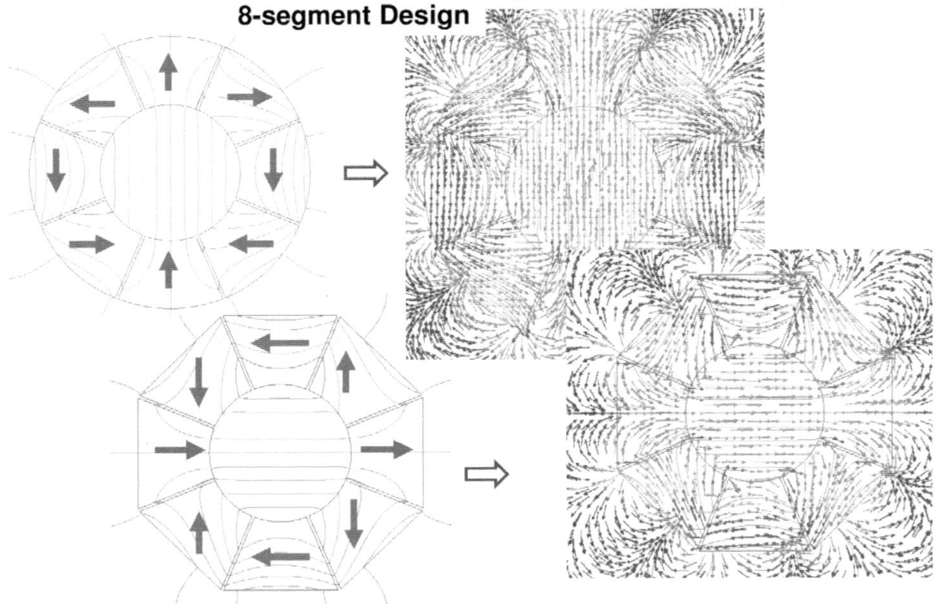

ELECTRON ENERGY CORPORATION
Magnet Expertise that Makes a World of Difference

Linear Halbach Array Design

Magnetic Type	Peak Field [T]
Alternating	1.075
Halbach	1.528

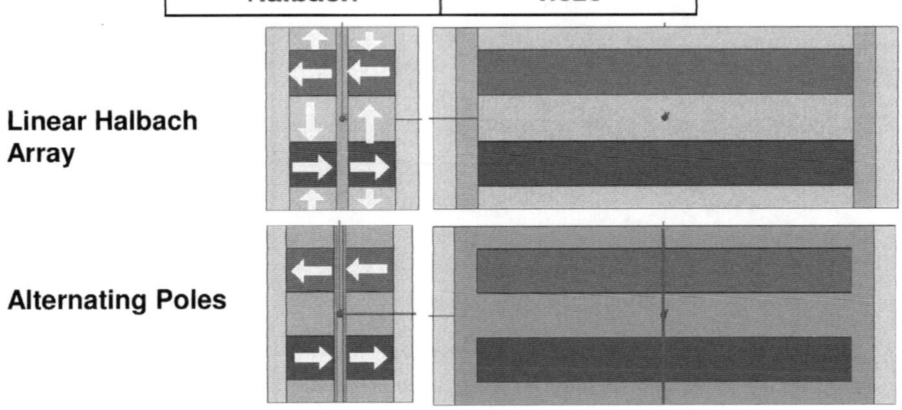

ELECTRON ENERGY CORPORATION

Magnet Expertise that Makes a World of Difference

Magnetic Coupler using Halbach Array

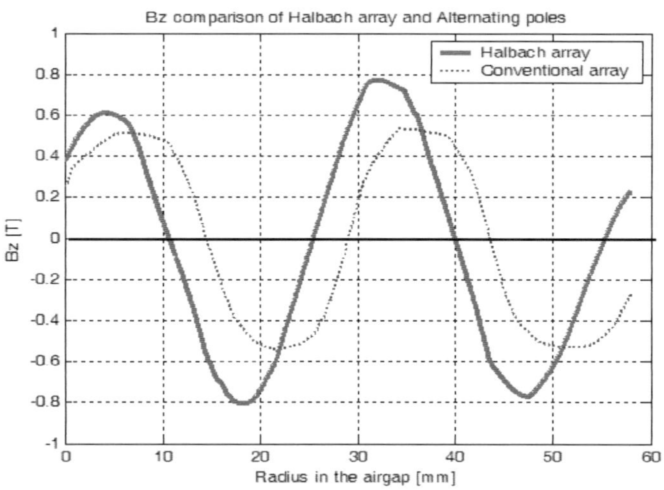

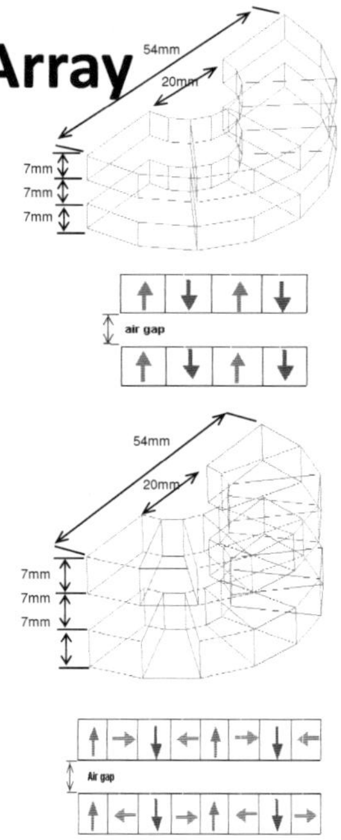

ELECTRON ENERGY CORPORATION

Magnet Expertise that Makes a World of Difference

Single Halbach Dipole Cylinder

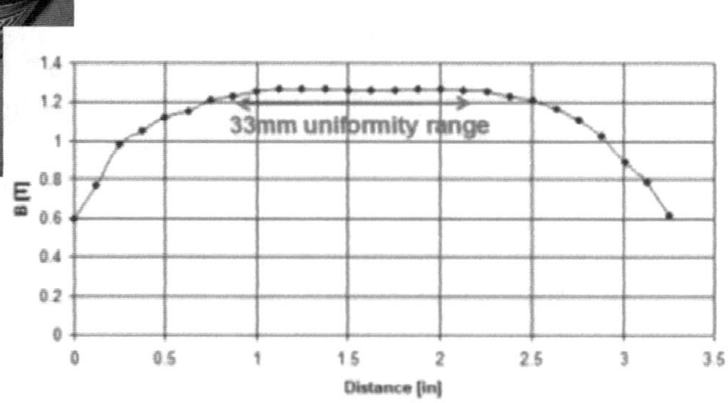

ELECTRON ENERGY CORPORATION

Magnet Expertise that Makes a World of Difference

Double Halbach Cylinder

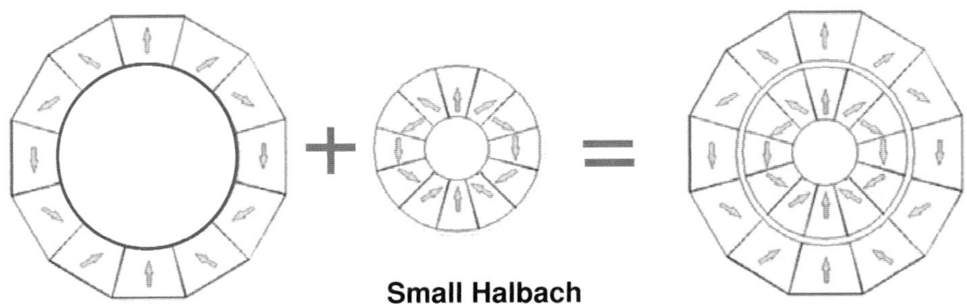

Small Halbach Dipole Cylinder

Large Halbach Dipole Cylinder

Double Halbach Cylinder

ELECTRON ENERGY CORPORATION

Magnet Expertise that Makes a World of Difference

Double Halbach Cylinder

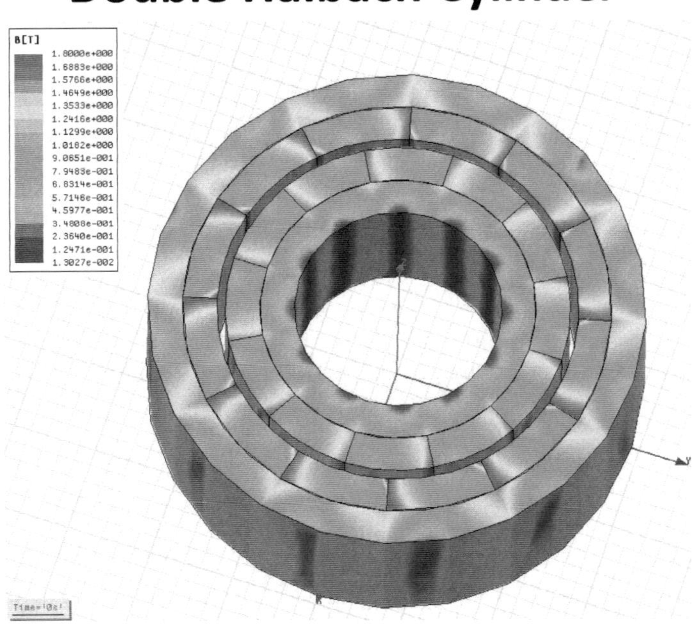

ELECTRON ENERGY CORPORATION

Magnet Expertise that Makes a World of Difference

Double Halbach Cylinder CAD

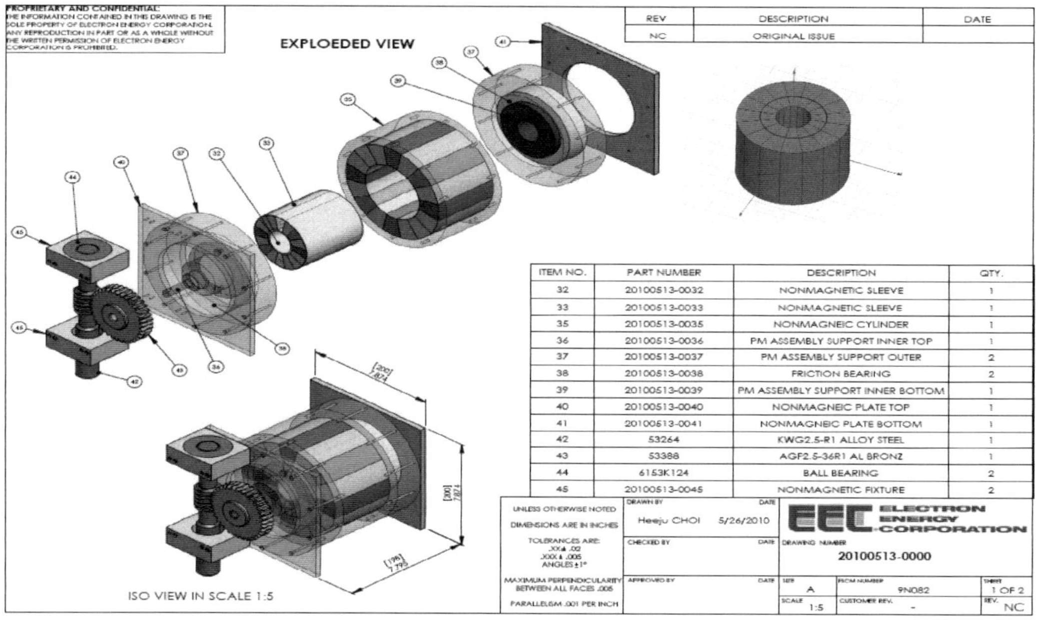

REV	DESCRIPTION	DATE
NC	ORIGINAL ISSUE	

ITEM NO.	PART NUMBER	DESCRIPTION	QTY.
32	20100513-0032	NONMAGNETIC SLEEVE	1
33	20100513-0033	NONMAGNETIC SLEEVE	1
35	20100513-0035	NONMAGNEIC CYLINDER	1
36	20100513-0036	PM ASSEMBLY SUPPORT INNER TOP	1
37	20100513-0037	PM ASSEMBLY SUPPORT OUTER	2
38	20100513-0038	FRICTION BEARING	2
39	20100513-0039	PM ASSEMBLY SUPPORT INNER BOTTOM	1
40	20100513-0040	NONMAGNEIC PLATE TOP	1
41	20100513-0041	NONMAGNEIC PLATE BOTTOM	1
42	53264	KWG2.5-R1 ALLOY STEEL	1
43	53388	AGF2.5-36R1 AL BRONZ	1
44	6153K124	BALL BEARING	2
45	20100513-0045	NONMAGNETIC FIXTURE	2

ELECTRON ENERGY CORPORATION

Magnet Expertise that Makes a World of Difference

Halbach Quadrupole Cylinder Example

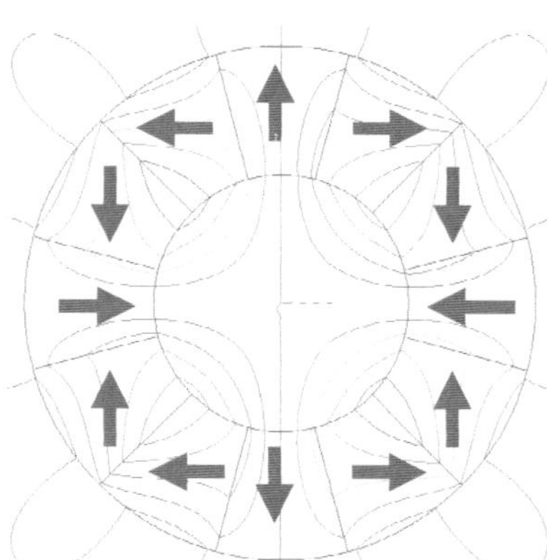

ELECTRON ENERGY CORPORATION

Magnet Expertise that Makes a World of Difference

Quadrupole Magnets for Proton Therapy

Proton Therapy:

- ✓ A precise delivery a **high dose of radiation** in a single treatment session to **a small target, such as a cancer tumor**
- ✓ **Less damage** to the surrounding healthy tissue
- ✓ This allows doctors to use **a higher dose of radiation** with proton therapy than they can use with X-rays
- ✓ Proton therapy can treat different type of **cancers, such as brain, eye, head and neck, lung, spine, and prostate cancer**

ELECTRON ENERGY CORPORATION

Magnet Expertise that Makes a World of Difference

Quadrupole Magnets for Proton Therapy

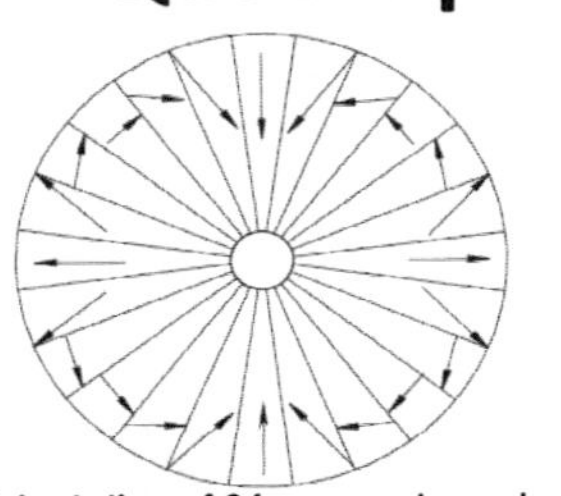

Orientation of 24 segment quadruple Halbach cylinder with the arrows representing the direction of the magnetization of each segment.

FEA Magnetic field distribution plot

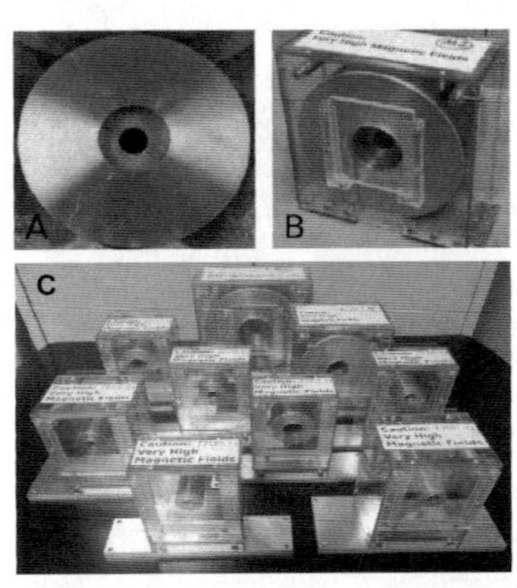

Focusing magnets consist of 24 segments of Sm_2Co_{17} material adhered into Halbach cylinders and encased in nonmagnetic stainless steel and placed in Lexan safety/mounting cases.

ELECTRON ENERGY CORPORATION

Magnet Expertise that Makes a World of Difference

DOE Fast Track Program

(DE-SC0015230)

Design and Manufacture of Tunable Permanent Magnet Based Quadrupole for Next Generation Electron Ion Colliders

PI: Heeju Choi

Electron Energy Corporation

Why Permanent Magnets?

1. **No Power consumption --- lower cost in construction, operation and maintenance.**
2. **Small volume ---- as compared to electromagnets.**

Principal Investigator:
Dr. Heeju Choi

ELECTRON ENERGY CORPORATION

Magnet Expertise that Makes a World of Difference

Quadrupole magnets for eRHIC

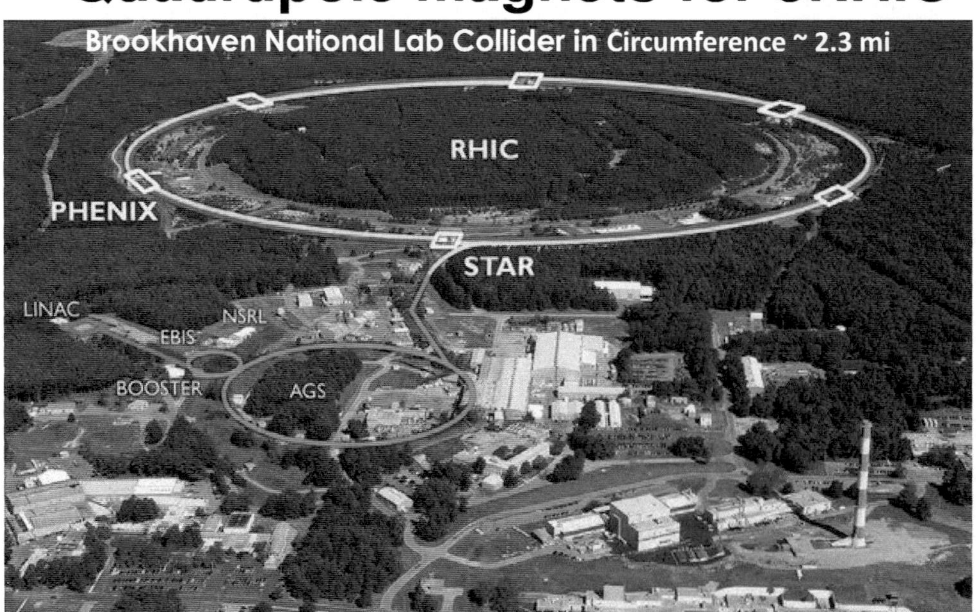

ELECTRON
ENERGY
CORPORATION

Magnet Expertise that Makes a World of Difference

DOE Fast Track Program

(DE-SC0015230)

Design and Manufacture of Tunable Permanent Magnet Based Quadrupole for Next Generation Electron Ion Colliders

What's the Objective?

1. Conduct design, construction, and testing of a <u>tunable</u> focusing quadrupole magnet prototype with high performance at low cost.

2. Meet specifications

Field gradients:	**34.42 T/m**
Field gradient error:	**≤ 0.1%**
Good field region:	**R13.4+2mm**

ELECTRON
ENERGY
CORPORATION

Magnet Expertise that Makes a World of Difference

300-mm Long Magnet Assembly with Adjusting Mechanism

Weight: 1,040 lbs (470 kg)

Size: 19.7" x 20.2" x 11.8"
(500 x 514 x 300 mm)

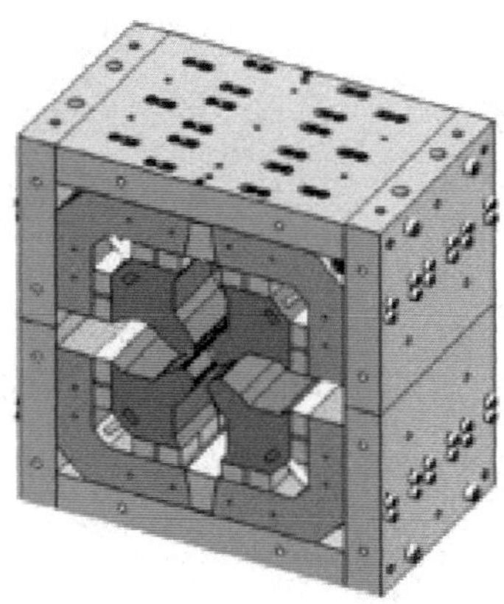

- In practice: modular assembly consisting of **12 x100** mm long units.
- Mechanical alignment is achieved within **±25μm**.

- FEA demonstrated that all targeted specifications were achieved:
  Field **gradient 34.42 T/m**
  Field gradient error ≤ 0.1%
  Good field harmonics

ELECTRON ENERGY CORPORATION

Magnet Expertise that Makes a World of Difference

3D Nonlinear FEA Field Contour Map of 300-mm Long Magnet Assembly

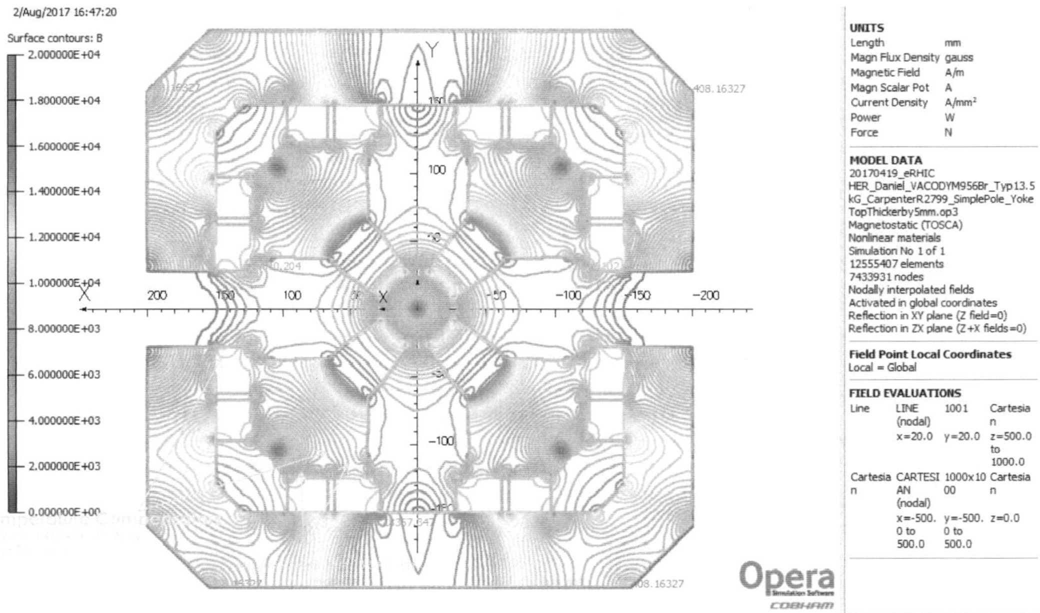

ELECTRON ENERGY CORPORATION

Magnet Expertise that Makes a World of Difference

3D Nonlinear FEA Field Contour Map of 300-mm Long Magnet Assembly

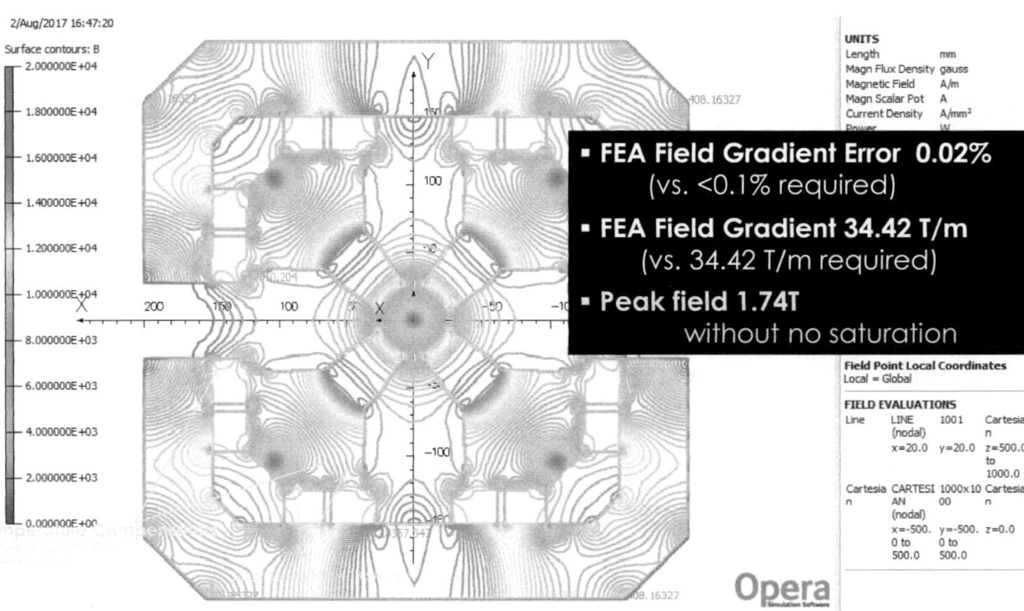

- **FEA Field Gradient Error 0.02%** (vs. <0.1% required)
- **FEA Field Gradient 34.42 T/m** (vs. 34.42 T/m required)
- **Peak field 1.74T** without no saturation

ELECTRON ENERGY CORPORATION

Magnet Expertise that Makes a World of Difference

Modular Magnet Assembly

Some Components for the assembly

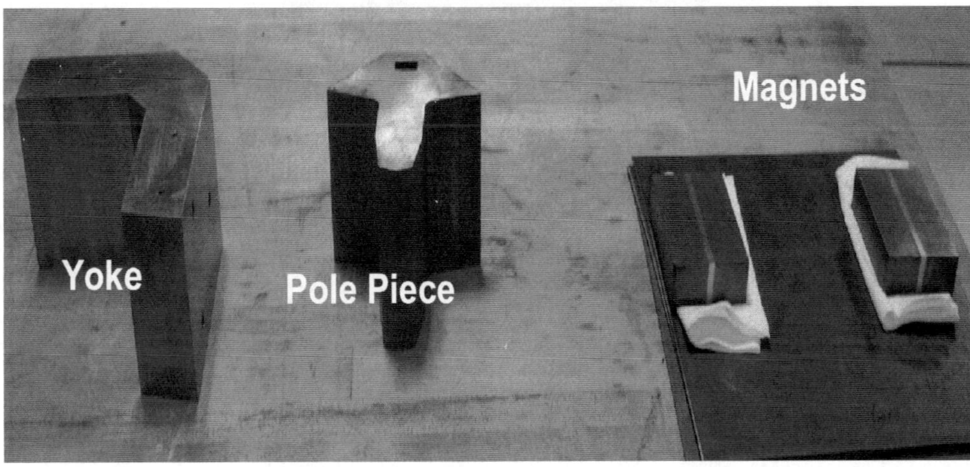

ELECTRON ENERGY CORPORATION

Magnet Expertise that Makes a World of Difference

100-mm Long, 12 Modular Magnets Uniformity Test

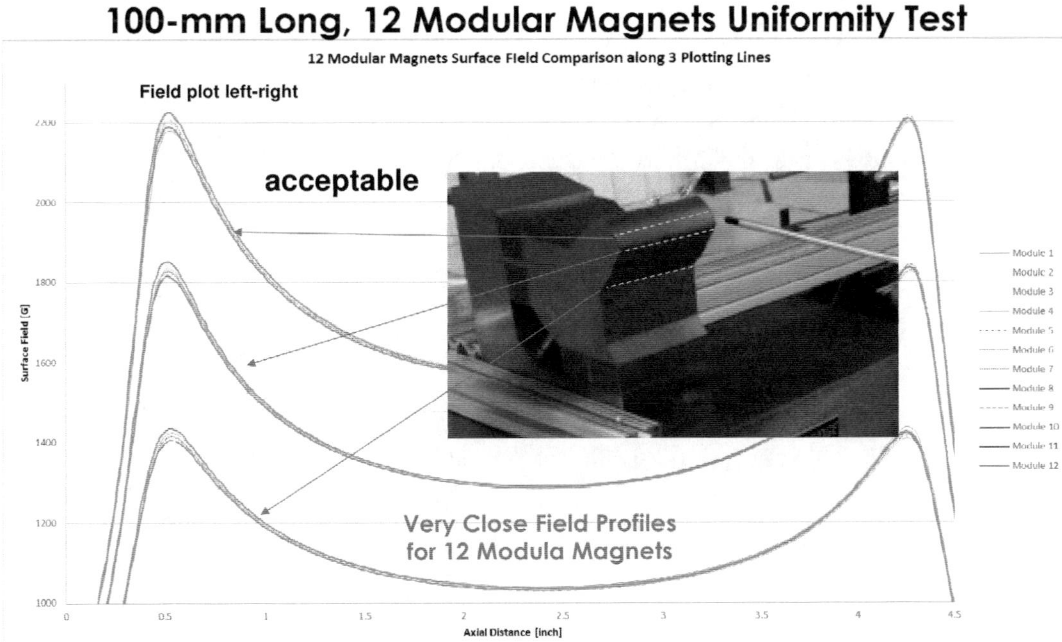

ELECTRON ENERGY CORPORATION

Magnet Expertise that Makes a World of Difference

Quadrupole Magnet Built by EEC

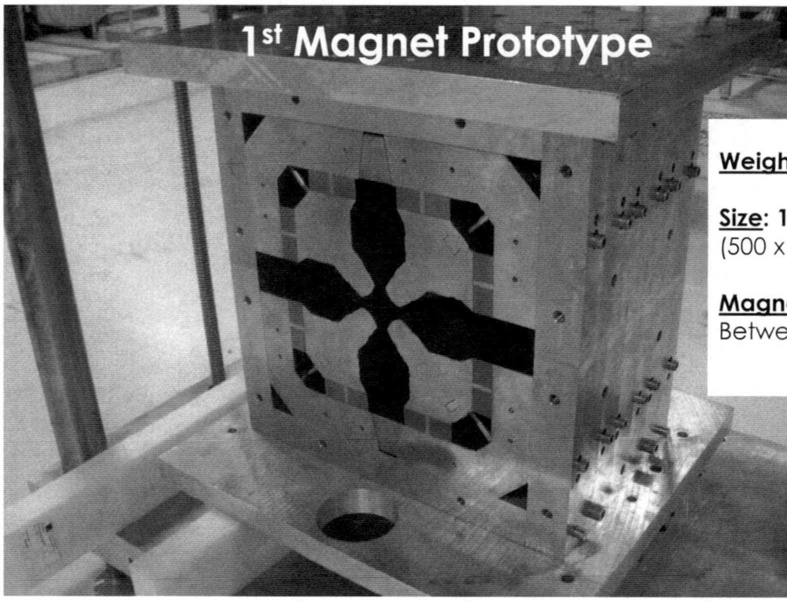

Weight: **1,040 lbs** (470 kg)

Size: **19.7 x 20.2 x 11.8"** (500 x 514 x 300 mm)

Magnetic Force: 1,200 lbs Between Top and Bottom

ELECTRON ENERGY CORPORATION

Magnet Expertise that Makes a World of Difference

Field Gradient Test Setup at EEC

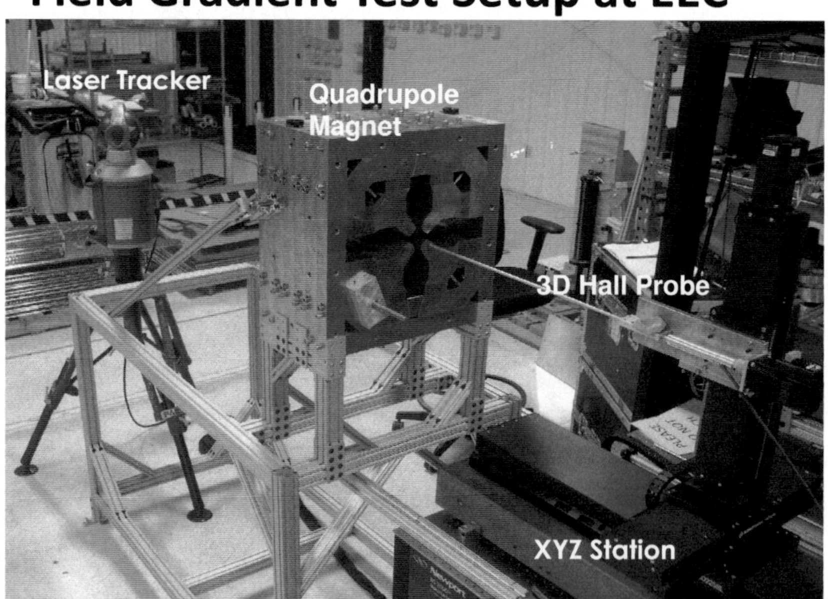

ELECTRON ENERGY CORPORATION

Magnet Expertise that Makes a World of Difference

Field Gradient Data of As-is Magnet without Adjustment

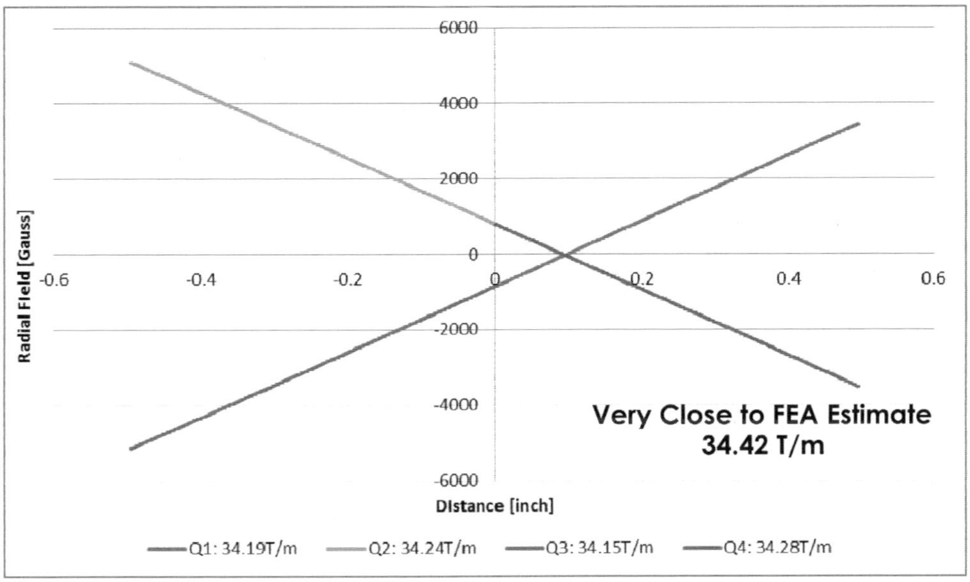

ELECTRON ENERGY CORPORATION

Magnet Expertise that Makes a World of Difference

The Field Harmonics of 1st magnet was tested using harmonic coil

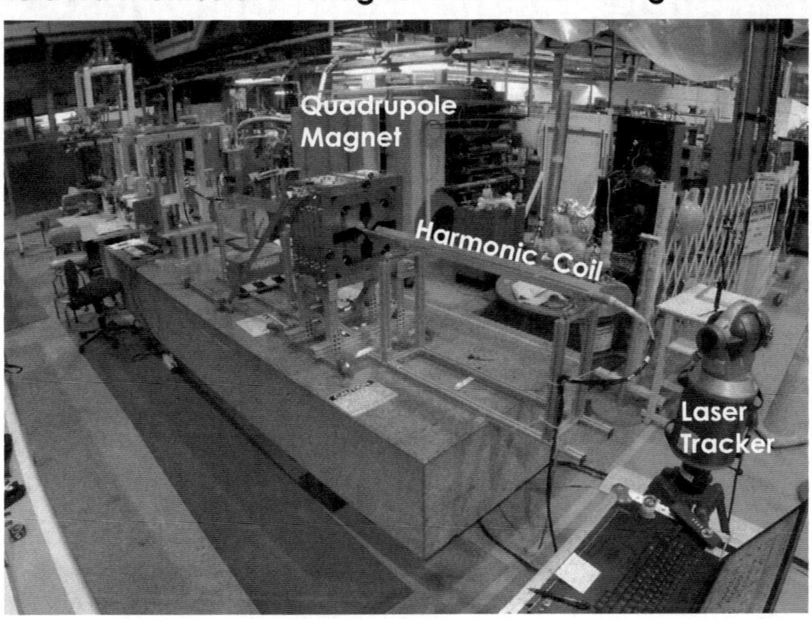

ELECTRON ENERGY CORPORATION

Magnet Expertise that Makes a World of Difference

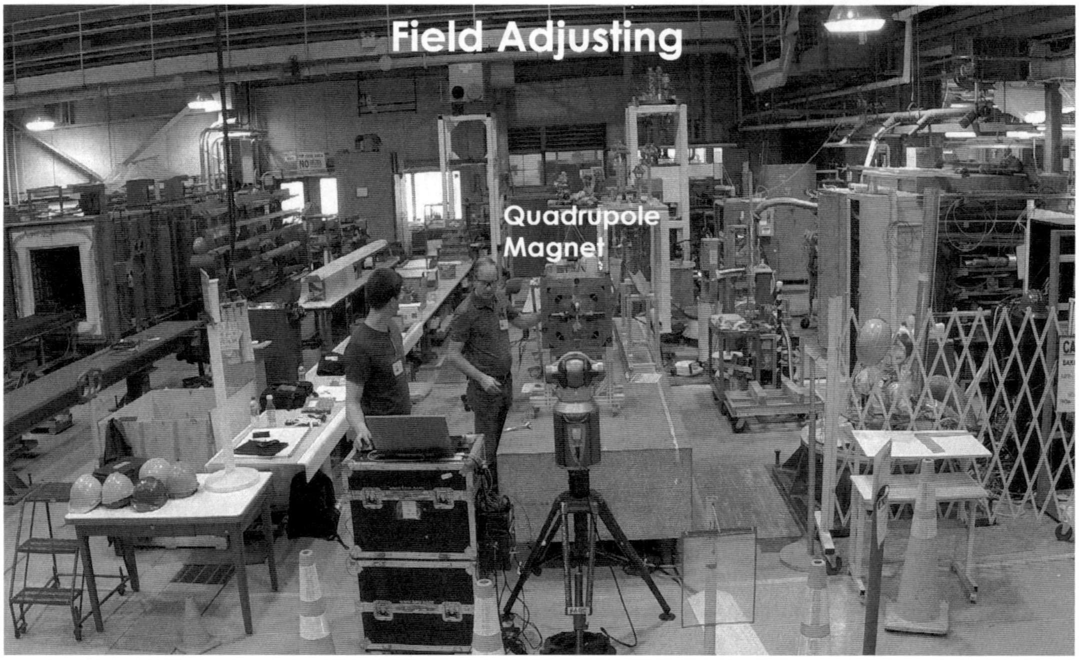

ELECTRON ENERGY CORPORATION

Magnet Expertise that Makes a World of Difference

1st Quadrupole Magnet Harmonics Test Results

Normal Harmonics

Real (Normal)		FEA	Run 4	Run 7	
Quadrupole	**b2**	**10,000**	**10,000**	**10,000**	
Sextupole	b3	1.84	-3.14	-0.74	*ok*
Octupole	b4	-2.67	-5.61	-5.67	*to be improved*
Decapole	b5	1.54	-0.48	-0.23	

✓Sextupole component comes from imbalanced poles and should be less than 1 unit out of 10,000.
Pole adjusting technique helped to reduce the Sextupole to 0.74 from 3.14.

✓ Octupole component comes from the geometrical non-symmetry of pole and should be less than 1.
Both adjusting and shunting methods didn't help to minimize the Octupole component.

ELECTRON ENERGY CORPORATION

Magnet Expertise that Makes a World of Difference

2nd Magnet Design for Better Harmonics

1st Magnet

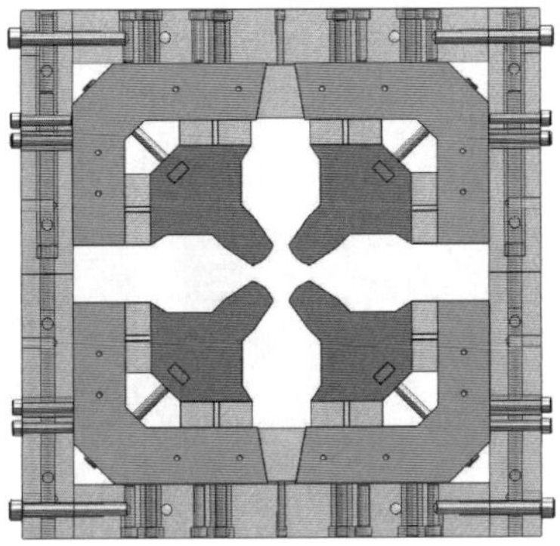

Symmetry

- Closed mid-plane

Pole Shape

- Removing unsaturated portion.

2nd Magnet

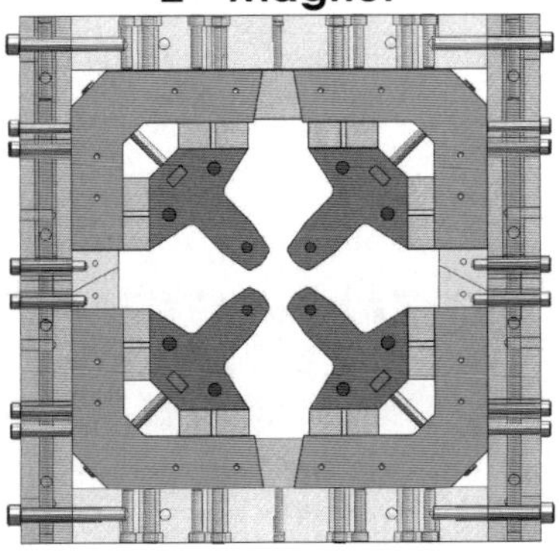

ELECTRON ENERGY CORPORATION

Magnet Expertise that Makes a World of Difference

Harmonics Comparison

Normal Harmonics		1st Magnet FEA	1st Magnet Test Run 7	2nd Magnet FEA
Quadrupole	**b2**	**10,000**	**10,000**	**10,000**
Sextupole	b3	1.84	-0.74	0
Octupole	b4	-2.67	-5.67	-0.49
Decapole	b5	1.54	-0.23	0

The 2nd magnet is designed to reduce the Octupole component

ELECTRON
ENERGY
CORPORATION

Magnet Expertise that Makes a World of Difference

Thank you!

Question?

Contact Information

Jinfang Liu, President & COO
Electron Energy Corporation
924 Links Ave
Landisville PA 17538 USA
liu@electronenergy.com

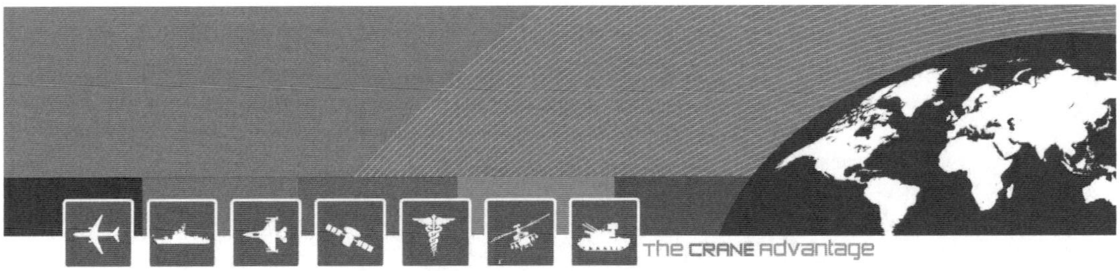

Significant Weight Reduction of Three-Phase Transformers through Advancements in Core Construction and Materials

Kaz Furmanczyk
Crane Aerospace & Electronics

2019 Magnetics Conference
Orlando, Florida, January 23-24, 2019

CRANE AEROSPACE & ELECTRONICS

CRANE AEROSPACE & ELECTRONICS

Introduction

- Three-phase transformers are commonly used for powering DC Brushless Motors from 3-phase AC power systems

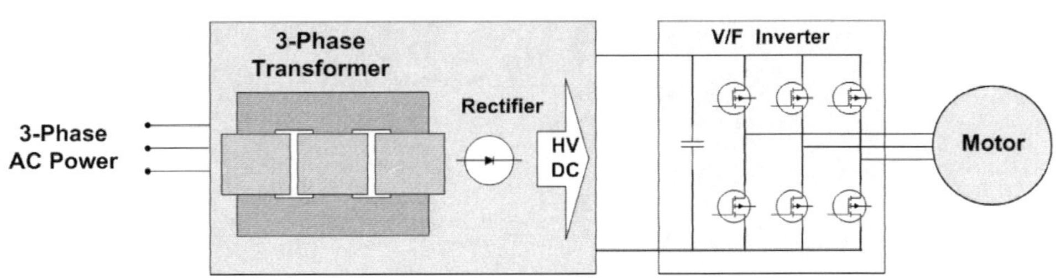

- The power transformer is a key component of the conversion system. Transformer design is critical to reducing weight and power dissipation of the motor driver
- This presentation covers key design elements influencing weight and efficiency of the transformer:
  - Core configuration and shape
  - Core materials
  - Winding materials and conductor shape

2

CRANE AEROSPACE & ELECTRONICS

Typical 3-Phase Transformer

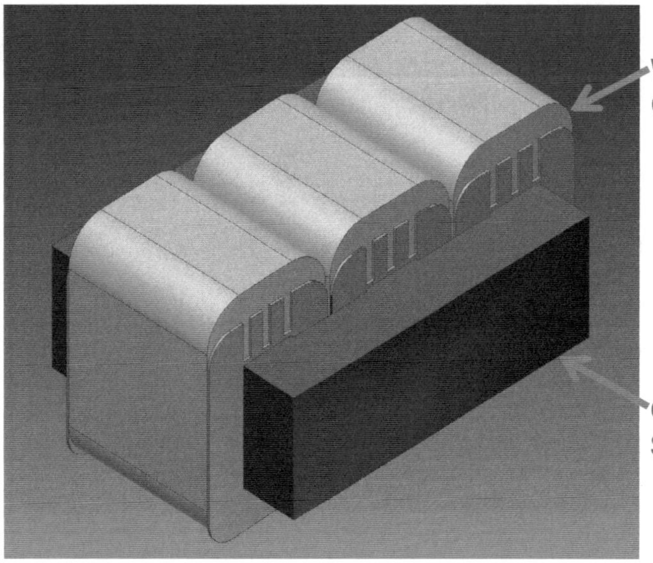

Windings:
Copper wires (round)

Core:
Silicon steel laminated

CRANE AEROSPACE & ELECTRONICS

Transformer Core

- Base line: Silicon steel, 3-legs, square laminated core

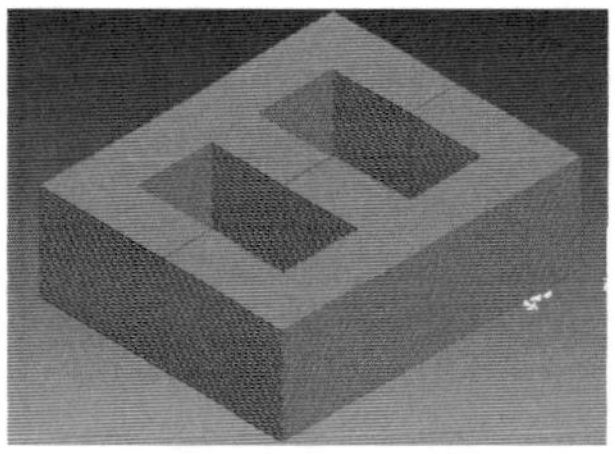

- Other options to consider:
  - Core shape:
    - Core cross section: square vs. round
    - Core form factor
  - Material:
    - High flux core
    - Cobalt base material

CRANE AEROSPACE & ELECTRONICS

Transformer Core Improvements

Core Cross Section

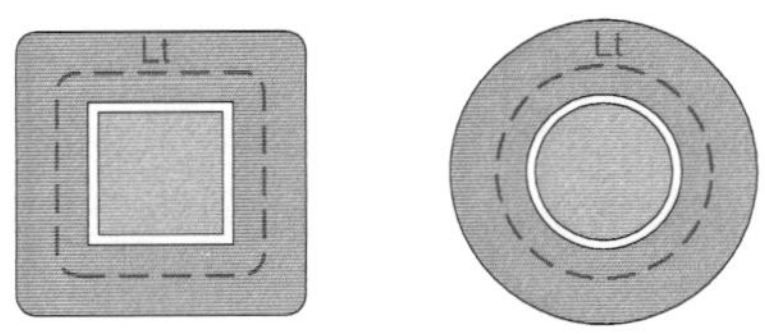

Base Line

Conductor length (Lt) for a round cross section core is 12% shorter than for a square cross section core with the same area

→ 12% saving in conductor weight and its power dissipation

Core Shape

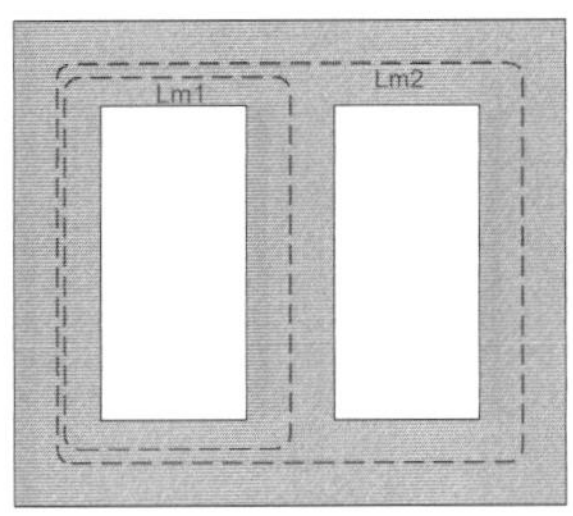

Traditional flat cores for 3-phase transformers have different magnetic paths (Lm) between center and outside core legs. This leads to differences in magnetizing currents in each phase and higher current distortion

→ Symmetrical and optimized core would benefit performance and further reduces transformer weight

CRANE AEROSPACE & ELECTRONICS

Transformer Core Improvements

Core Form Factor

Flat Core; Square Legs | Flat Core; Round Legs | Symmetrical Core; Round Legs (3-Windows Transformer)

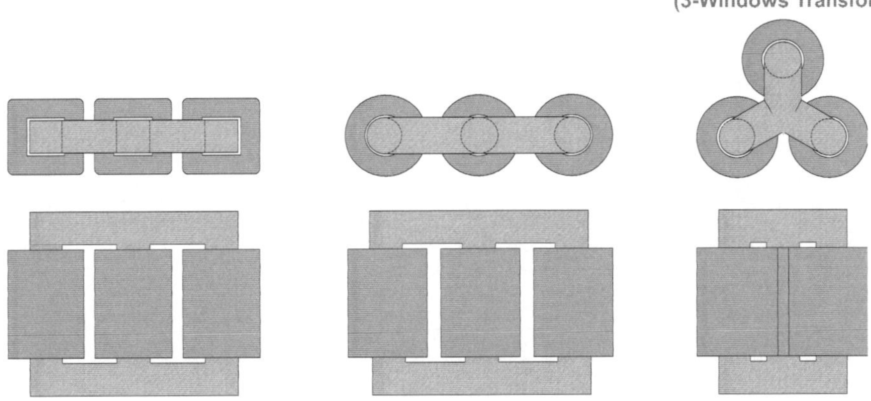

Base Line

Improvements:
- 12% Weight
- 12% Power Dissipation

Improvements:
- 18% Weight
- 14% Power Dissipation
- Lower current distortion

CRANE AEROSPACE & ELECTRONICS

Examples of 3-Windows Transformer

Standard C-Cores Construction

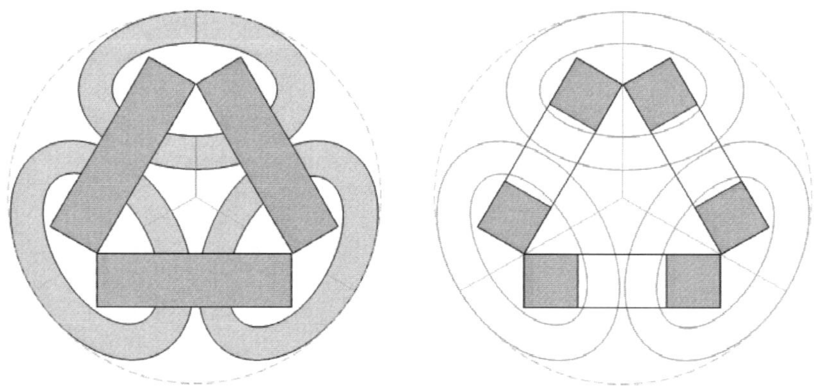

- The core is made up of 3 standard C-Cores
- Magnetizing current is identical in each phase – current distortion is minimized
- Coils are oversized

7

CRANE AEROSPACE & ELECTRONICS

Examples of 3-Windows Transformer

Custom C-Core Construction

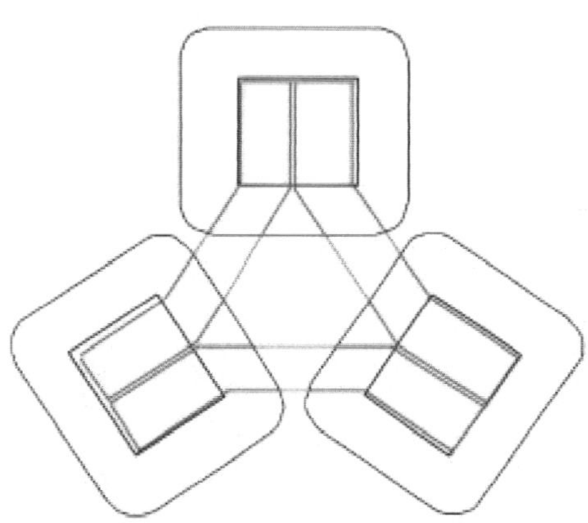

- The core is made up of 3 bent C-cores
- Magnetizing current is identical in each phase – current distortion is minimized
- Coils have square shape

8

CRANE
AEROSPACE & ELECTRONICS

Examples of 3-Windows Transformer

Optimum Core Construction*

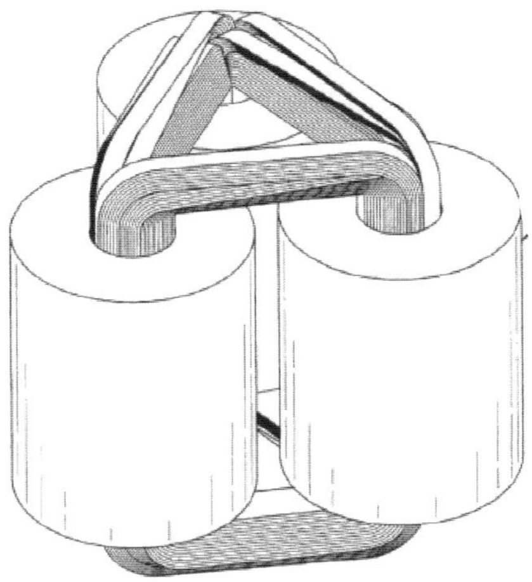

Optimum core and coils shape for the highest efficiency, best performance and lowest weight transformer

- Symmetrical core
- Round legs

***Transformer core construction and manufacturing method details are covered by U.S. Patent No. 6, 683,524.**

The core is made up of rings rolled from strips of constant width

CRANE
AEROSPACE & ELECTRONICS

Transformer Core Improvements

Core Material

B-H Loops of Saturable Materials

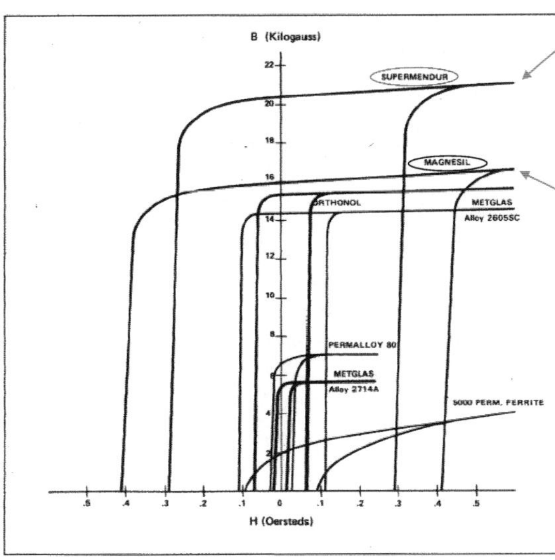

High Flux Core

Cobalt Base Steel – Flux Density 21.5 kGs

- **17% Weight Improvement**
- **(5-10)x Higher Cost**

Base Line

Silicon Steel – Flux Density 17.8 kGs

CRANE AEROSPACE & ELECTRONICS

Transformer Windings

- Base line: Copper wires (round) - currently used in most transformer designs
- Other options to consider:
  - Material:
    - Copper
    - Aluminum
  - Conductor shape:
    - Square wire
    - Foil

CRANE AEROSPACE & ELECTRONICS

Transformer Windings

Comparison between copper and aluminum

Parameter	Unit	Material Property at 20 deg. C Copper [CU]	Aluminium [AL]	Ratio CU/AL
Conductivity	[m/O mm^2]	57	34.8	**1.6**
Resistivity	[O mm^2/m]	0.01754	0.0287	**0.6**
Temp. Coeficient	[1/C]	0.00393	0.0036	**1.1**
Mass Density	[g/cm^3]	8.93	2.7	**3.3**
Term. Conducivity	[W/cm C]	3.86	2.18	**1.8**

- Aluminum has losses 60% higher than Copper
- Aluminum weighs over three times less than Copper
- In practice, a transformer with aluminum windings is about 20% lighter than one with copper windings with the same electrical performance

CRANE
AEROSPACE & ELECTRONICS

Transformer Windings

Conductor Shape

Window utilization: **62%** | Window utilization: **78%** | Window utilization: **90%**

Base Line | **26% Improvement** | **45% Improvement**

- Round wires give poor transformer window utilization → leads to larger and heavier transformer
- Square wires may not be practical for lower power units, where small wires are needed
- The best transformer window utilization is achieved by using foil for windings
- Weight saving of foil wound completed transformer is about 10% as compared to standard (round) wires

13

CRANE
AEROSPACE & ELECTRONICS

Transformer Improvements Summary

Improvements	Action Taken	Expected Weight Improvements
Transformer Core	Use symmetrical core with rounded legs in place of flat core with square legs	18%
	Use High Flux core material in place of silicon steel	17%
Transformer Windings	Use foil in place of round wires	10%
	Use AL in place of CU	20%

14

CRANE
AEROSPACE & ELECTRONICS

The Crane Advantage!

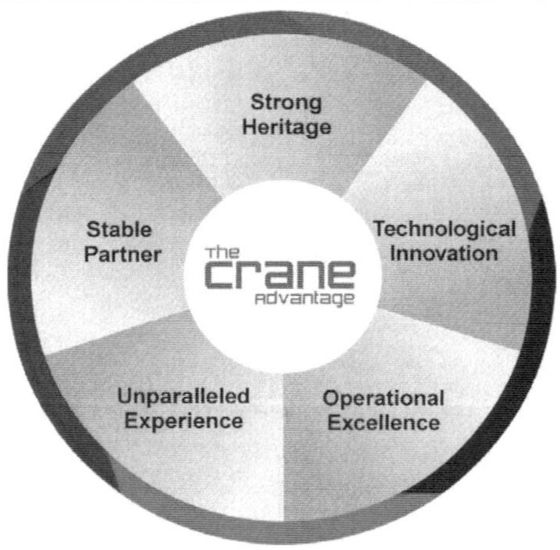

For more information please visit CraneAE.com

Technical Assistance:
Kaz Furmanczyk, Principal Engineer
Tel. +1 425.743.8106
Email: kaz.furmanczyk@craneae.com

15

Comparison of Numerical and Analytical Methods for the Design of Permanent Magnets

Thomas Schliesch
Max Baermann GmbH, Bergisch Gladbach
Germany

- **Permanent magnetic design – What does it mean ?**
- **Numerical approaches - Overview**
- **Analytical approaches - Overview**
- **More detailed explanation of FEM**
- **FEM - Step by step**
- **FEM - More advanced**
- **More detailed explanation of analytical approaches**
- **Systems that can be handled analytically**
- **Software and examples for analytical calculations**
- **Comparative summary**

From user's perspective

Permanent Magnetic Design – What Does It Mean ?

Customer provides detailed specification:
- **Magnetic material**
- **Pole pattern**
- **Magnetic performance of single magnet**

A N

Design Task:
- **Simulation of single magnet**
- **Comparison of e.g. field components in air with customer demands**

Customer has no idea about magnet:
- **Performance of application is demanded**
- **Could be a motor or sensor or clamping system or many other**

N A

Design Task:
- **Partial system simulation of customers system**
- **Trying to find the optimum magnet, like pole pattern, material, pole shape etc.**

N

Design Task – Tooling
(especially isotropic or bonded magnets)
- **Optimization of magnetizing coils**
- **Optimization of injection molding tools**

Numerical Approaches - Overview

FDM (Finite Differences Method)

- Differential equations of problem are transferred into a system of linear equations by substitution of differential quotients into difference quotients on a regular mesh
- Due to the regularity demand for the mesh, geometric flexibility is poor

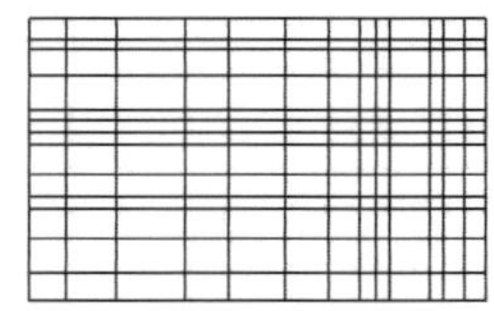

regular mesh

FEM (Finite Element Method)

- Differential equations of problem are transferred into a system of linear equations via minimizing a related functional on an arbitrary mesh
- High geometric flexibility
- Most widely spread

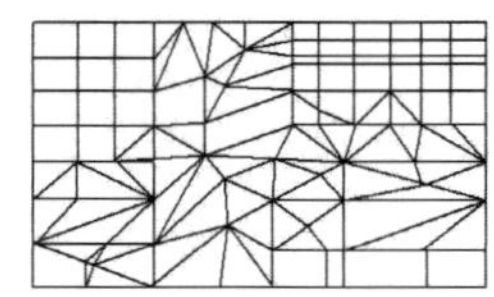

irregular mesh

FI (Finite Integration Technique)

- Discretization of Maxwell's equations in integral form, determined by regular meshes in the past
- Due to the regularity demand for the mesh geometric flexibility was a problem, but now enhancements have been made

BEM (Boundary Element Method)

- Uses integral equations which follow from Maxwell equations. Solutions have to be calculated only on discretized boundaries
- Basic structure of solution has to be known. Not usable for arbitrary problems

Analytical Approaches - Overview

Poisson's Equation

- Describes mainly permanent magnets in free space. Can be solved by the evaluation of integrals when distribution of magnetization is known. 3D
- Simple soft magnetic parts can be included by magnetic mirror model
- Very fast when implemented into software

Laplace's Equation

- Describes magnet free areas like air gaps in electrical machines. Can be solved under specific circumstances with boundary conditions for H and B
- In combination with Poisson's equation in the presence of permanent magnets close to the airgap
- L eq. and P eq. are solved simultaneously, parameters are calculated by boundary conditions
- Only applicable for specific problems, mostly 2D
- Very fast when implemented into software

Magnetic Circuit Method

- Direct application of Amperes law and the law of flux conservation to *nearly closed magnetic circuits*
- Empirical parameters like magnetomotive force loss coefficients and flux leakage coefficients are needed
- Mainly useful to describe known systems, like e.g. a motor, to study the impact of slight design variations
- Fast when implemented into software

Finite Element Method (FEM) – General Scheme

E.g. rigid permanent magnets and current in air, 2D (a more complex situation would include e.g. time, other materials etc.):

$$\Delta A_z = -\mu_0 \cdot (j_z + \vec{\nabla} \times \vec{M}) \qquad \vec{B} = \vec{\nabla} \times \vec{A} \qquad \vec{\nabla} \cdot \vec{A} = 0$$ **+ boundary conditions**

Discretization, use of nodal functions of nodes s inside finite elements E_i

$$A_i = \sum_s f_{is}(x, y) A_s$$ **(similarly for j and M)**

Transfer to an element functional of energy

$$W_i(A_i) = \frac{1}{2}\int |\Delta A_i|^2 ds - \mu_0 \int A_i (j_i + \nabla_x M_{iy} - \nabla_y M_{ix}) ds$$

Assemble global functional of energy to be minimized

$$W(A) = \sum_i W_i(A_i) = \min$$

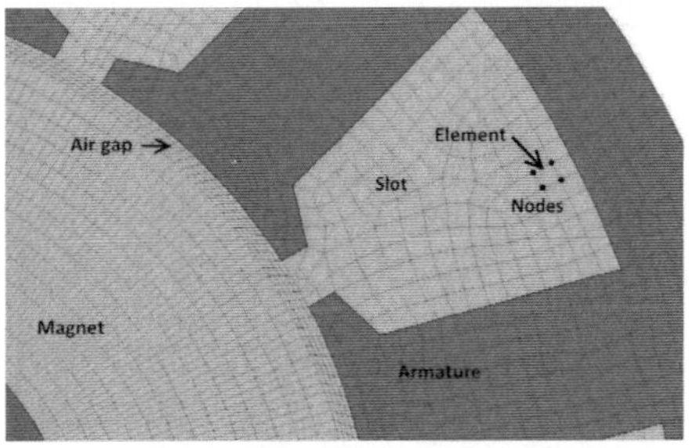

(Discretization of a PM motor, including soft magnetic armature here)

Large system of linear equations. To be solved by iteration when nonlinear materials are present

$$\begin{pmatrix} & & \\ & & \\ & & \end{pmatrix} \begin{pmatrix} A_1 \\ \cdot \\ A_s \\ \cdot \end{pmatrix} = \begin{pmatrix} \\ \\ \\ \end{pmatrix}$$

A basic and handy description of FEM can be found e.g. in: E.P. Furlani, Permanent Magnet and Electromechanical Devices, Academic Press 2001

Finite Element Method (FEM) – Step by Step

1. Materials

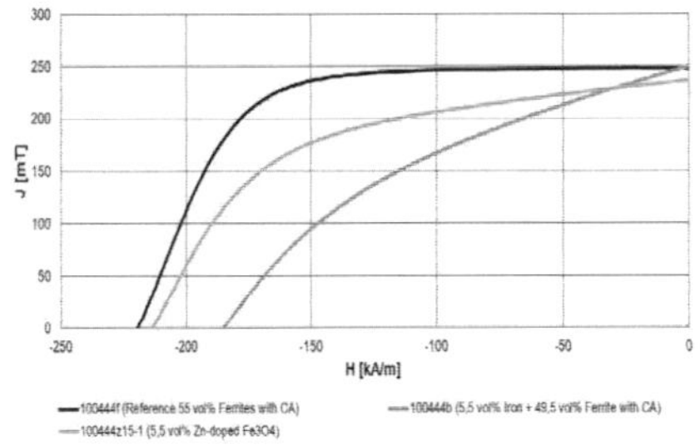

Demagnetization curves: Rigid and non rigid permanent magnetic materials

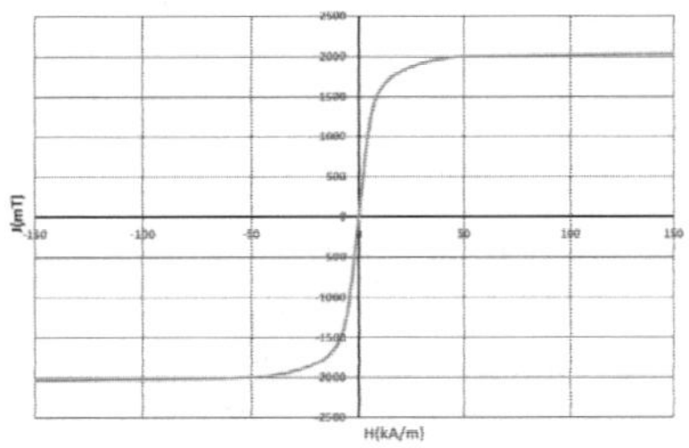

Soft magnetic steel

Nonlinearities are handled by iterative solution of matrix equations

Finite Element Method (FEM) – Step by Step

2. Geometric Models

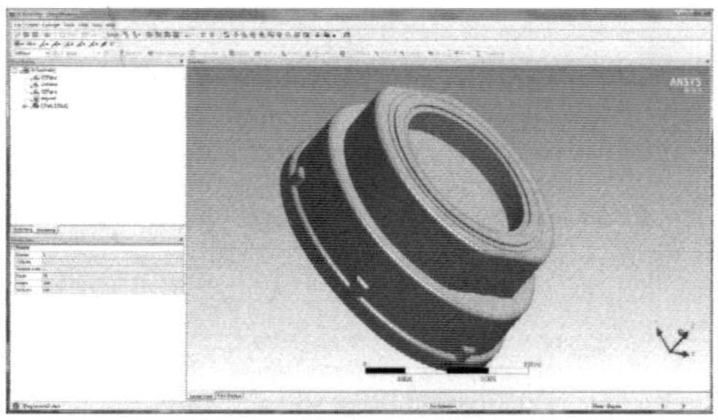

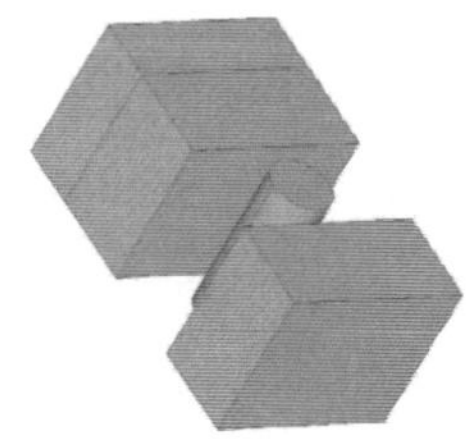

A. From CAD models

- provides most complicated geometries
- can be cumbersome due to imperfections
- sewing, repairing, simplification is often needed

B. Manual input

- From primitives
- From points, lines, faces, volumes
- Less problems
- Time consuming for fastidious systems

Finite Element Method (FEM) – Step by Step

3. Meshing

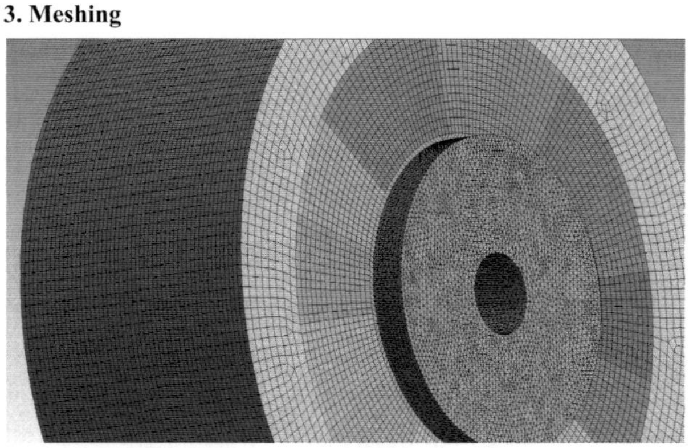

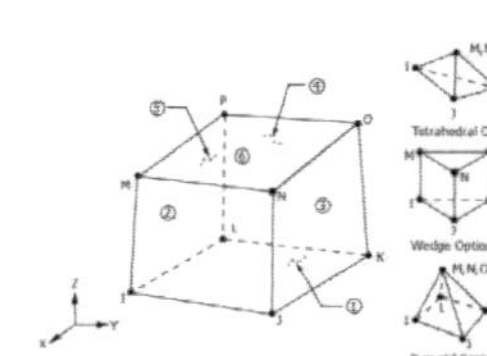

* **Elements with corner nodes**

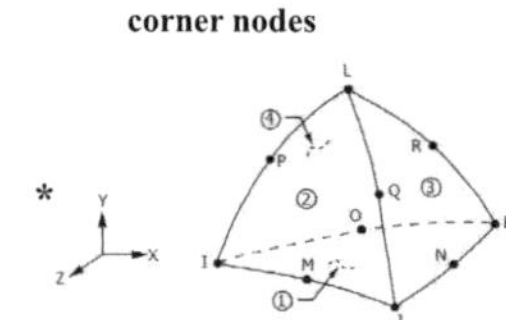

* **Elements with additional edge nodes**

* *ANSYS help system, version 19.0*

It is beneficial when software has cube, tetrahedron and prism/wedge elements

- Cube elements are usually most accurate
- Some software packages have only tetrahedron elements
- In electromagnetics all materials including air have to be meshed !

Finite Element Method (FEM) – Step by Step

4. Boundary Conditions

In electromagnetics all locations where fields can emerge have to be meshed.
By this its is advantageous to reduce the size of simulation by boundary conditions.

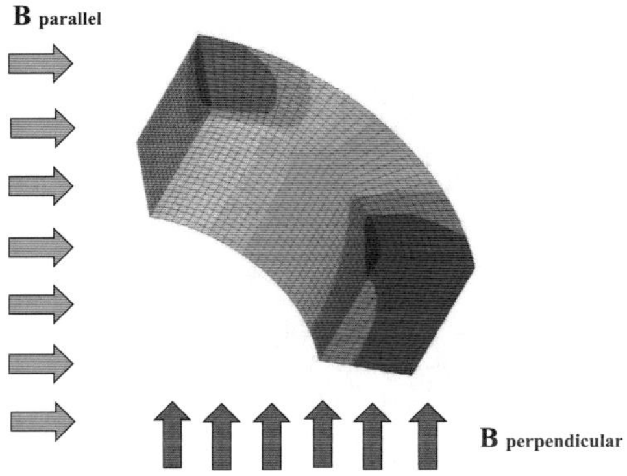

Boundary conditions can be e.g. B-parallel, B-normal, periodic or antiperiodic coupling, far field decay

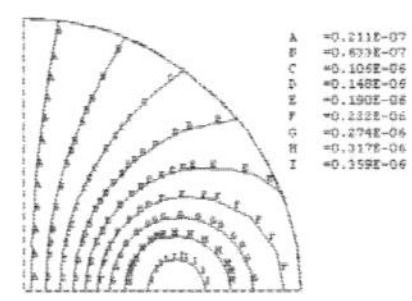

Impact of far field elements

(ANSYS help system, version 19.0)

Comparison of Numerical and Analytical Methods for the Design of Permanent Magnets
Magnetics 2019, Orlando, FL - Thomas Schliesch, Head of Research and Development

Email: t.schliesch@max-baermann.de, Phone: +49(0)22048309141

Finite Element Method (FEM) – Step by Step

5. Solution

- **Solving the system of matrix equations can be done by various approaches**
- **Decreasing the system size by boundary condition reduces computation time lot**
- **When nonlinear materials are included, solution is done iteratively**

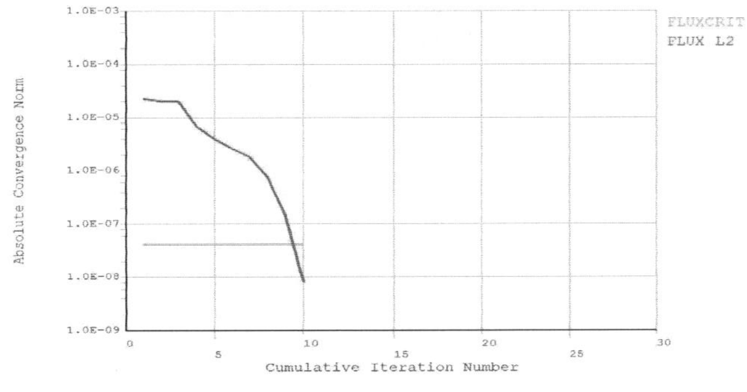

Comparison of Numerical and Analytical Methods for the Design of Permanent Magnets
Magnetics 2019, Orlando, FL - Thomas Schliesch, Head of Research and Development

Email: t.schliesch@max-baermann.de, Phone: +49(0)22048309141

Finite Element Method (FEM) – Step by Step

6. Post processing and general capabilities

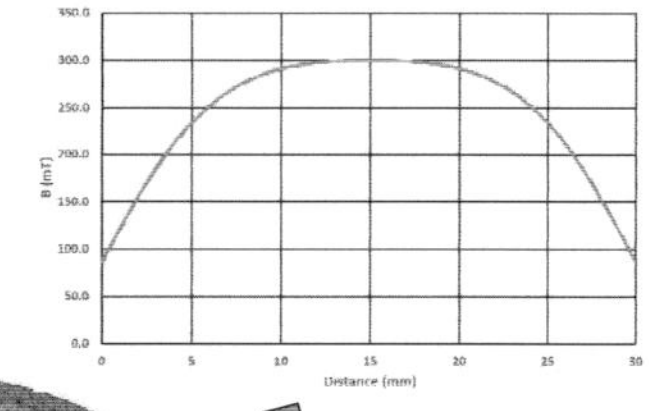

All kinds of FEM software provide

- **Contour plots of B and H fields in volumes and areas**
- **Field components on given paths**
- **Forces or torques or energies on specified volumes**

All software packages can handle simple, i.e. uniform directions of magnetization as being shown here for a calibration unit

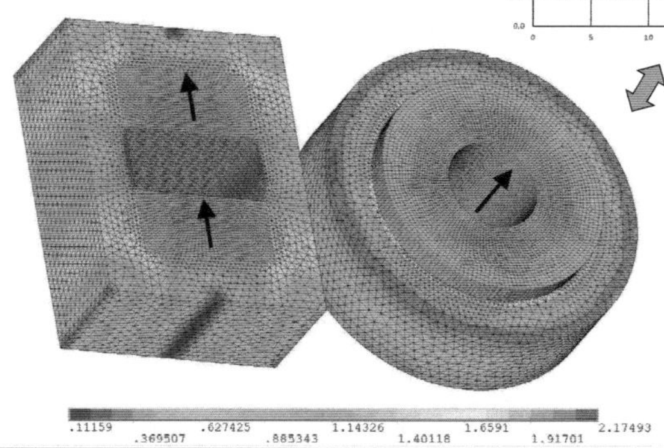

Finite Element Method (FEM) – More Advanced

A few FEM packages can handle more complicated distributions of polarization when its is known by a formula as the one below.

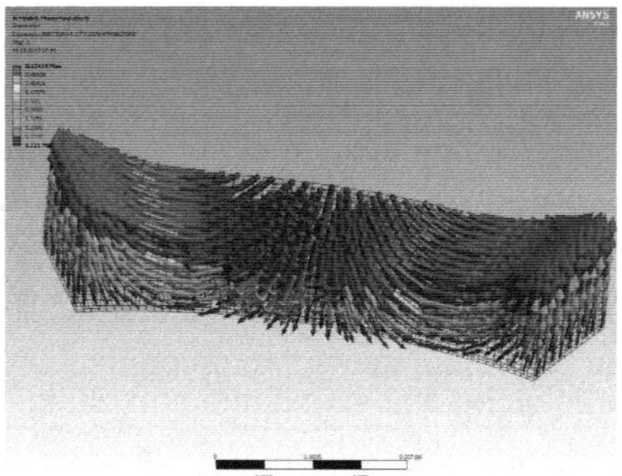

Formula for a multipolar cylinder magnet with bow shaped axial magnetization

$$M_r(\varphi,z)=0$$

$$M_{r_\varphi}(\varphi,z)=M_{r_0}\cdot\exp\left(-\frac{1}{4}\cdot\frac{n_p{}^2\cdot(z_0-z)^2}{r_m{}^2}\right)\cdot\cos\left(\frac{n_p}{2}\cdot(\varphi+\varphi_0)\right)$$

$$M_{r_z}(\varphi,z)=M_{r_0}\cdot\exp\left(-\frac{1}{4}\cdot\frac{n_p{}^2\cdot(z_0-z)^2}{r_m{}^2}\right)\cdot\sin\left(\frac{n_p}{2}\cdot(\varphi+\varphi_0)\right)$$

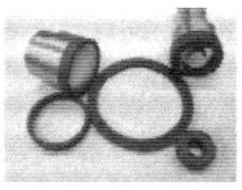

Results on a circular path above a 16 pole magnet compared with measurement

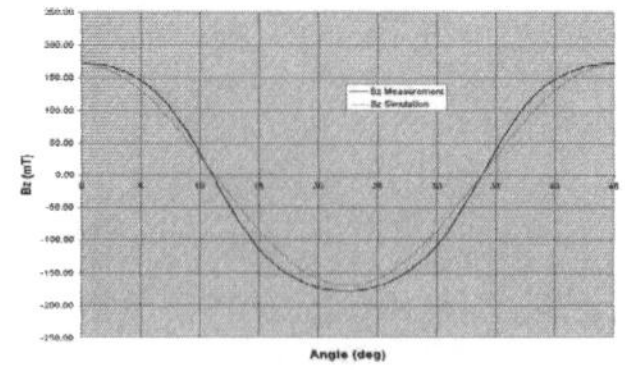

Finite Element Method (FEM) – More Advanced

General methods to handle sophisticated magnets:
Multiple step simulation needed

Simulation magnetizing device

Simulation magnet

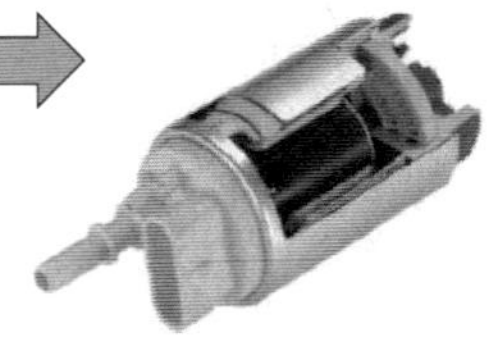

Simulation applikation

H

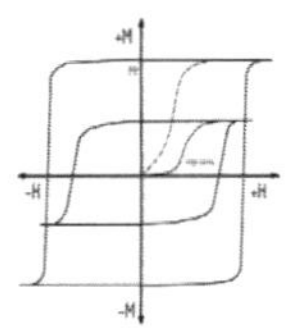

M

Hysteresis

- **Data transfer into single finite elements is profitable**
- **Alternatively subdivision of magnet into many subunits (cumbersome)**

Finite Element Method (FEM) – More Advanced

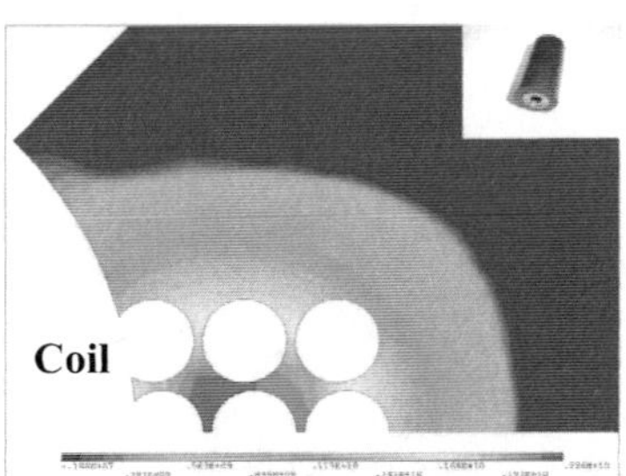

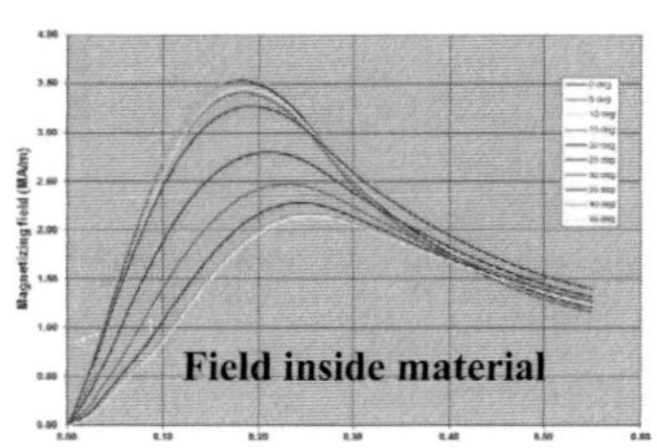

Magnet

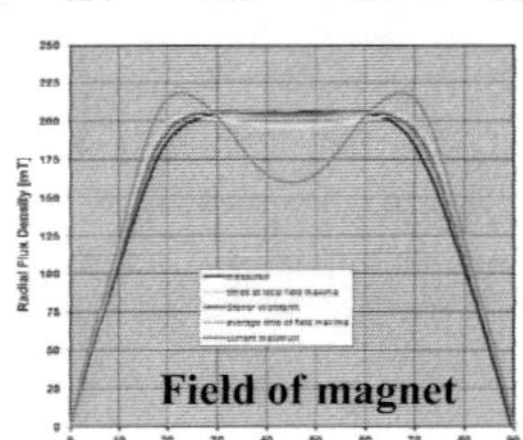

Magnetization with pulse coils of isotropic magnets:
- **Coils are feed by condenser discharge**
- **Electrical circuit has to be modelled**
- **Improved hysteresis model**

Finite Element Method (FEM) – More Advanced

Mold

Direct magnetization of injection molded magnets inside mold by static fields from permanent magnets or dc coils

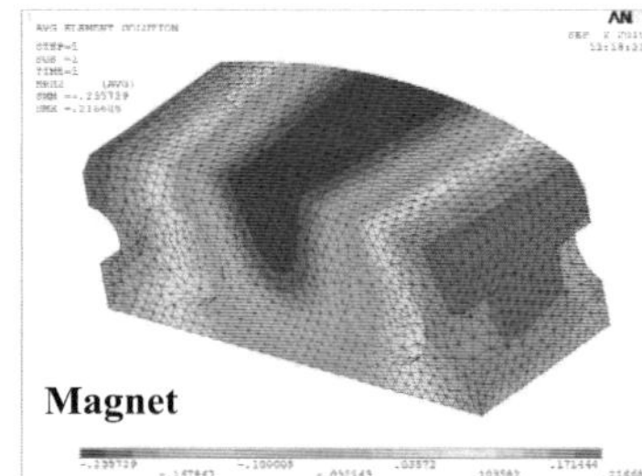

Magnet

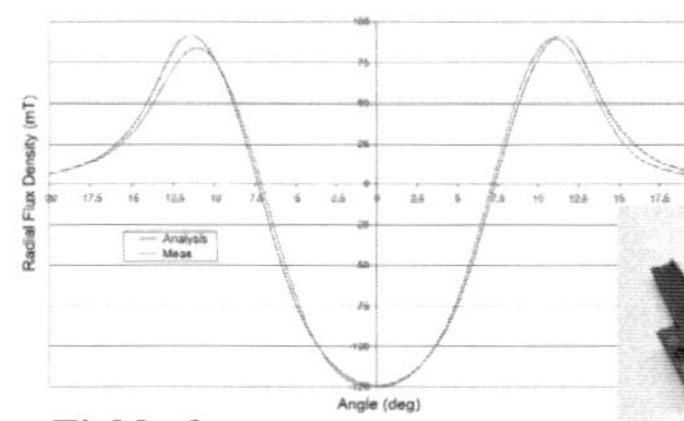

Field of magnet

Finite Element Method (FEM) – More Advanced

Other advanced features of some software packages are/can be:

- **Full scripting** **
- **Design optimization**
- **Circuit elements** **
- **Coupling to system simulation software**
- **Sub modelling**
- **Direct access to finite elements** **
- **Implemented hysteresis models**
- **Implemented stability calculations**
- **Interfaces to other pre- or post-processors or solvers**
- **Interface to other CAD software**
- **Different potential formulations** **

Permanent magnet with sub modelling volume above to model sophisticated sensor structures

Four-pole magnet model with submodelling space for axial sensor distance 1.5mm

** = very important for PM magnet design

Finite Element Method (FEM) – Summary

- **With FEM by principle all kind of permanent magnets and related application systems can be designed**
- **All sorts of materials can be handled**
- **Tools for manufacturing can be designed**
- **Many sophisticated features are implemented in many software packages**

- **Not every package has all needed features**
- **FEM is expensive**
- **FEM needs high training efforts**
- **FEM is slow compared to analytic methods**

It is inevitable to use FEM or other numerical methods for designing magnets, related tools and related applications.

But: By analytical methods one can safe a lot of time and costs. And: A majority of daily problems do not need FEM and can be handled analytically !

Analytical Methods

What can analytical methods provide for the PM design ?

- **Exact results for <u>single permanent magnets</u> or magnets with simple soft magnetic environment**
- **First estimates also for more complicated systems**
- **Plausibility check of numerical simulations**

e.g. sensors !

Which additional advantages do analytical methods have ?

- **Results can be achieved within seconds when methods are implemented into software**
- **Problem input can be very easy and super fast**
- **No special training needed to handle respective software**
- **Related software packages are extremely cost effective**

Poisson's and Laplace's Equation

Maxwell equation, divergence free B-field

$$\vec{\nabla}\cdot\vec{B}=0 \qquad \textbf{(M1)}$$

Constitutive relation for magnetic material

$$\vec{B}=\mu_0(\vec{H}+\vec{M}) \qquad \textbf{(M2)}$$

(M1) and (M2) lead to:

$$\vec{\nabla}\cdot\vec{H}=-\vec{\nabla}\cdot\vec{M} \qquad \textbf{(M3)}$$

The H-field is curl free due to Amperes law, neither macroscopic currents nor electric displacement fields are present:

$$\vec{\nabla}\times\vec{H}=\vec{j}+\frac{\partial\vec{D}}{\partial t}=0 \qquad \textbf{(M4)}$$

So H can be expressed by a scalar potential:

$$\boxed{\vec{H}=-\vec{\nabla}\Phi} \qquad \textbf{(M5)}$$

(M3) and (M5) lead finally to Poisson's equation for permanent magnetic fields:

$$\boxed{\Delta\Phi(\vec{r})=\vec{\nabla}\cdot\vec{M}(\vec{r})} \qquad \textbf{(M6)}$$

In areas where M=0 we get Laplace's equation:

$$\boxed{\Delta\Phi(\vec{r})=0} \qquad \textbf{(M7)}$$

Poisson's Equation – Description of Single Magnets

General Solution of Poisson equation with boundaries at infinity:

$$\vec{H}(\vec{r})=\frac{1}{4\pi}\oint_A\frac{(\vec{M}\cdot\vec{n}')(\vec{r}-\vec{r}')}{\left|\vec{r}-\vec{r}'\right|^3}dA'-\frac{1}{4\pi}\int_V\frac{(\vec{\nabla}'\cdot\vec{M})(\vec{r}-\vec{r}')}{\left|\vec{r}-\vec{r}'\right|^3}dV'$$

Formula see e.g. in: E.P. Furlani, Permanent Magnet and Electromechanical Devices, Academic Press 2001

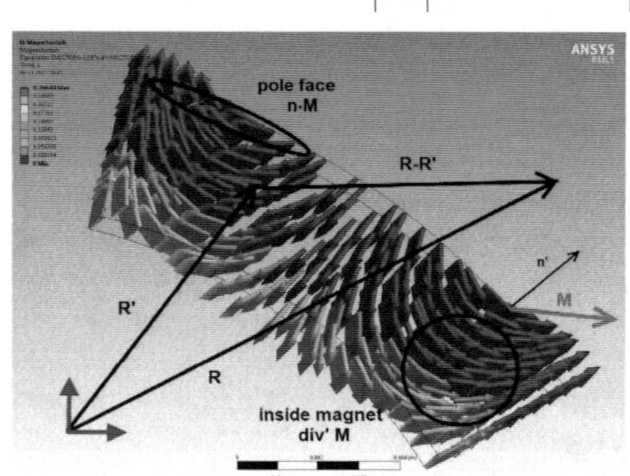

Permanent magnets originate magnetic fields by:
- **Polarization vectors at pole faces**
- **Sources or sinks of polarization inside magnetic body**

Even the most complicated magnetic structures only need the solution of face and volume integrals

Poisson's Equation - Materials

Materials which can be handled:
All modern magnetic materials with rigid or nearly rigid magnetization.

Materials with less rigid M like some sorts of bonded NdFeB: Calculate H inside the magnet near pole faces and correct remanence to sheared remanence B_{rs}

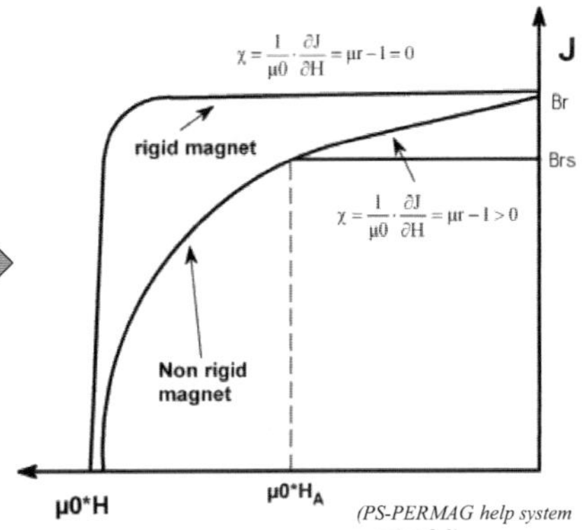

(PS-PERMAG help system version 3.1)

Not covered:
Alnico or semi hard materials

Poisson's Equation – Examples for Applicable Systems

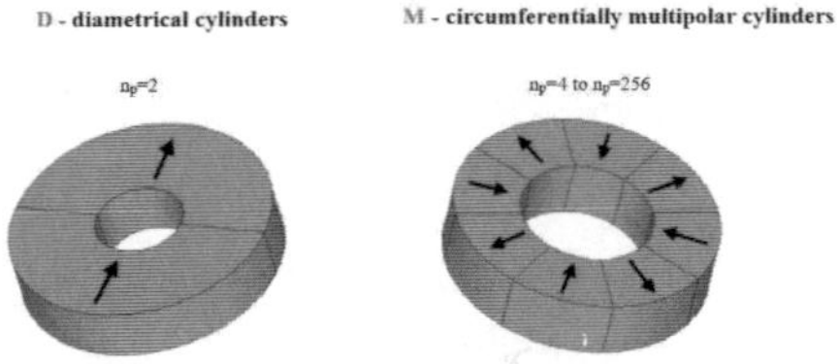

Homogeneous magnetization inside each pole segment

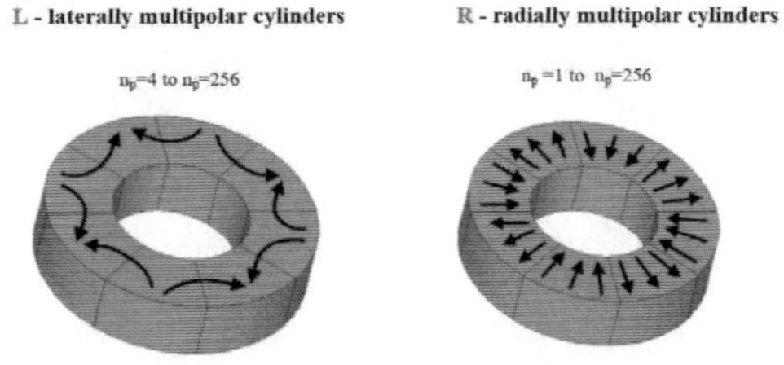

Source of example geometries:
www.permagsoft.com/english

Bow shaped and radial magnetization at outer circumference

Poisson's Equation – Examples for Applicable Systems

C - Homogeneously multipolar cuboids, also with soft magnetic plates of adjustable distance and computation of attracting forces (n_p=1 to n_p=256)

Example: axial cube, n_p=1

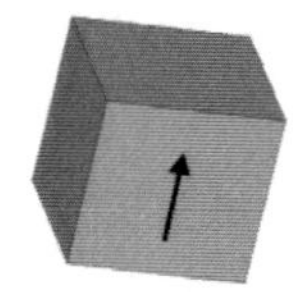

Example: 8 -polar magnetized plate

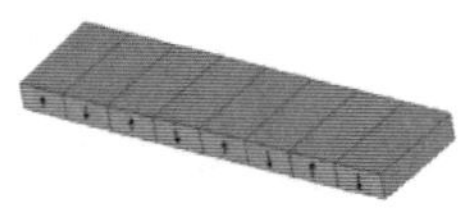

Magnetization is homogenous within each single pole

soft magnetic plates calculated by magnetic mirror method

Example: Four pole magnet above soft magnetic plate

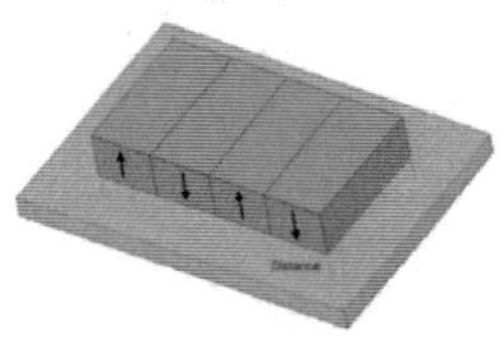

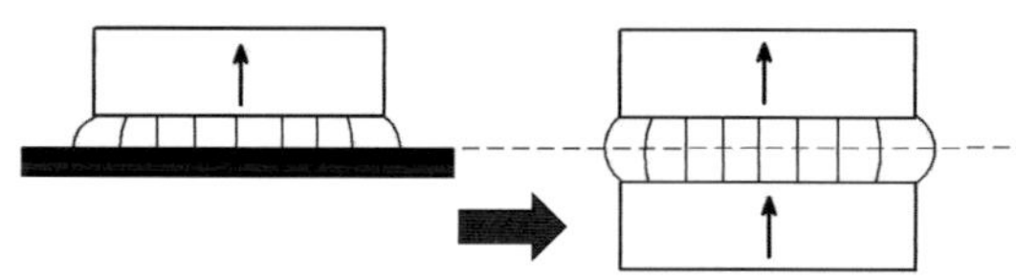

Poisson's Equation – Examples for Applicable Systems

A - axially multipolar cylinders, also with soft magnetic plates of adjustable distance and computation of attracting force (n_p=1 to n_p=256)

Example: n_p=10

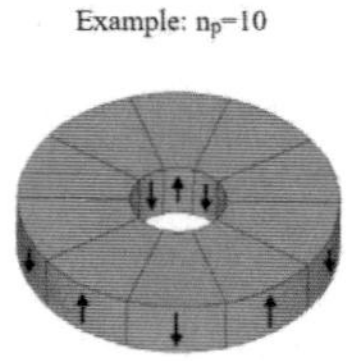

Example: n_p=6 with soft magnetic plate

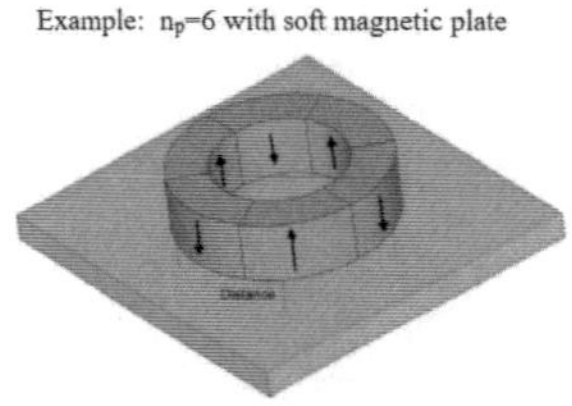

CS - multipolar bar segments with irregular poles, also with soft magnetic plates of adjustable distance and computation of attracting force (n_p=1 to n_p=8)

Example: Magnetic strip n_p=3

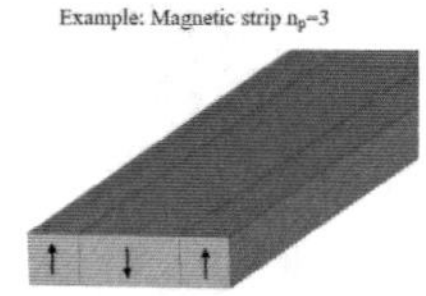

Example: two cuboids with n_p=2 each

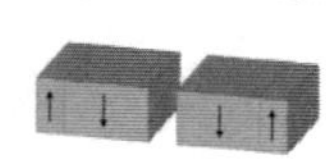

Example: Irregularly poled segements with gap above soft magnetic plate

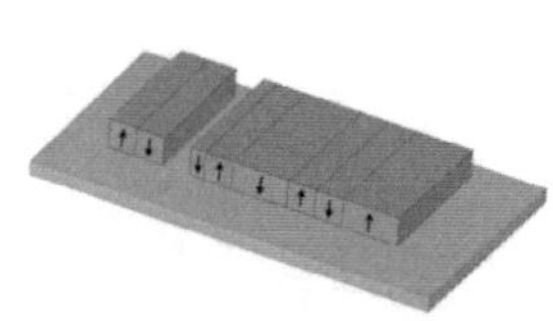

Poisson's Equation – Examples for Applicable Systems

II - multipolar cylinders due to the Hallbach principle, continuous or segmented magnetization (n_p=2 to n_p=120, number of segments per pole 1 to 40)

Example: n_p=2 with 8 segments per pole

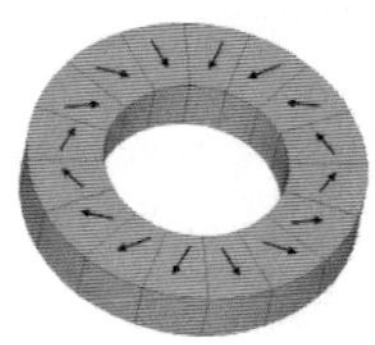

AL - Axially lateral (bow shaped) magnetized cylinders oder cylinder rings (n_p=4 to n_p=256)

Example: Cylinder ring n_p=8

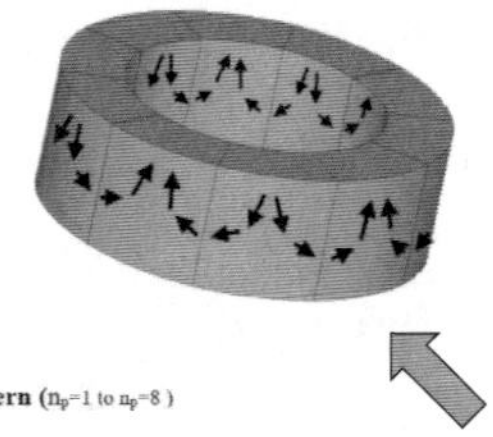

Bow shaped magnetization in axial direction

RS - radially magnetized cylinder segments of irregular pol patthern (n_p=1 to n_p=8)

Example: Two segments of different size separated by an air gap

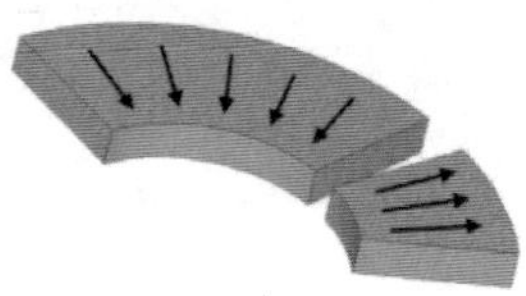

Comparison of Numerical and Analytical Methods for the Design of Permanent Magnets
Magnetics 2019, Orlando, FL - Thomas Schliesch, Head of Research and Development
Email: t.schliesch@max-baermann.de, Phone: +49(0)22048309141

Max Baermann GmbH Kunststoffgebundene Dauermagnete

Poisson's Equation – Examples for Applicable Systems

SD - Two pole diametrical sensormagnet with up to four rotationally symmetric ledges or depressions (np=2)

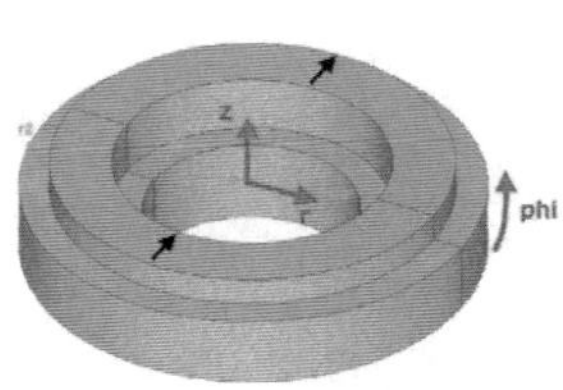

SA - Two pole axial sensormagnet with up to four rotationally symmetric ledges or depressions (np=2)

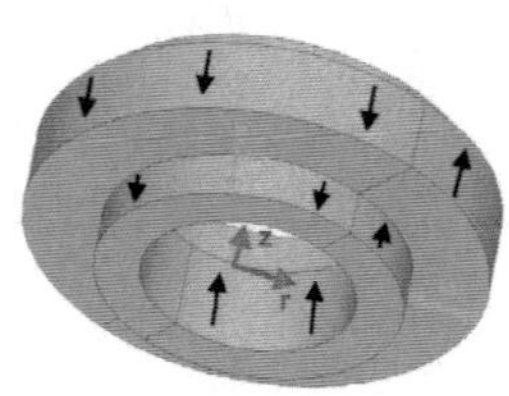

SL - Two pole axial-lateral sensormagnet with up to four rotationally symmetric ledges or depressions (one sided bow shaped magnetization) (np=2)

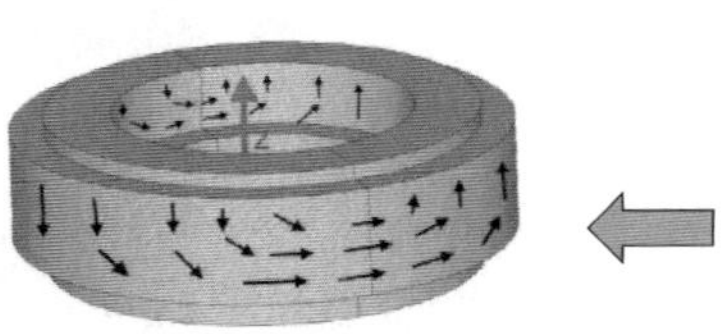

Bow shaped magnetization in axial direction

Comparison of Numerical and Analytical Methods for the Design of Permanent Magnets
Magnetics 2019, Orlando, FL - Thomas Schliesch, Head of Research and Development
Email: t.schliesch@max-baermann.de, Phone: +49(0)22048309141

Max Baermann GmbH Kunststoffgebundene Dauermagnete

Software for Analytical Calculations

Solution of Poisson's as well as Laplace's equations lead to huge and complicated formulas. But when implementing them into respective software, problems can be handled easily and results are available within seconds.

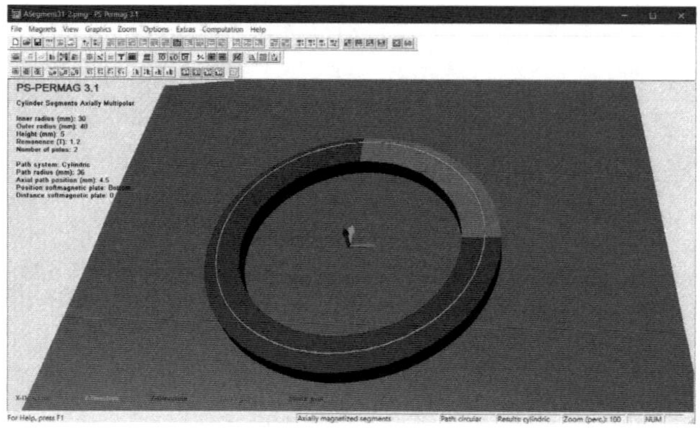

Circular path above magnet ring and steel plate

Source of software screenshots:
www.permagsoft.com/english

Software for Analytical Calculations

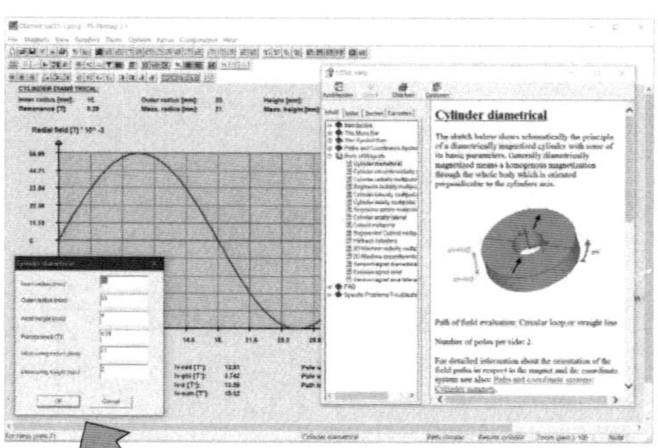

Easy input by dialog masks

Most easy problem definition, minutes in comparison to hours with FEM

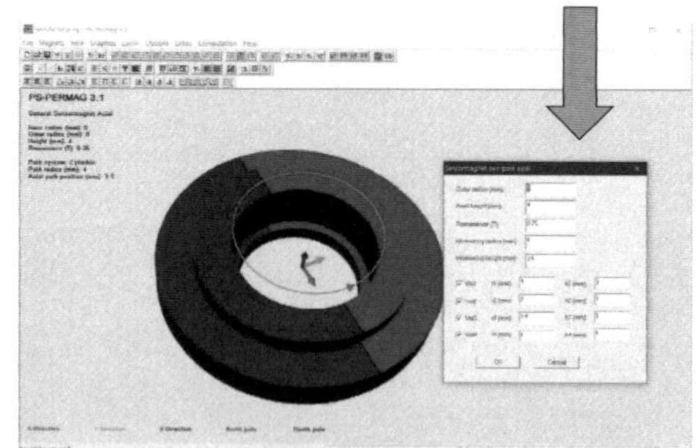

Software for Analytical Calculations

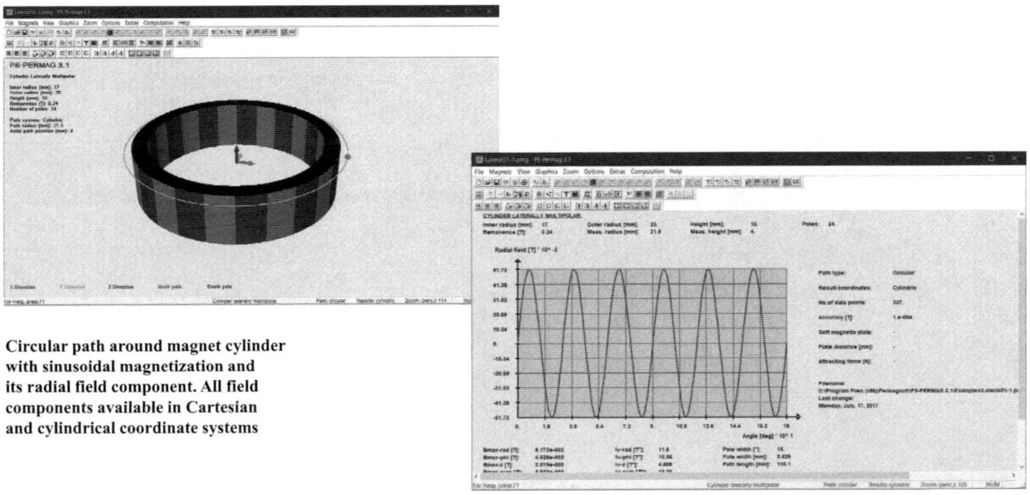

Circular path around magnet cylinder with sinusoidal magnetization and its radial field component. All field components available in Cartesian and cylindrical coordinate systems

Software for Analytical Calculations

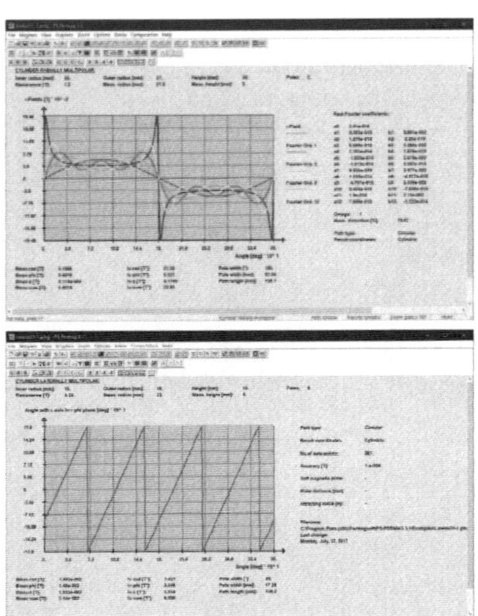

Derived results like Fourier analyses of field components, adhesion forces, field integrals etc. are easily available

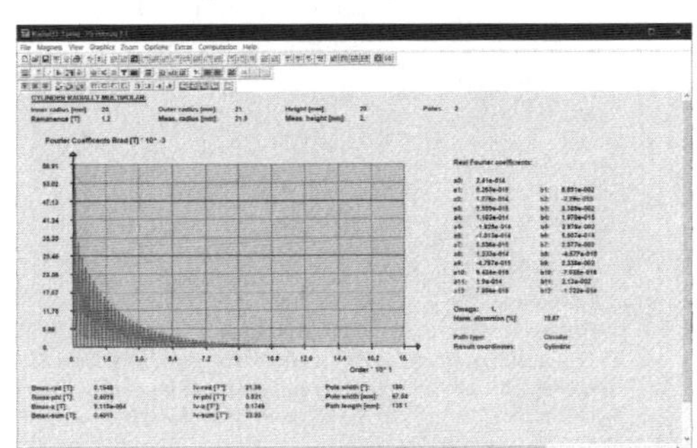

Derived results: Field angles

Software for Analytical Calculations

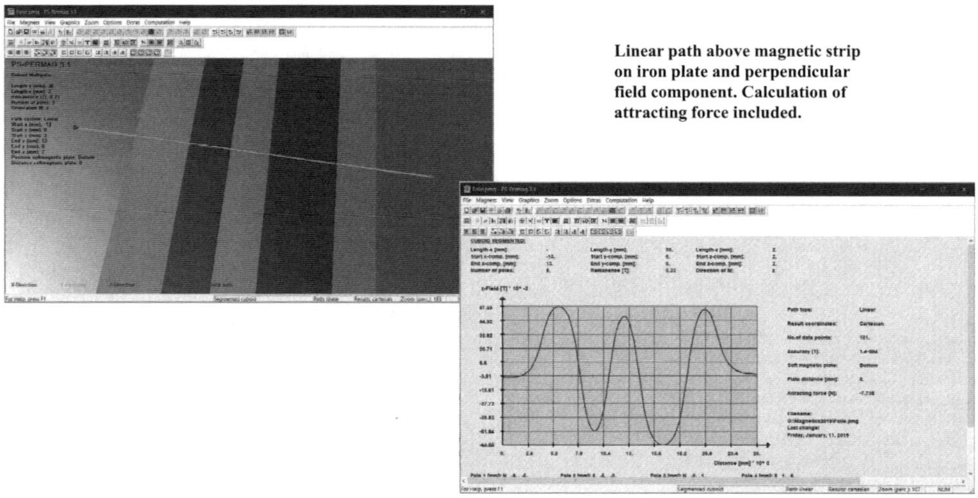

Linear path above magnetic strip on iron plate and perpendicular field component. Calculation of attracting force included.

Description of Magnetic systems – Laplace's Equation

- **Describes mainly periodic systems where unique boundary conditions can be set**
- **Often used for calculating fields in airgaps near iron and permanent magnets with simple magnetization (there in combination with Poisson's equation)**
- **Mainly 2D**

2DM, 2DR - 2D-Models for electrical machines, magnetization circumferentiallly multipolar and radially multipolar, inner and outer rotor assemblies (n_p=2 to n_p=256)

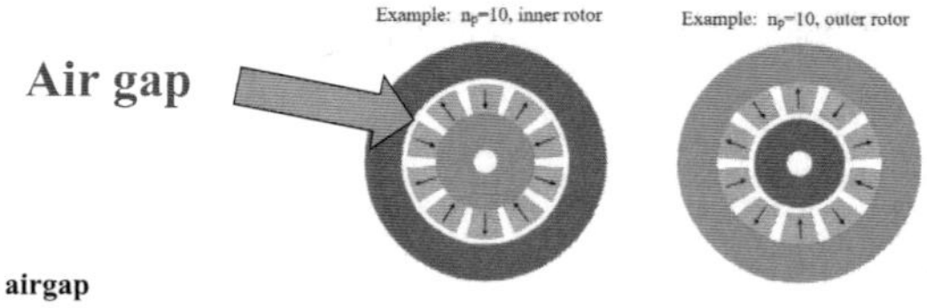

Sketch of solution for a motor system:

- **General solution for Laplace's equation in airgap**
- **Perform an angular Fourier series expansion for periodic magnetization**
- **General solution for Poisson's equation in magnet area**
- **Set equations from boundary conditions at airgap iron boundary**
- **Set equations from boundary conditions at airgap-magnet boundary**
- **Calculate unknown parameters from all sorts of boundary conditions**

(*see e.g. at Z.Q. Zhu. D. Howe, C.C. Chan: Improved Analytical Model for Predicting the Magnetic Field Distribution in Brushless Permanent-Magnet Machines, IEEE Trans. On Magnetics, Vol 38, No 1, Jan. 2002, pp. 239*)

Description of Magnetic systems – Laplace's Equation

Systems like motor assemblies or similar can also be implemented into software, problem input and solution are also very fast

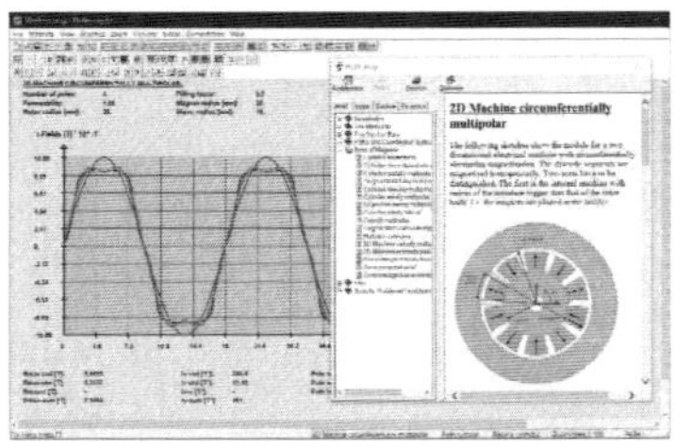

Radial field in airgap due to solved Laplace's equation

Source: *www.permagsoft.com/english*

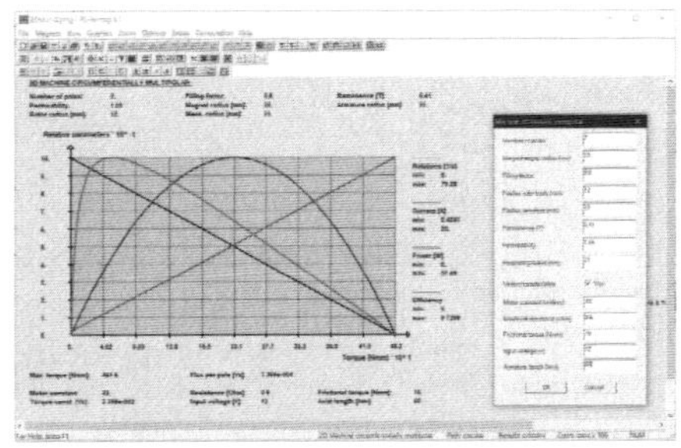

Problem definition and resulting parameters of a DC motor when motor constant is known

Method can be used to predict air gap flux densities in periodic systems, to study the impact of pole pattern or magnet size or of material grade. For DC motors from air gap distributions even motor characteristics can be deduced when the coupling to armature (motor constant) can be estimated. Method can be extended to slotted iron areas to predict e.g. cogging torque.

Analytical Methods - Summary

- **Single magnets or magnets with simple soft magnetic configurations can be calculated by using Poisson's equation**
- **Calculations are constricted to rigid or nearly rigid materials, i.e. no Alnico**
- **Resulting formulas can be very complicated, but implementing them into respective software makes their use very easy and fast**
- **Software implementation constricts problem treatment to given geometries and pole configurations**
- **Models based on Poisson's equation are 3D**

- **Periodic systems with iron can be handled by Laplace's equations (together with Poisson's equation), which provides fields in airgaps of motors or similar systems. 2D !**
- **Also from Laplace's equations resulting formulas are complicated, but practical application can be made very handy by implementing into software**

- **Magnetic circuit method is constricted to nearly closed magnetic systems where stray field and magnetomotive force losses have been evaluated experimentally or by other methods**
- **Magnetic circuit method is fine for studying the impact of small design variations, 2D mainly**

Summarizing Comparison Numerical vs Analytical

Numerical Methods:

- **Are inevitable when treating universal problems of magnet design**
- Covers all kinds of materials
- Covers all kinds of systems

- Many software packages can only treat simple sorts of magnetization without problems
- **Advanced packages can even treat magnetizing or demagnetizing processes and hysteresis models**
- Even more advanced packages permit the user to perform free programming of own models and simulation sequences or provide finite element access

- Numerical methods need elaborate training
- Numerical methods are time consuming
- **Respective software is widely spread but usually expensive**

Analytical Methods:

- Are constricted to predefined classes of problems
- **Are well suited when only magnets or magnets near simple soft magnetic entities have to be treated**
- **Cover 2D and 3D problems but usually** no nonlinearities like saturation effects

- Are extremely fast and easy to use when implemented into software
- Can cover 70% to 80% of daily simulation work at magnet development
- **Can be very impressing to customers when problem solution is directly done at phone**

- Do not demand laborious user training
- **Respective commercial software is less widely spread but very cost effective**

Pro - con

Comparison of Numerical and Analytical Methods for the Design of Permanent Magnets

Thank you for your attention !

KOLEKTOR

Anisotropic injection moulding of multipole radial rotors for IPM

M. Ohm
Kolektor Magnet Technology GmbH, Essen, DE

KOLEKTOR

Locations Worldwide – Magnetics (in bold)

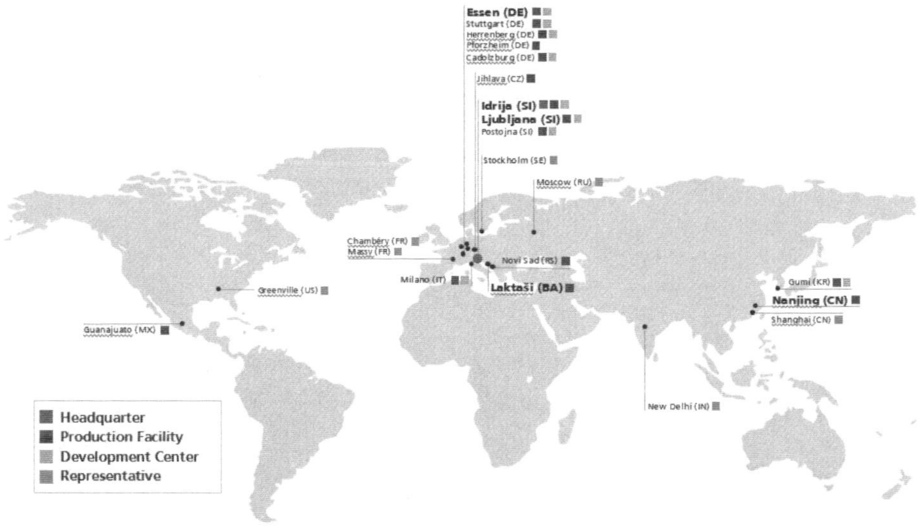

Locations Worldwide – Magnetics (in bold)

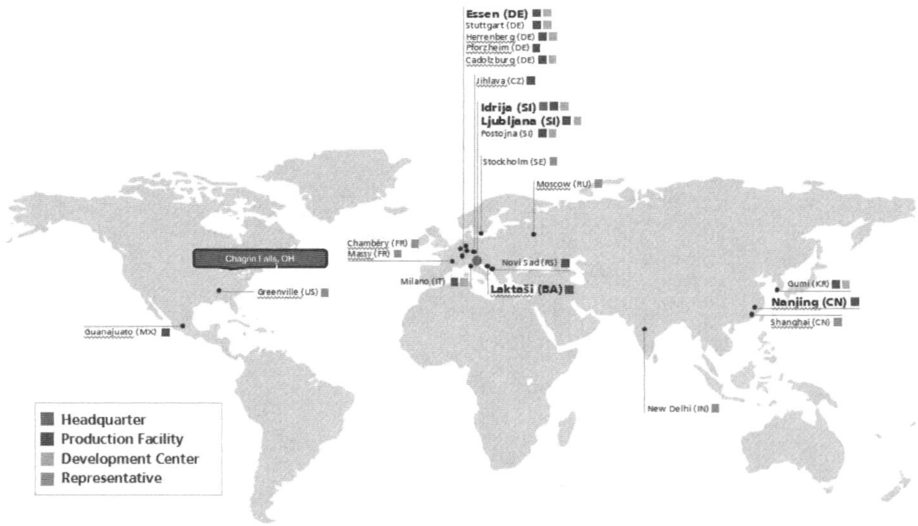

Strategic Business Units
Components & Systems
Commutators
Magnetics
Hybridics
Electronics & Drives
Automation
Equipment
Tools
Machine Vision
Electrical Power
Small Hydro Plant
Hydro Equipment
Power Transformers
Electrical Power Systems
Engineering & Technology Systems
Civil Works
Water Treatment
Automation & Electrical Engineering
Insulation Solutions
KOLEKTOR
Magnetics 2019, Orlando, FL
23. 1. 2019 • All rights reserved by KOLEKTOR® • www.kolektor.com
5

Products
Rotors
Sensor magnets
Stators
Inductive components
FUNCTION
Transfering electrical energy into mechanical movement
Sensing position, torque, speed, proximity etc.
Transfering electrical energy into mechanical movement
• Sensing
• DC/DC transformation
• Antennas
COMPETITIVE ADVANTAGE
• Inhouse production of compound
• Media tight overmoulding
• Production of tools inhouse
• In process magnetization
• Supply rotor and stator
• Experience with thermoseth overmoulding
• Producing soft ferrites inhouse
• Flexible production from low volumes to high series
KOLEKTOR
Magnetics 2019, Orlando, FL
23. 1. 2019 • All rights reserved by KOLEKTOR® • www.kolektor.com
6

Kolektor KMT

Structure of the presentation

- Motivation
- Application and Motor requirements
- Rotor requirements
- Magnetic and core stack
- Simulations
- Manufacturing Process
- Magnetic properties
- Conclusion

Introduction

Anisotropic injection insert or over - moulding of ferrite permanent magnetic materials in thermoplastic matrix is well established technology.

It enables:

- manufacturing of complex shapes
- highly automated processes
- net shaped products magnetised to desired level
- complex magnetic pattern
- one processing step to final part

In this work, we would like to present utilisation of RE anisotropic injection moulding of a multipole rotor for IPM motor.

The application is for a road sweeper motor.

Motivation

Main advantages of in-stack injection molding for IPM rotors would be the following:

- **High degree of freedom** in a pole configuration construction for flux concentration which enables low ripple/torque ratio.
- **One step process** of aligned rotor manufacturing which enables highly automated manufacturing.
- **Aligning in radial** as opposed to diametral (as with sintered Neo)

In the presentation, following results are disclosed:

- Anisotropic moulding technology design for RE-based material
- Comparison of magnetic properties to isotropic NdFeB rotor
- Magnetic properties of anisotropic 8-pole radially oriented rotor

Motor/rotor requirements

- Power: 10 to 15 kW
- Moment: 50 Nm
- Flux in 0,7 mm gap: 700 mT
- Note nearly perfect radial alignment

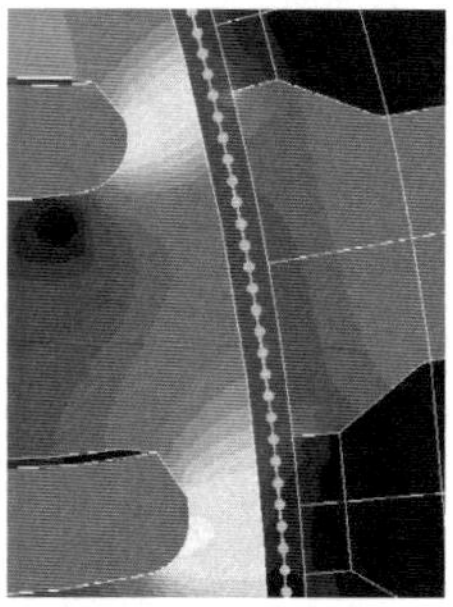

Air gap

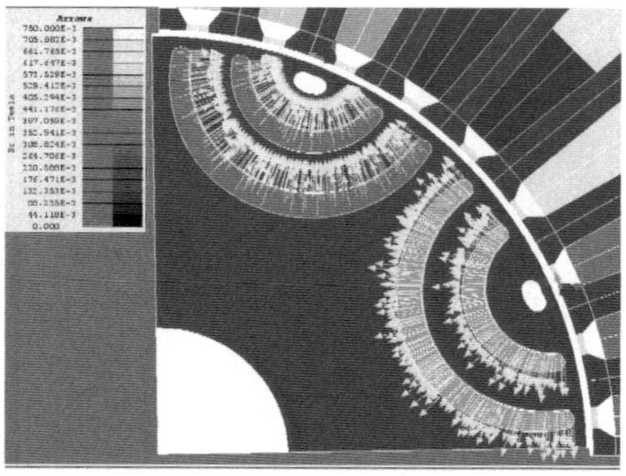

Motor simulation (8-36 topology)

Diametral alignment @ sintered RE-based

Two materials (Br=550 mT and Br=750 mT Flux) gives flux in gap 260 and 475 mT respectively.

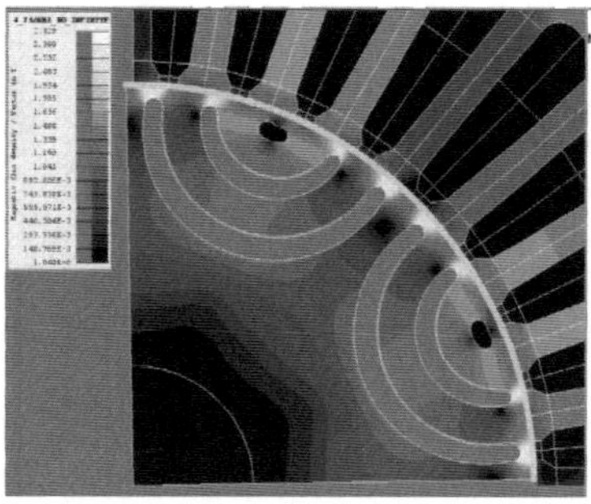

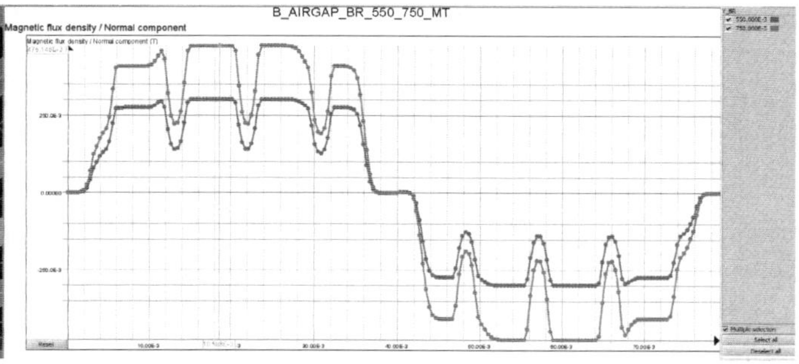

Radial alignment @ polymer bonded RE

Two materials (isotropic (Br = 550 mT) and anisotropic (Br = 750 mT) gives Flux in gap 500 and 750 mT respectively (by value nearly the same as remanence)

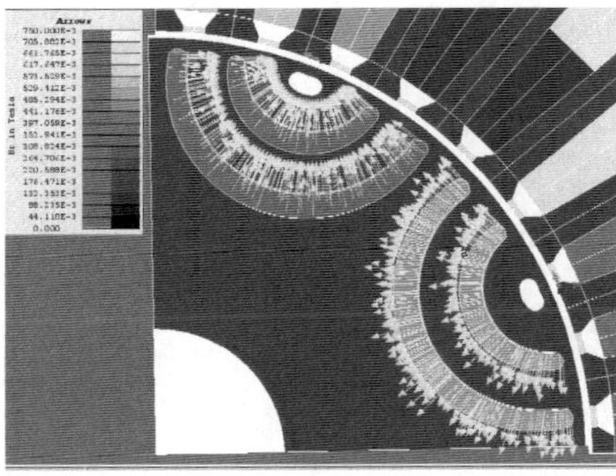

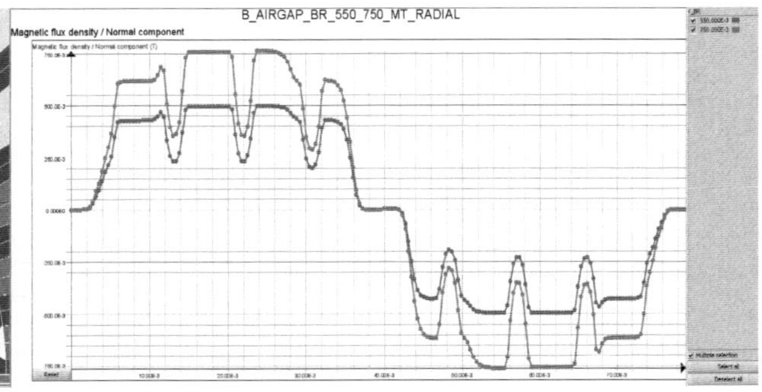

Target

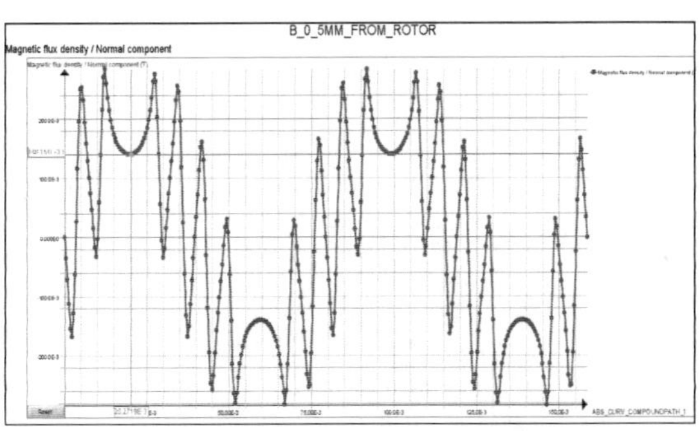

Simulated flux distribution on the surface of the rotor

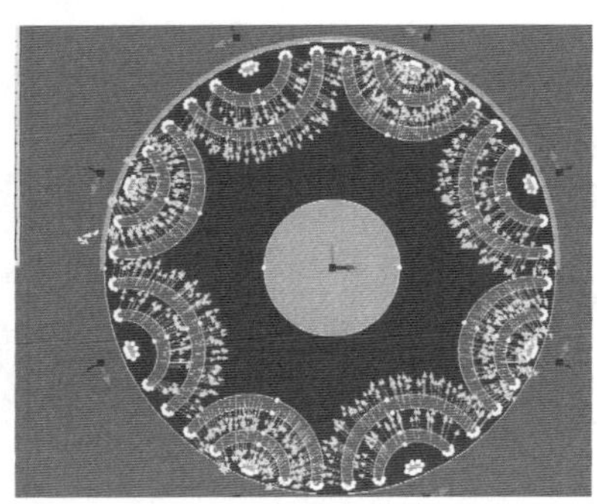

Radial magnet alignment

Core stack topology

Core stack topology for IPM rotor

Laser cutting of individual lamellas

Core stack manufacturing

Possible Technology:

- Laser welding
  - Power
  - Spot size
  - timing
- Lamination bonding (Back Lack)
  - Pressure
  - Temperature

IPM rotor core stacks

Result of tool simulation

Requirements (material dependent):

- Material specific data
  - Isotropic NdFeB
  - Anisotropic NdFeB
  - Anisotropic SmFeN
  - Fe sheet metal
- Alignment field

Method used:

- FEM Ansys

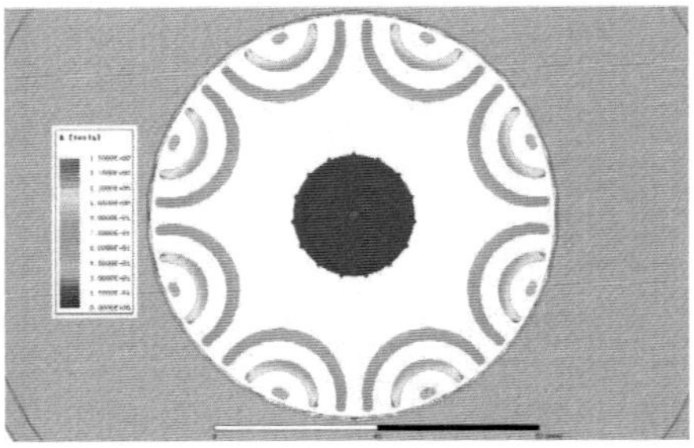

Alignment magnetic field for 8-pole radial IPM rotor.

Magnetic properties of material used

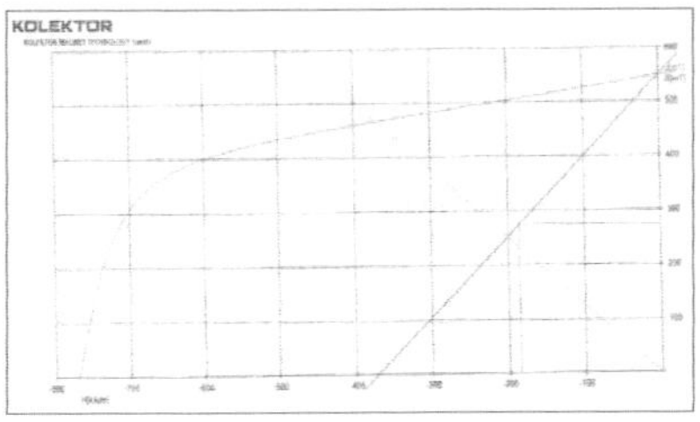

Isotropic NdFeB
(Br=540 mT, Hcj 760 kA/m)

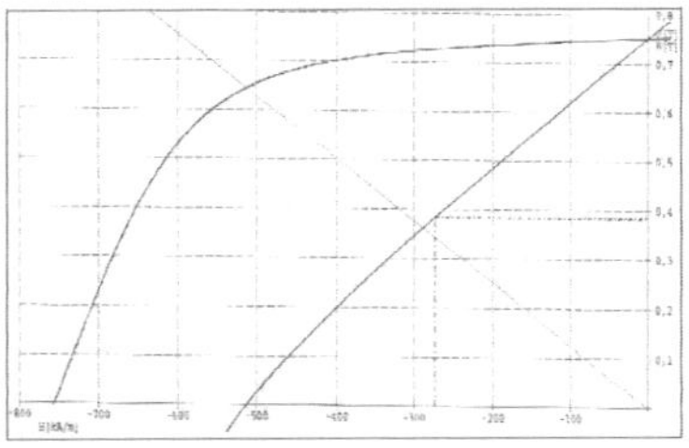

Anisotropic SmFeN
(Br=750 mT, Hcj 760 kA/m)

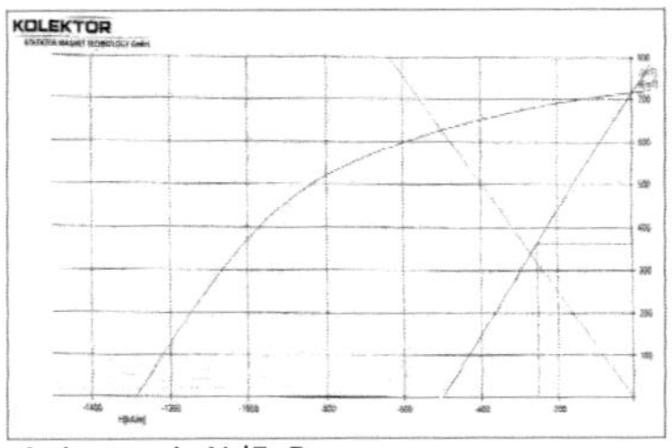

Anisotropic NdFeB
(Br=710 mT, Hcj 1280 kA/m)

Magnetic properties of material used (example of SmFeN)

Alignment trial:

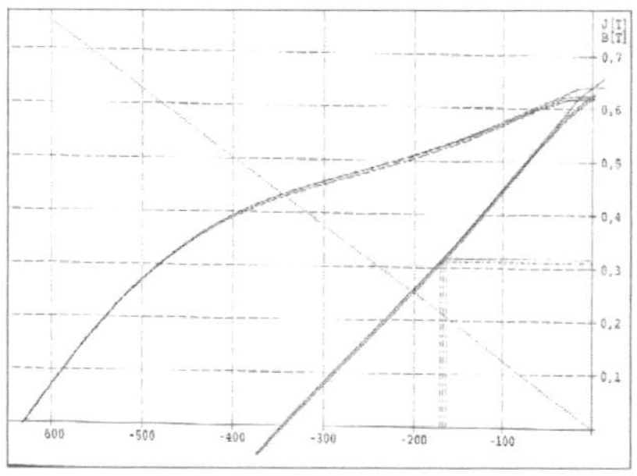

Demag curve as molded in magnetic field
(axial test sample, 500mT)

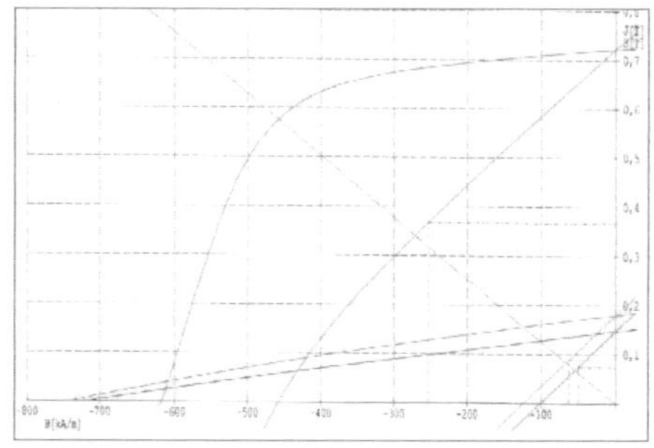

Demag curves in x,y,z direction indicating alignment
(after re-magnetisation)

Friendly note: Please do not use homepage magnetic material characteristics. They are produced in ideal conditions as to aligning and magnetising fields. Realistic values are normally lower than that.

Manufacturing process

Compounding: PA12 plus magnetic filler

Production process: injection moulding

Alignment: in-build permanent magnetic field arround 1 Tesla

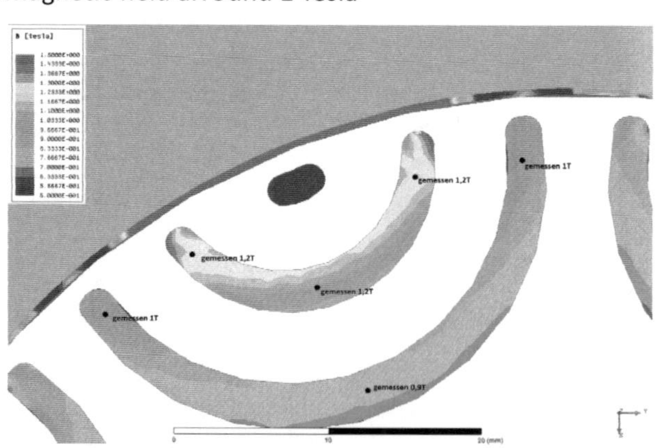

Aligning field distribution

Injected rotor (100 mm OD)

Gauss reading of isotropic NdFeB rotor

average tot. pole amplitude	403,91	mT
total RMS flux density	321,19	mT
max. amplitude deviation	20,06	mT
max. polewidth deviation	2,10	°

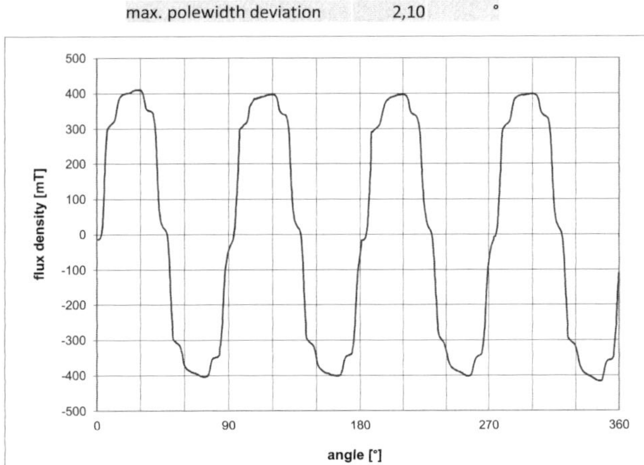

Test 8 pole iso NdFeB sample, in-gap flux density

Gauss reading of anisotropic NdFeB rotor

average tot. pole amplitude	591,16	mT
total RMS flux density	462,35	mT
max. amplitude deviation	22,70	mT
max. polewidth deviation	12,46	°

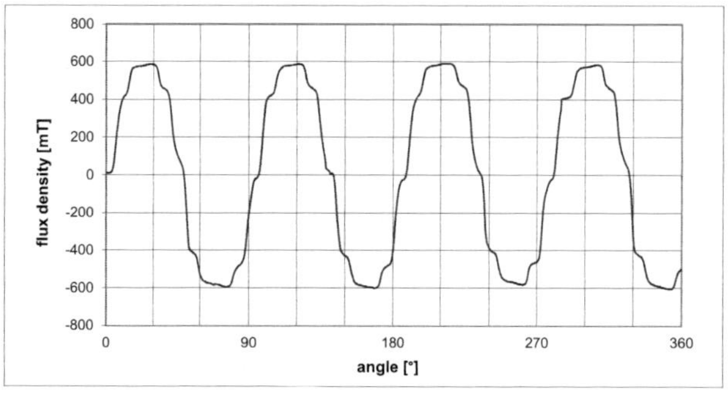

Test 8 pole aniso NdFeB sample, in-gap flux density

Gauss reading of anisotropic SmFeN rotor

average tot. pole amplitude	627,75	mT
total RMS flux density	493,53	mT
max. amplitude deviation	25,13	mT
max. polewidth deviation	11,49	°

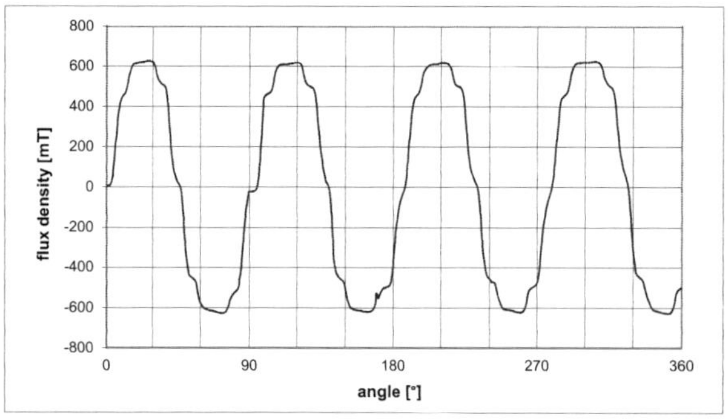

Test 8 pole aniso SmFeN sample, in-gap flux density

Conclusions:

- IPM anisotropic moulding technology proved feasible
- Promising magnetic results
- Still not enough aligning field to saturate (calculating from test sample measurement, enhancement possible)

Further steps:

- Magnetically saturate (additionally pulsed field after moulding)
- Test in a motor

Contact:

Boris.Saje@Kolektor.com
Wolfgang.Stass@Kolektor.com

Thank You

&

Enjoy The Cocktails

MAGNETICS 2019

Impact of New Tariffs and a Looming Trade War

So who, you may ask, am I?

My name is Mike Miller and amazingly I have spent the last 50 years in the magnet industry. Starting straight from school at 16 in 1968 as a tool making apprentice designing and making the tools for Sintered Alnico magnets, I eventually ended up selling all magnet materials around the world.

In a nut shell, I tell my grandchildren that I was a traveling salesman who sold magnets!

When I started work in 1968

- Robert Kennedy and the Rev. Martin Luther King were both assassinated
- **A gallon of gas cost 34 cents in the US and 5 shillings and 5 pence in the UK (28 new pence)**
- **Phone calls meant staying in one place tethered by a cord**
- Richard Nixon was elected President of the US
- Harold Wilson was the PM of the UK
- Mao Zedong was still the leader in China
- **The year end Dow Jones stood at 943**
- The Vietnam War raged
- The first successful heart transplant was performed by Dr. Christian Barnard

- The Big Mac was introduced by McDonalds for $0.49
- **The 747 made its maiden flight**
- The Beatles were still a group and just released the White Album
- The Rolling Stones released Jumping Jack Flash
- Intel was founded by Robert Noyce and a few friends
- **The first desktop computer was released by Hewlett-Packard (9100A)**
- Personal computers were still a thing for the future
- **Most companies used telex as the fastest means of communication overseas**

Commercially Available Permanent Magnets

1968	2018
Sintered Alnico	Sintered Alnico
Cast Alnico	Cast Alnico
Sintered Ferrites (Ceramics)	Sintered Ferrites (Ceramics)
Cunife	Cunife
	Bonded Ferrite as well Rare Earth (Compression & Injection)
Lodex	
	Flexible Ferrite
	Flexible Neodymium
	Sintered Samarium Cobalt
	Sintered Neodymium

Today's trade dispute between the US and China is a result of 2 issues.

1. It is a result of the current round of protectionism, not only in the US but around the world.

2. The emergence of China as a potential threat to the US's current top position both economically and politically in world trade.

The Thucydides Trap:

There have been many wars fought over trade, especially when one great power threatens to take over from another super power. This is not a new situation. 2,500 years ago Thucydides first identified this as what we came to know it as "the Thucydides Trap." Thucydides said it was inevitable that any new rising power could only be met by war from the existing top power.

From the early classical days of the empires of Phoenicia and Mesopotamia to the Egyptians, Greeks and Romans to the wars fought over the New World by England, France, Portugal and Spain this has been true.

Then in the 19th century the Opium wars were fought between the Qing dynasty and the British Empire between 1839 and 1842 over the ban on trafficking of the substance by the British East India Company to China. This led to China losing Hong Kong to Britain during the second Opium war between 1856-1860. Britain along with France forced China to open all of China to foreign merchants and exempt foreign import duties. Both the wars weakened the Qing dynasty and led eventually to the struggle for independence and the modernization of China.

The above examples were all armed regional conflicts but todays trade war between the US and the People's Republic of China, poses a much more threatening disruption to world trade.

First some background information leading up to the current Trade War with China.

- In 1968 the GDP of the USA, ranked 1st ,was $901B and China, ranked 7th was $70B – **7.77%**
- In 2000 the GDP of the USA, ranked 1st ,was $9,764B and China, ranked 6th was $1,198B - **12.27%**
- By 2018 the expected GDP of the USA, ranked 1st ,was $20,412B and China, ranked 2th was $14,092B - **69.04%**
- There are conflicting GDP estimates of where China will be in the future!
- China now has the highest share of exports (13.8%) of any country since 1968 when it was the USA
- In 2017 the USA imported approx. 19% of the total Chinese export volume and is China's largest export market

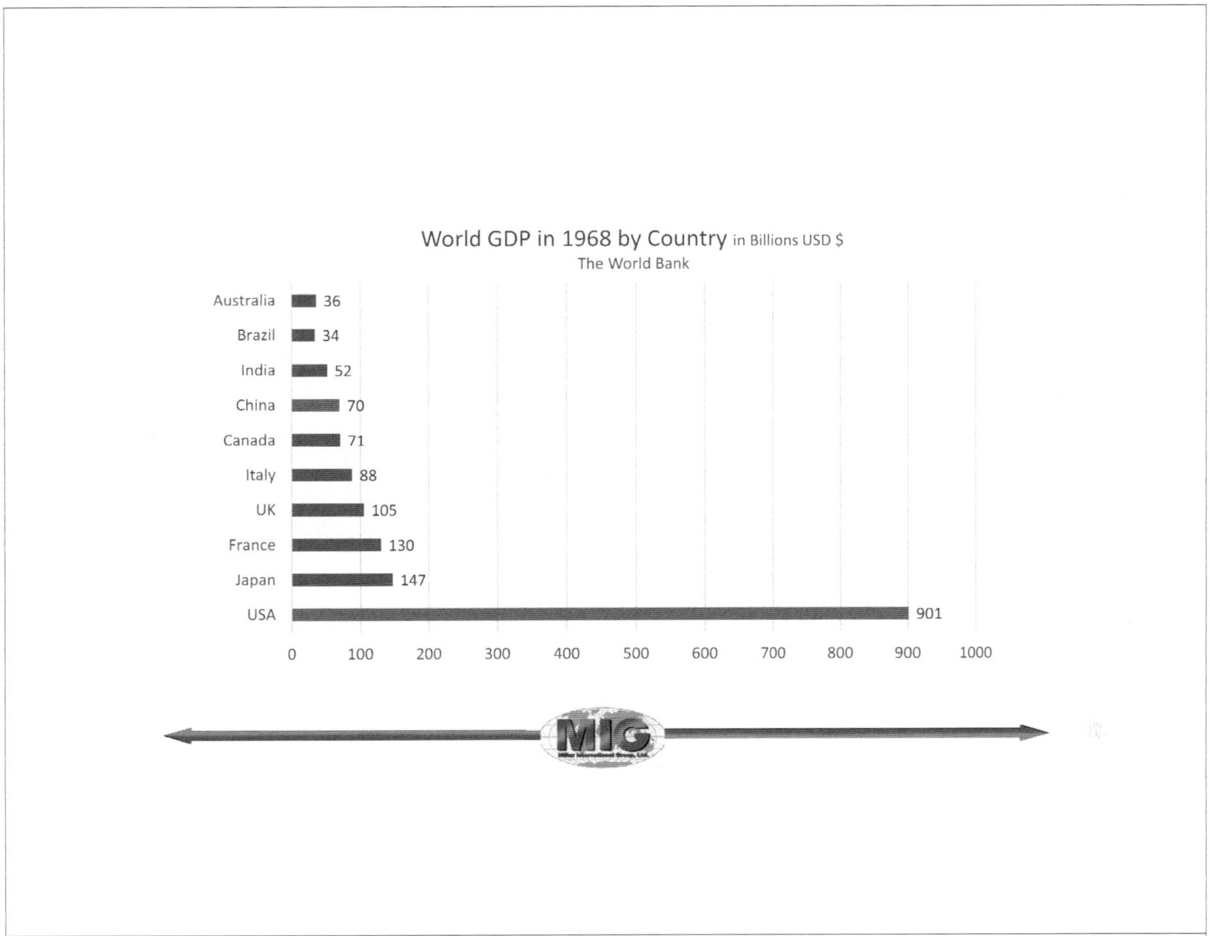
World GDP in 1968 by Country in Billions USD $
The World Bank
Australia 36
Brazil 34
India 52
China 70
Canada 71
Italy 88
UK 105
France 130
Japan 147
USA 901
0 100 200 300 400 500 600 700 800 900 1000
MIG

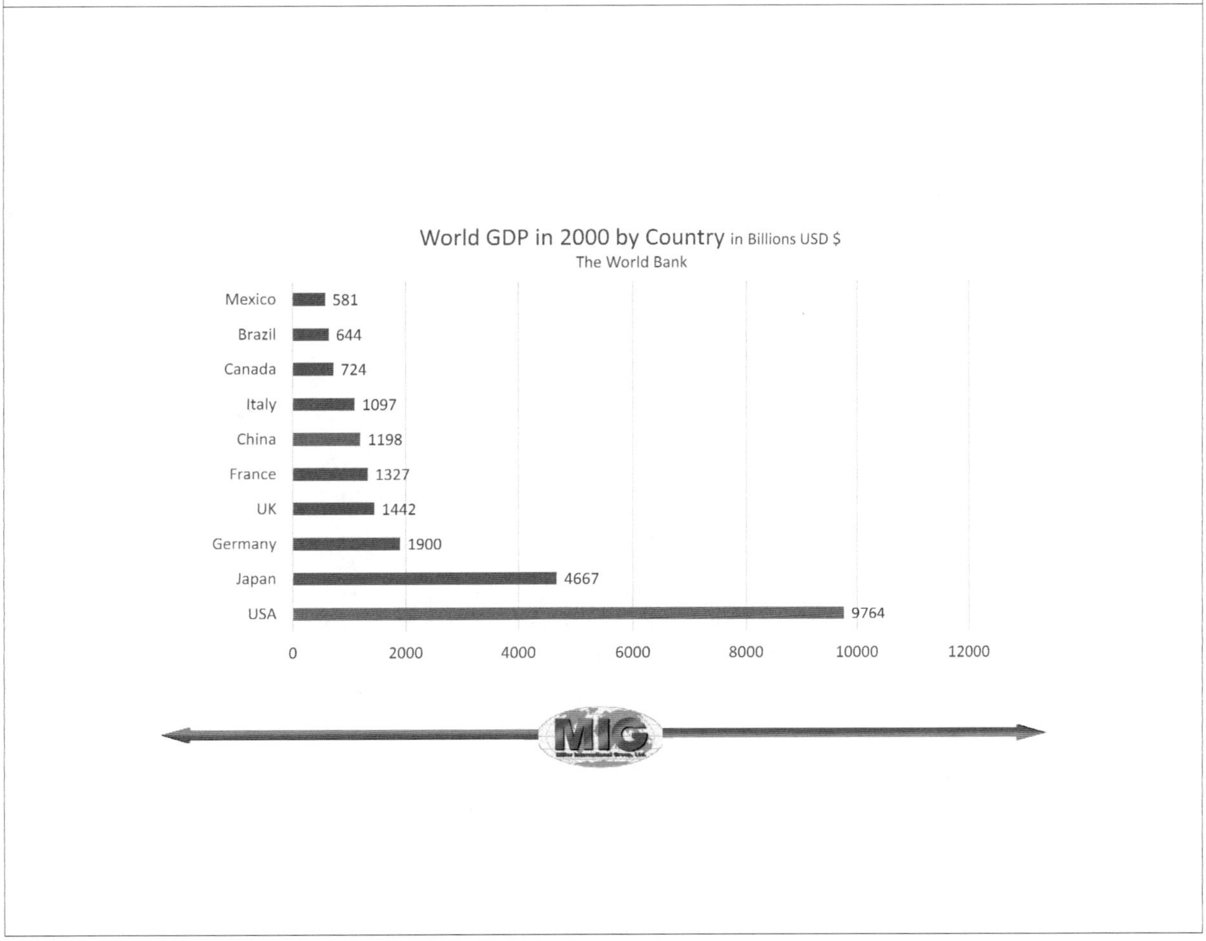
World GDP in 2000 by Country in Billions USD $
The World Bank
Mexico 581
Brazil 644
Canada 724
Italy 1097
China 1198
France 1327
UK 1442
Germany 1900
Japan 4667
USA 9764
0 2000 4000 6000 8000 10000 12000
MIG

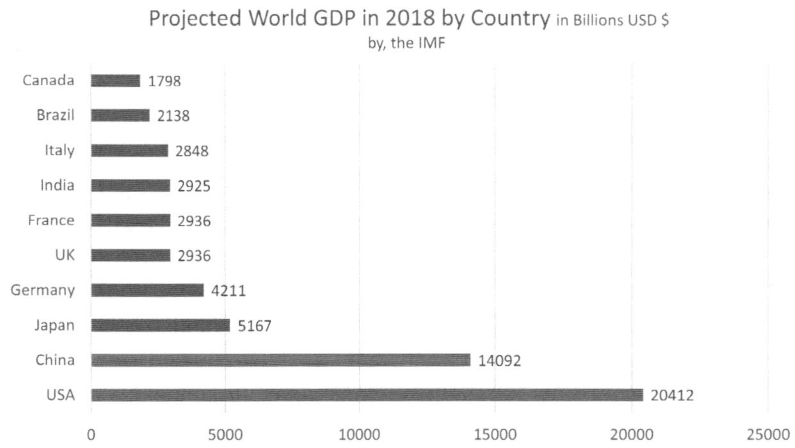

According to the US Census Bureau – US trade in Goods from China

	US Exports	US Imports	Balance
1985	3.86	3.86	0
2000	16.18	100.02	-83.84
2017	129.89	505.47	**-375.58**

All figures $B

While Chinese figures show a record surplus with the U.S. for 2018 of $323.32B, China's figures routinely show a smaller imbalance than U.S. ones. The countries' trade figures don't match due to different calculation methods.

China's Five-Year Plans (五年计划)

A series of social and economic development initiatives issued since 1953.

Since 1949 the communist party has helped shape the economy of China through the plenary sessions of the Central Committee and national congresses. The Plans map the strategies for economic development, setting growth targets, and launching reforms.

There has always been a long-term national interest goal in the evolution of the specifics of the medium-term strategy via the five-year plans. One of the key areas identified has consistently been **new materials**. Many of these new materials include Rare Earth elements.

In the case of Rare Earths (RE) there seems to have been close links between Xu Guangxian, the father of the Rare Earth Chemistry/Industry in China and Deng Xiaoping the Chairman of the Chinese People's Political Consultative Conference and the de facto head of the Politburo.

Program 863

In 1986 he approved Program 863 – a Program promoted by three key scientists from the strategic Nuclear Program. The plan revealed major gaps in Chinese technology that Xiaoping saw as needing to be fixed.

Program 863 which was funded and administered by the central Chinese government to develop and advance 7 key technologies of which New materials was one. Rare Earth materials and magnets fell under this area. The plan called for stimulation to make China independent in these areas.

In 1987 China set up the State Key Laboratory of Rare Earth Chemistry and Physics to help development of these materials.

China's Five-Year Plans (五年计划)

We are now in the Thirteenth Plan (2016 – 2020,) which now includes "Made in China 2025." Some highlights of draft plan are:

- Value-added output of emerging strategic industries accounting for 8% of GDP
- Inviting foreign investment in modern agriculture, high-tech, and environmental protection industries
- Moving coastal regions from being the "world's factory" to hubs of research and development, high-end manufacturing, and the service sector

Made in China 2025 (中国制造2025)

Is a strategic plan of China issued by Chinese Premier Li Keqiang and his cabinet in May 2015.

The goals of Made in China 2025 include:

- Increasing the Chinese-domestic content of core materials to 40% by 2020 and 70% by 2025
- The plan focuses on high-tech fields with the stated objective of China becoming a major competitor in advanced manufacturing, including biotechnology, space, information, laser, automation, energy and New Material Technologies
- Creating champions in Artificial Intelligence (AI), Electric Cars and other key high-tech industries
- Encourage foreign companies to enter into joint ventures, including the transfer of technology to Chinese companies

This Made in China strategy maps out how China will upgrade its industries to become "Champions" in key industries.

Made in China 2025 (中国制造2025)

Made in China 2025 seems to be in direct competition to President Trump's Made in America and as a direct response to the 13th and made in China 2025 plan. The US saw this as an attack on their current world trading position and technological leadership.

The Center for Strategic and International Studies describes it as an "initiative to comprehensively upgrade Chinese industry." It is an attempt to move the country's manufacturing up the value chain and become a major manufacturing power in direct competition with the United States.

The US think tank Council on Foreign Relations stated in 2018 that it is a "**real existential threat to U.S. technological leadership.**"

The Chinese government maintains that the plan is in line with the country's WTO obligations. On 15 June 2018, the Trump administration imposed a higher tariff on Chinese goods, and escalated the trade tensions between China and the U.S. The tariff list mainly focuses on the products included in Made In China 2025 plan, including IT and robotics related products.

From China's view point the two main grievance's against the US are:

- The US limits its exports of "dual use" technology with possible military applications
- Chinese companies are treated unfairly in US security reviews of proposed corporate acquisitions

President Trump kicked off his presidency by targeting, what he said were unfair trading conditions with its 4 largest trading partners, Europe, Canada, Mexico and China. He started the current round of "Trade Wars" with Mexico and Canada:

NAFTA was relatively "quickly" and "painlessly" re-negotiated and settled with the new U.S.-Mexico-Canada (USMCA) Agreement signed at the G20 summit in Buenos Aires, Argentina, December 2018.

The largest trading partner, China, is the subject of this presentation, which has been neither a quick nor painless process!

President Trump and President Xi Jinping - Friend or Foe?

Photo curtesy of Andy Wong/AP news

From their first warm meetings at Mar-a-Lago and then in Beijing in 2017, to the cold light of day in 2018 with President Trump imposing an escalating series of trade tariffs:
How did we get here and what is next in 2019?

April 2017 Mar-a-Largo, USA

"Tremendous progress" has been made in talks with Chinese President Xi Jinping, President Trump said on the summit's second and final day.

President Xi told President Trump: "We have a thousand reasons to get China-US relations right, and not one reason to spoil the China-US relationship."

November 2017 Beijing, China

President Trump is quoted as saying, "As far as China is concerned, my relationship, as you know, with President Xi is also excellent. I like him a lot. I consider him a friend. He considers me a friend".

Move on almost 1 year!

March 2018

USTR released its latest edition of the 1974 US Trade Act, Section 301* findings of China's acts, policies and practices related to technology transfer, intellectual property and innovation are unreasonable and discriminatory and burden or restrict US commerce.

*Section 301 of the Trade Act of 1974 provides the United States with the authority to enforce trade agreements, resolve trade disputes, and open foreign markets to U.S. goods and services. It is the principal statutory authority under which the United States may impose trade sanctions on foreign countries that either violate trade agreements or engage in other unfair trade practices. When negotiations to remove the offending trade practice fail, the United States may take action to raise import duties on the foreign country's products as a means to rebalance lost concessions.

Caitlain Devereaux Lewis Legislative Attorney
March 29, 2018

As to the USTR's findings, following an analysis of the evidence it received, the USTR concluded that certain "acts, policies, and practices of the Chinese government related to technology transfer, intellectual property, and innovation are unreasonable or discriminatory and burden or restrict U.S. commerce." Specifically, the USTR determined that:

1. China's use of foreign ownership restrictions (such as joint venture requirements and foreign equity limitations), foreign investment restrictions, and administrative licensing and approval processes to pressure technology transfers from U.S. to Chinese companies is unreasonable and burdens or restricts U.S. commerce.
2. China's use of licensing processes to transfer technologies from U.S. to Chinese companies on terms that favor Chinese recipients is discriminatory and burdens U.S. commerce.
3. China's facilitation of systematic investment in and acquisition of U.S. companies and assets by Chinese entities to obtain technologies and intellectual property, thereby generating large-scale technology transfer, is unreasonable and burdens U.S. commerce.
4. China's cyber intrusions into U.S. computer networks to gain access to valuable business information are unreasonable and burden U.S. commerce.

Having made this determination, the statute directs that the USTR "shall take all appropriate and feasible action authorized under subsection (c) [of Section 301], subject to the specific direction, if any, of the President regarding any such action."

July 2018

Chinese imports set to get new trade tariffs made public, the list contains 6,031 tariff lines and is about half of what China sends to the US. The US government stated that $50 Billion worth of Chinese imports will get a 25% tariff and up to another $250 Billion, a 10% tariff.

August 2018

A nine-member delegation from Beijing, led by Vice Commerce Minister Wang Shouwen, held meetings with U.S. officials led by the Treasury undersecretary, David Malpass.

"The international community is a global village and should not engage in zero-sum games," Xi was quoted as saying. "China's door to the outside world will open even wider, rather than being closed."

Also in August 2018 and as a side issue:

A new US Defense Law Bans Magnets from China:

US President Donald Trump, on 08/13/2018, signed into law the John S. McCain National Defense Authorization Act which sets an increased budget for US defense expenditures for fiscal year 2019. Section 871 of the act prevents purchase of rare earth magnets, specifically Samarium Cobalt and Neodymium Iron Boron magnets from prohibited countries, like China, Russia, North Korea and Iran. An exception to this is any Neodymium Iron Boron magnet manufactured from recycled material if the milling of the recycled material and sintering of the final magnet takes place in the US.

The law explicitly prohibits rare earth magnets from being "melted or produced" in China as well as the other 3 countries. That means the production of the magnet can not be in those countries, so importers and distributors can not simply bring in magnet blocks and cut/finish them to final size and specification as they do with current DFAR and ITAR rules &regulations.

September 2018

As part of its continuing response to China's theft of American intellectual property and forced transfer of American technology, the office of the United States Trade Representative (USTR) released its list of 5,745 full or partial lines of the original 6,031 tariff lines. Worth approx. $200 billion worth of Chinese imports. Effective starting 24th September 2018 the new tariffs will initially be in the amount of 10%. Starting 1st January 2019, unless an agreement has been made, the level of the additional tariffs will increase to 25%.

The US **did not** include rare earth elements metals used in magnets, radars and consumer electronics in the final list.

However, there is still some confusion with the following sections from the new tariffs announced which seem ambiguous.

HTS Subheading 8505.19.20: "Composite goods containing flexible permanent magnets, other than of metal."

HTS Subheading 8505.19.30: "Permanent magnets and articles intended to become permanent magnets after magnetization, other than of metal."

September 2018

In retaliation China announces a new tariff of between 5 and 10% on $60 billion of US goods.

September 2018

President Trump announces that if there is no progress with China on the trade imbalance, he will look to add another $257 billion in additional Chinese imports from February 2019. This would mean tariffs on all Chinese goods sold to the US. **This equate's to 4% of world trade**.

September 2018

As per Andrew Hecht, Seeking Alpha: China retaliated by imposing protectionist measures on many US agricultural products and exports of liquified natural gas.

October 2018

China's Vice-Minister Wang Shouwen at the Bloomberg New Economy Forum in Singapore seemed to suggest that China is open to restart high level bilateral talks which were suspended in June. This may be an opening to try to solve the trade dispute before the 2 leaders meet in Argentina for the G20 meeting.

October 2018

Ford President and CEO Jim Hackett said in an interview that the tariffs on imported steel and aluminum will cost the company $1 billion through 2019.

From Ford to Walmart to Procter & Gamble, a growing number of iconic American companies are warning of having to raise their costs and prices to offset the new tariffs.

December 2018 Buenos Aires, Argentina – G20 Meeting

In the next meeting of the 2 leaders over dinner on December 1st, Chinese President Xi Jinping and US President Trump agreed to a 90-day truce. The US agreed to hold off plans to raise tariffs on January 1st on $200 billion in Chinese goods. This would have raised the tariffs from 10% to 25% (there is another $50 billion already getting a 25% tariff). There were mixed signals from both sides but the Chinese appeared to agree to buy additional agricultural, energy and industrial products. There were conflicting reports on whether China had agreed to drop its 40% tariff they currently add to US autos.

Some movement was made on the US government's accusation of Chinese using predatory tactics in its drive to secure world dominance in technology. Both sides agreed to begin immediate negotiations on this issue and agreed to complete the negotiations within the 90-day window.

HUAWEI

In December, in fact on the same day President Trump and President Xi Jinping sat down for dinner together! Meng Wanzhou , chief financial officer and also the daughter of the founder of Huawei, a major world power in global information and communications technology was detained and arrested in Canada at the request of the US.

It appears that the US believe that Huawei are guilty of breaking sanctions that the US set against Iran. This seems to ratchet up the issue of China and the US over Trade and all the other associated complicated issues. .

In a telephone interview with a high-ranking person in one of China's premier rare earth magnet companies, I asked the following questions:

1. How is the current trade/tariffs situation affecting your business?

"We have to be prepared for any events due to the current trade war or barriers set before us. We must share information with our immediate domestic as well as export customer's for magnets or assemblies. We must also understand our customer's customer for the end product and how this affects their programs. We must be ready for anything.

2. Would/will you lower prices to allow for any future tariffs on magnets or your customer's end products?

"We will take an overall look at each market and each customer from our company strategic point of view as well as looking at what our competitors are doing. We understand we will have to do something. In our view, no one can make money at a 25% tariff without a price increase. We believe under 15% will cause no major problems however 25% will have a major effect."

3. What is your opinion of the current trade dispute between China and the USA.

"We believe that this is a political issue with neither side wanting to take the lead. We also believe that Europe and Japan are influencing the US in their trade discussions and talks with China. This is a very serious situation not only for US ~ China relationships but also for the world. It is completely understandable that the US wants to protect its intellectual property rights, but it should not change the current trade relations between China and the USA. This is a very negative move forward concerning our relationship."

4. What is the perception of the Chinese people to the tariffs and negative speeches of the USA government about China?

"It is very unfortunate that these politicians increase the tension between our two nations and **we in China want to see a return to normal relations with the USA as quickly as possible."**

5. What is the current situation with the rare earth supply from the raw materials suppliers in China? And is there any current shortfall in supply or rationing?

"Firstly, there is no rationing or any current problems in getting rare earth material from any of our sources within China even while the government is still closing some illegal mines. The environment is still very important to us in China and we are in agreement to close these mines as it is in everybody's best interest. We may see a slight increase in price over the coming months due to demand and we are watching very closely rare earth mines of foreign competitors in Australia and other countries."

6. Finally what is your opinion of the long-term viability of the supply source out of China? With your domestic Chinese market climbing and electric car and other green energy sources being supplied around the world, is this going to mean a shortfall in supply from China in the future?

"We believe we have no problems until maybe 2023 at which time there may be some disruption due to increased demand but not too much to give a short fall. There is a shortsighted view by our government regarding the supply in China of rare earth materials and we believe they should be storing more material for the future. They must at once increase our future rare earth reserves."

This from another source within China:

"We see everything in the news. I think China does ask foreign companies to transfer their technology to China, but I think it's all legal. It's a deal. It's a technology-for-market. It's what China does in Africa. China also teaches African technology, all of which is voluntary".

"Most Chinese don't care about politics. They only care about how much money they will make tomorrow.
Some of them don't even know that the United States is fighting a trade war with China".

Ways China can influence or direct the current trade war apart from tariffs is by:

1. Devaluing the Chinese Yuan.
2. China is the leading holder of US government debt! If China were to stop buying or were to sell off some of its US bond holdings it could result in US interest rates increasing!
3. The other important weapon up China's sleeve is its current world dominance of rare earth materials (15 Lanthanide metallic elements plus the metals Scandium and Yttrium making up 17 elements) as well as magnets.

1. The Devaluation of the Chinese Yuan as a Tool.

Since the 15th August, 2015 when China devalued its currency by over 3%, we had seen a relatively stable rate.

In 2018 President Trump said that China is manipulating its currency and we have seen the Chinese yuan fall by almost 5% to its lowest level in more than a year against the dollar.

The remarks, in a tweet and an interview with CNBC, suggested that the U.S.-China trade war is now broadening to include currencies, putting fresh scrutiny on Chinese management of the yuan.

Wang Tao at UBS Group AG is among those predicting China will use tools other than the exchange rate to "cushion the blow" from the trade war.

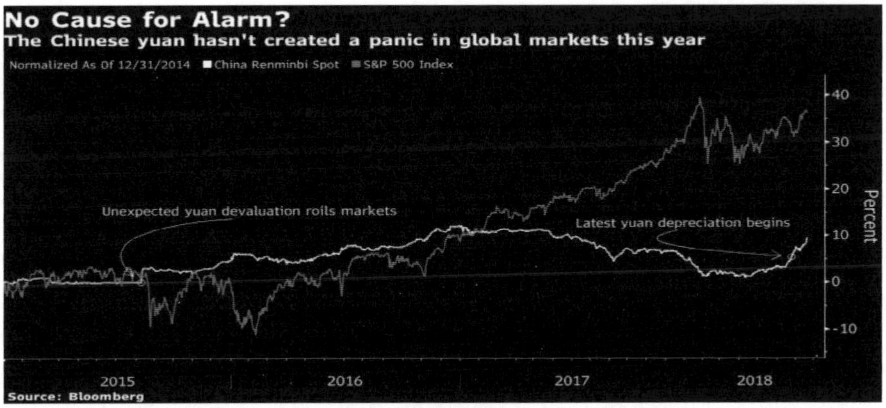

Courtesy of Bloomberg
In white – China RMB spot
In Blue – S&P 500 Index

2. China's $1.17 trillion weapon

- China holds $1.17 trillion of U.S. government debt.
- Economists and investors worry if there is a trade war, China could reduce its U.S. debt holdings as a political weapon against the Trump administration tariffs proposal.
- If that happens, the dollar could fall and other countries could follow suit and sell their holdings.
- If China reduces its buying at a time when the U.S. is increasing its supply of new Treasuries into the market, that could lead to a rout in the bond market.

3. China has world dominance of rare earth materials

- In the 1990's China became the worlds leading producer of rare earth materials
- Several times in the past, China has flexed its muscles to force rare earth prices higher
- China is also the world's leading consumer of these materials
- China effectively controls between 85% to 95% of the annual production of these RE materials

This control extends all the way from mining to the production of key intermediate products such as magnets. Many of these intermediate products are critical inputs for high growth industries such as electric and hybrid cars, windmills, other green technologies, energy storage and lighting. These are also the industries in which China is trying to build scale for future dominance.

China has been flexing its muscles during this period:

According to Reuters, the Chinese government limited domestic production of RE materials in the second half of 2018:

- Cutting its RE separation and smelting by 36%.
- Limiting its domestic RE production to 45,000 tonnes. It was 70,000 in the first half of 2018.
- According to Ryan Castilloux from Adams Intelligence, prices for key RE elements, including PrNd Oxide could increase by 10 to 50% over the next 12 months. However as of yet we have not seen this kind of movement.

These new quotas are likely to be tied very closely to the closing of illegal mines in Jiangxi province as well as the clean up in Baiyun Obo during 2018.

- As already noted, the US did not include rare earth elements as well as magnets (8505.11.00 code) in its final list of products to be faced with the increased tariffs. This maybe a sign of how much the US currently relies on China for these strategic products. They are critical in many of today's key industries and technologies. So as of today the tariffs are not a factor with magnets produced in China.
- However in the short term, China could severely disrupt the US economy as it did to Japan in 2010 by reducing or stopping the export of raw materials as well as magnets to US companies.
- Rare Earth elements/metals as well as finished magnets could become a critical part of the negotiations over the next 90 days.
- However, although China does have a huge competitive advantage in these materials, it does not have a total stranglehold on the markets. There are other sources of supply outside China that may not be as cost-effective today, but they are becoming more readily available.

In January 2019, trade talks resumed in Beijing and at the end of 3 days of negotiations both sides said the outcome was positive.

As we convene here in Orlando, another meeting is taking place in Switzerland!

22nd to 25th January 2019 Davos-Klosters, Switzerland

The world Economic Forum's annual meeting will convene to discuss global, regional and Industrial agendas. President Trump is set to attend as is the Chinese Vice President Wang Qishan. If this meeting does take place, lets hope they discuss the current trade dispute between the US and China and come to a settlement.

Stay Tuned!

THANK YOU

SENIS
magnetic & current measurement

Accurate 3-Axis Magnetic Field Measurements

Remo Ughini, Application Engineer

Magnetics 2019, Orlando

Requirements

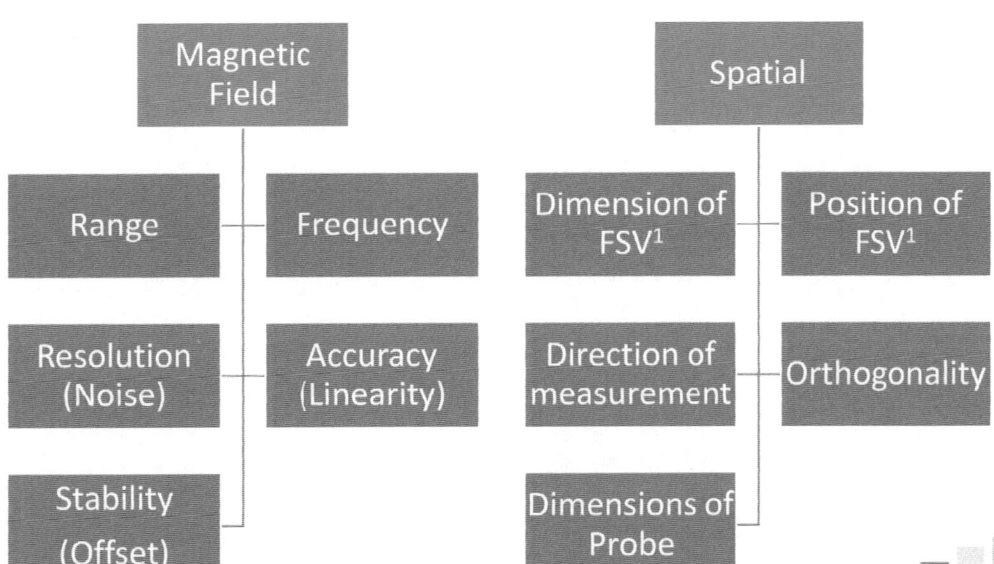

[1] FSV: Field Sensitive Volume

2

3MH6 Digital Teslameter

SENIS
magnetic & current measurement

3 axis
100x100μm
2ppm RES
50ppm ACC
2μ - 20T
Multirange
DC to 10kHz

Low noise and resolution

- 4 selectable ranges:
  - ± 20mT, 200mT, 2T, 20T
- Low noise:
  - 2μT peak to peak
  - 2μT @ 2T range: 2ppm
  - Hall voltage 100nV
- Bandwidth DC to 10kHz

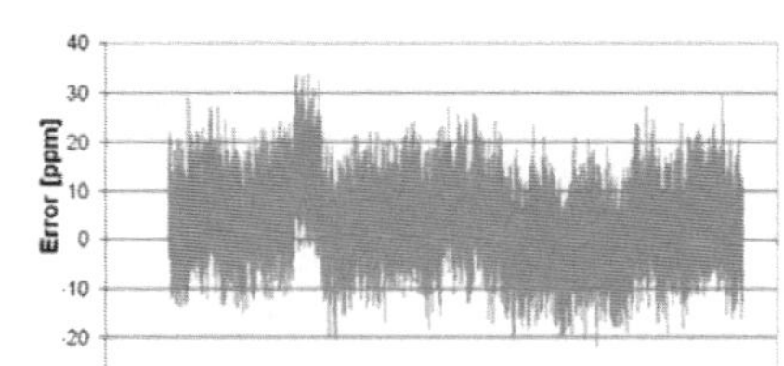

4

3 Axis Integrated Hall Sensor

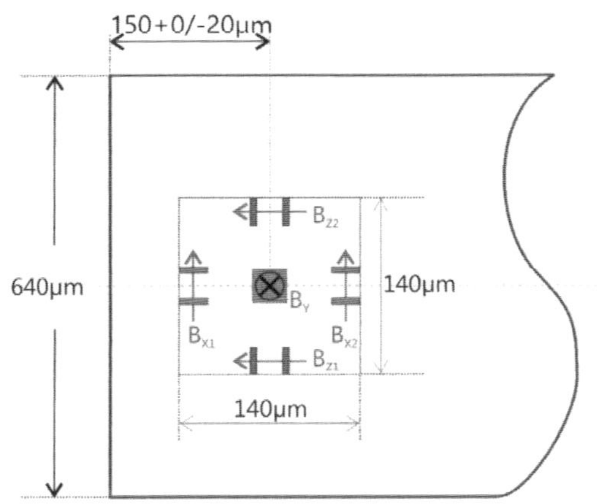

CMOS Technology

- Sliding current
- Signal Amplification
- Linearization
- Temperature sensing and compensation
- Digital output (SPI/PWM)

5

3 axis fully integrated Hall sensor

CMOS Technology

- Sliding current
- Signal Amplification
- Linearization
- Temperature sensing and compensation
- Digital output (SPI/PWM)

6

Planar Hall Element

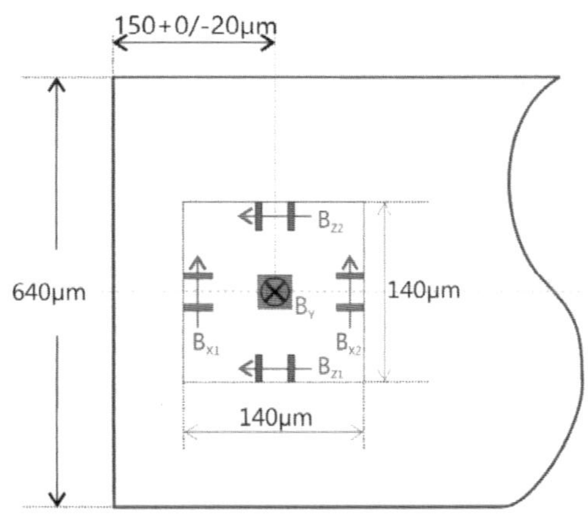

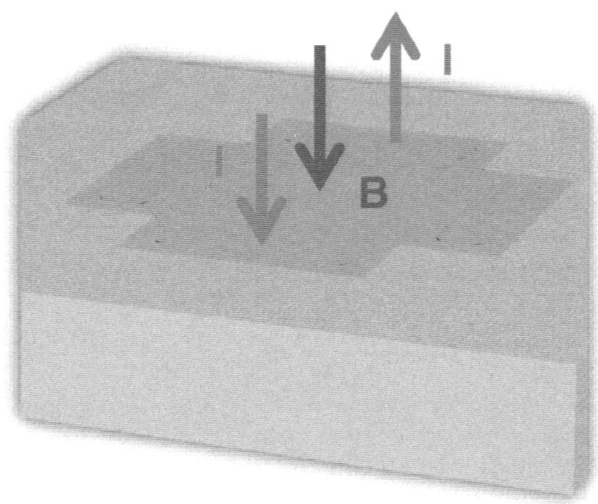

7

Planar Hall Element

- Lorentz force

$$\bar{F} = \bar{v}q \times \bar{B}$$

- Sensitive to the perpendicular component of $\bar{B}$

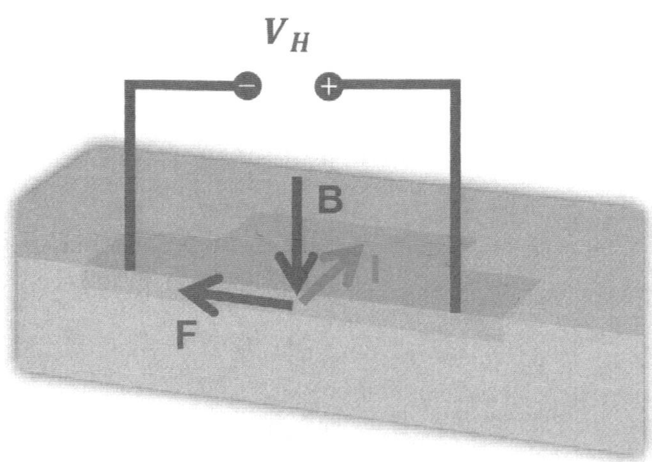

8

Vertical Hall Element

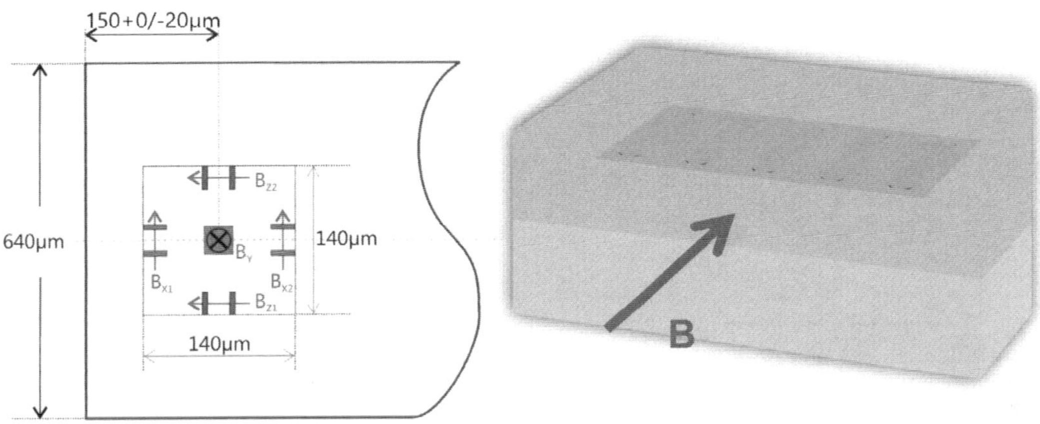

9

Vertical Hall Element

- Invented 1994 by Prof. Popovic
- Sensitive to the in-plane component of B
- Highest sensitive vertical Hall elements

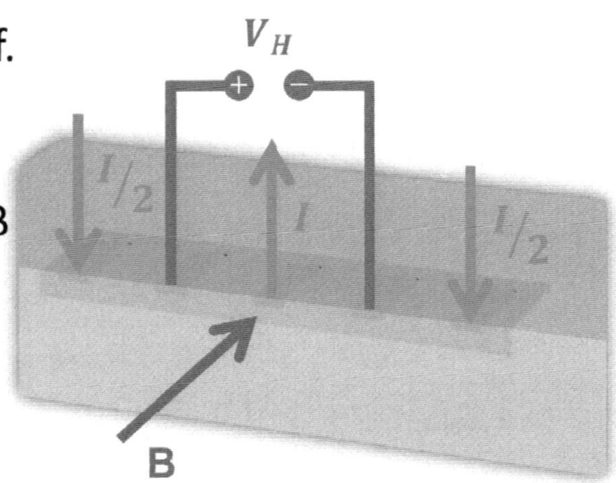

10

Sliding Current

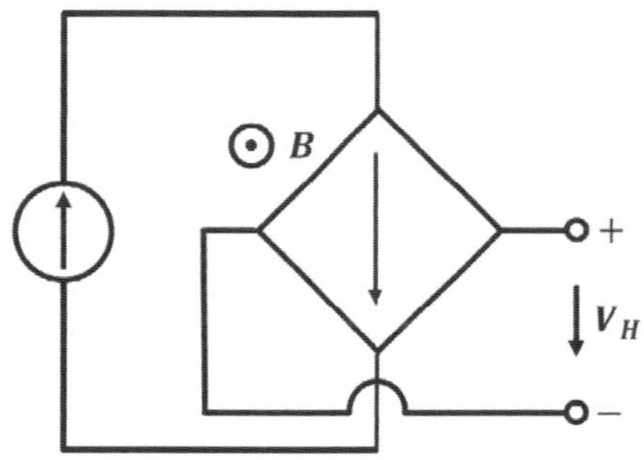

- Biasing current is rotated
- Reducing
  - Planar Hall Effect
  - Offset
  - 1/f Noise

11

Sliding Current

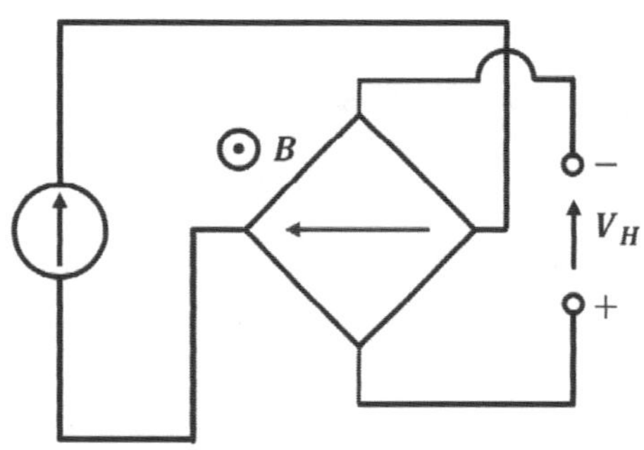

- Biasing current is rotated
- Reducing
  - Planar Hall Effect
  - Offset
  - 1/f Noise

12

Sliding Current

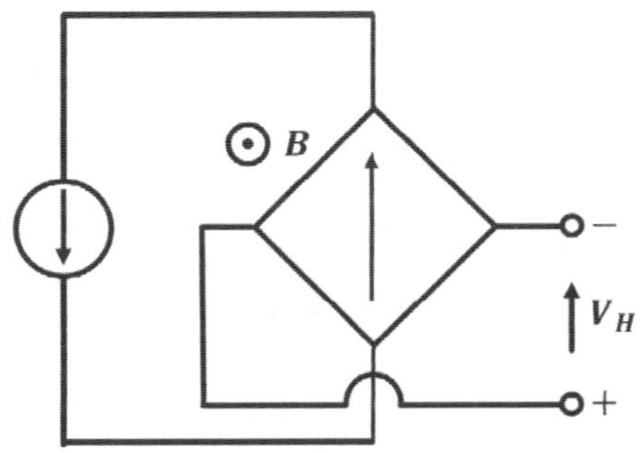

- Biasing current is rotated
- Reducing
  - Planar Hall Effect
  - Offset
  - 1/f Noise

13

Sliding Current

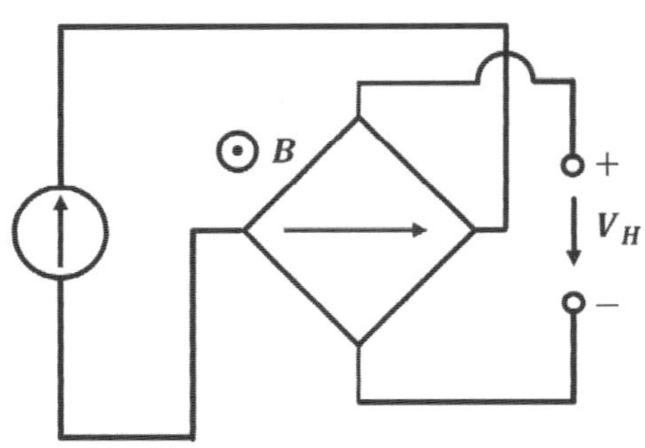

- Biasing current is rotated
- Reducing
  - Planar Hall Effect
  - Offset
  - 1/f Noise

14

Calibration and Accuracy

SENIS
magnetic & current measurement

- 3xElectro-magnets
- Helmholtz Coils
- Zero Gauss chambers
- Up to 3T
- 2xNMR Magneto-meters
- Temperature chambers

Calibration and Accuracy

- Reference field: Electromagnets
- Calibration reference: NMR[1] magnetometer
- Characterization
  - Nonlinearity
  - Offset dependency of temperature
  - Sensitivity dependency of temperature
  - Electronics temperature influence
- Compensation of the above
  - All three axis separately
  - Up to 5th order polynomials
- 50 ppm accuracy

[1] NMR: Nuclear Magnetic Resonance

16

Measuring high gradient fields

- Field of a dipole: $\bar{B}(\bar{r}) = \frac{\mu_0}{4\pi}\left(\frac{3\,\bar{n}\,(\bar{n}\cdot\bar{m})-\bar{m}}{|\bar{r}|^3}\right)$
  - Decrease with r^3 -> High gradient
- Field Sensitive Volume
  - Acts as an averaging filter
  - Dimension corresponds to the window size
- Requirements
  - High accuracy positioning
  - A small FSV for a high spatial resolution
  - A small probe

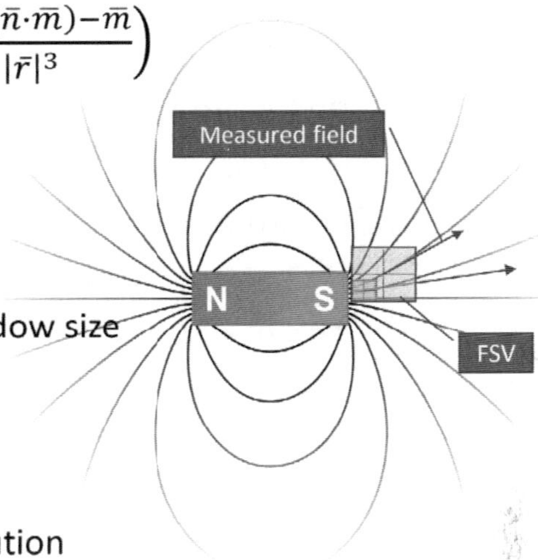

17

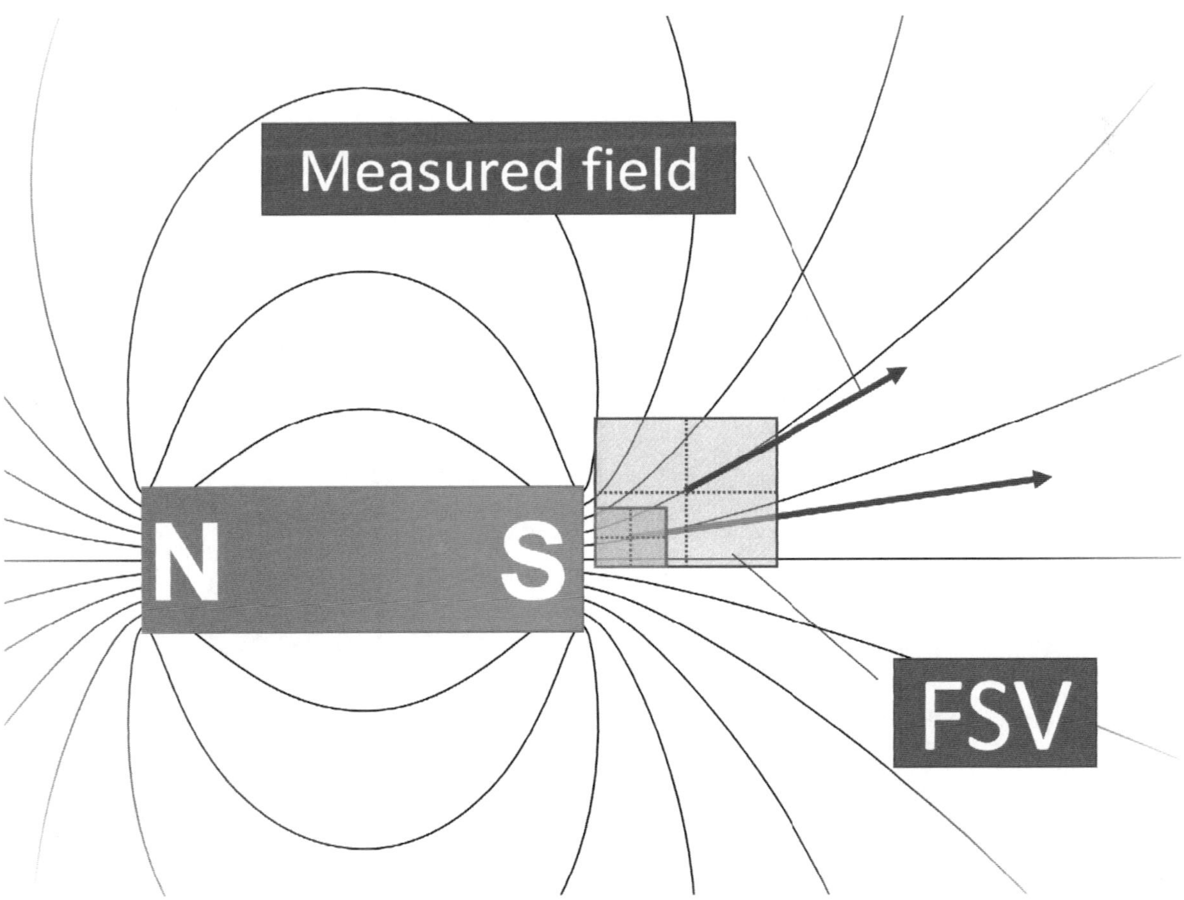

Measuring high gradient fields

- Field of a dipole: $\bar{B}(\bar{r}) = \frac{\mu_0}{4\pi}\left(\frac{3\,\bar{n}\,(\bar{n}\cdot\bar{m})-\bar{m}}{|\bar{r}|^3}\right)$
  - Decrease with r^3 -> High gradient
- Field Sensitive Volume
  - Acts as an averaging filter
  - Dimension corresponds to the window size
- Requirements
  - High accuracy positioning
  - A small FSV for a high spatial resolution
  - A small probe

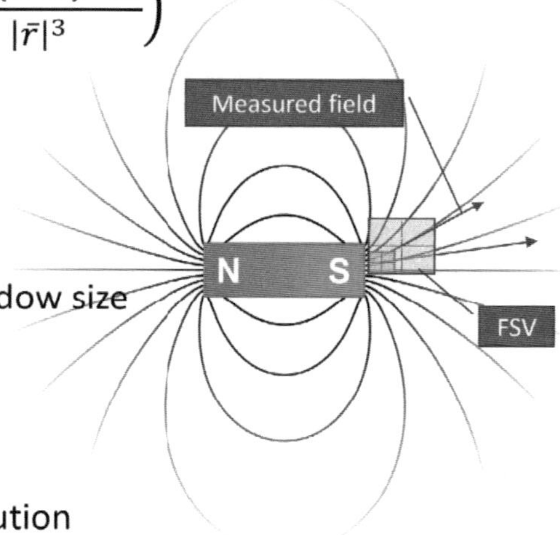

19

Orthogonality

- Orientation
  - CMOS process precision
    Orthogonality: 1-2°
  - Patented calibration method
    Orthogonality: 0.1°

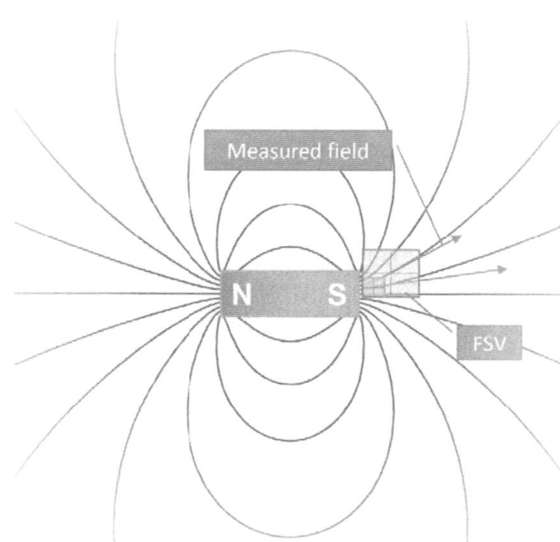

20

Senis Mapping Systems

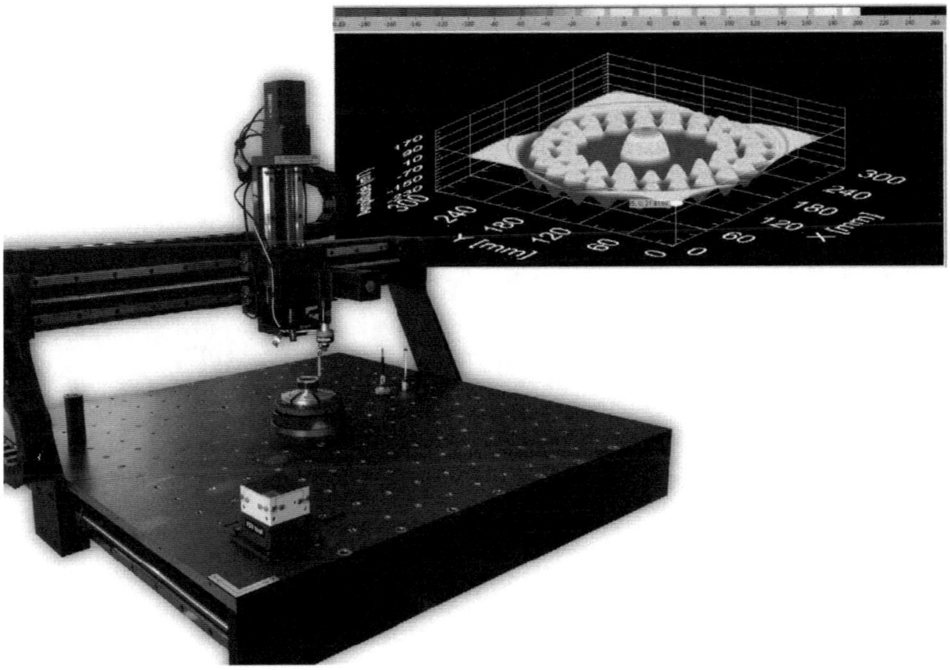

4 axis platform

0.5x0.5x0.5 m

Exact positioning <10μm

Extensive analysis tools

Hall sensor packaging

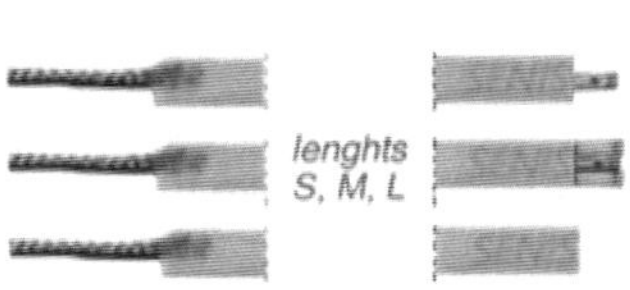

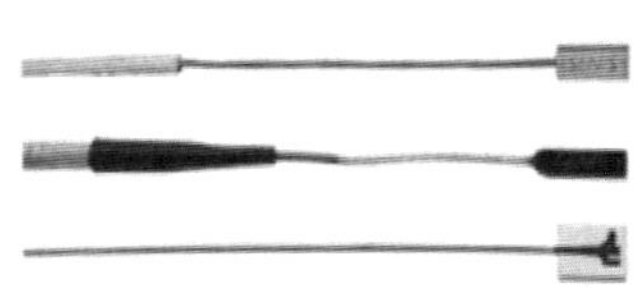

Ceramic package

-40...+155°C

Hall sensor packaging

SENIS
magnetic & current measurement

Ceramic package

-40...+155°C

Height 0.9

Width 4.0

Length 8.0

Hall sensor packaging

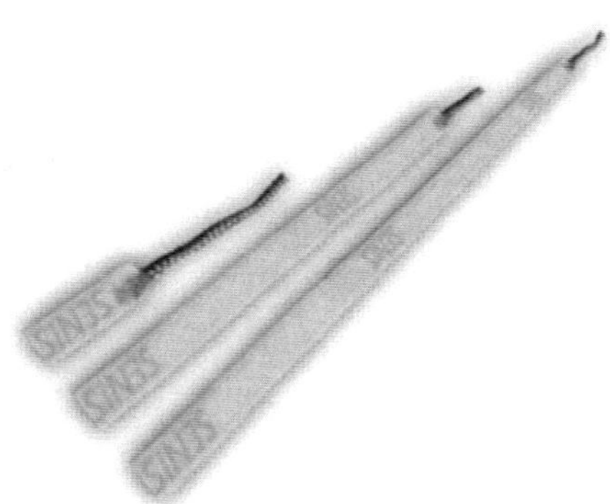

SENIS
magnetic & current measurement

Ceramic package

-40...+155°C

Height 0.5

Width 2.0

Lengths

8.0, 47, 71

Closed

Hall sensor packaging

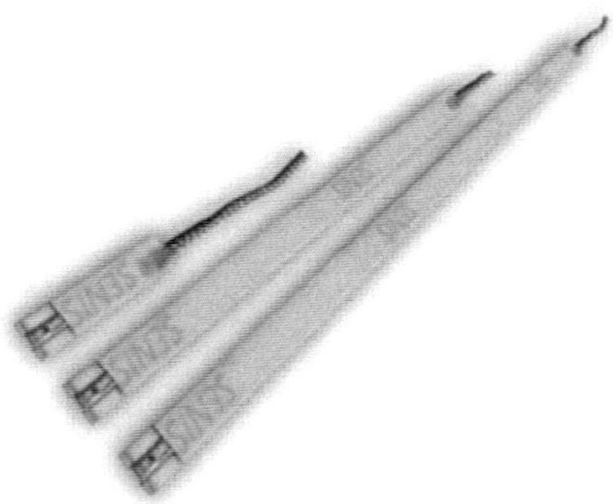

SENIS
magnetic & current measurement

Ceramic package

-40...+155°C

Height 0.5

Width 2.0

Lengths

8.0, 47, 71

Open

Hall sensor packaging

SENIS
magnetic & current measurement

Ceramic package

-40...+155°C

Height 0.5

Width 2.0

Lengths

8.0, 47, 71

Free

Hall sensor packaging

SENIS
magnetic & current measurement

Ceramic package

-40...+155°C

Height 0.25

Width 3.0

Length 8.0

3MH6 Digital Teslameter Functionality

28

3MH6 Digital Teslameter Functionality

- Embedded computer (GUI on Android) with TFT LCD graphic display
  - Bx, By, Bz, Btot
  - Hall Probe temperature
  - Numerical, graphical and statistical visualisation
  - Magnetic vector visualisation

29

3MH6 Digital Teslameter Functionality

- 24-bit A/D convertor
- Selectable sampling rate 10...30’000 S/sec
- Averaging filter: 10...500 samples
- Four selectable ranges: 20mT, 200mT, 2T, 20T (autorange)
- Zeroing, hold reading, MAX/MIN values
- Internal and external triggers
  - Single shot and continuous (up to 4kS/sec)

SENIS
magnetic & current measurement

3 axis
100x100μm
2ppm RES
50ppm ACC
2μ - 20T
Multirange
DC to 10kHz
20ppm/°C

3MH6 Digital Teslameter Functionality

- Measured data logging
  - 0.5– 60 S/sec, i.e. 2.5 - 300 days
- Units in gauss (G), tesla (T)
- Analog output (not calibrated)
- Data acquisition & visualisation software for Windows

SENIS
magnetic & current measurement

3 axis
100x100μm
2ppm RES
50ppm ACC
2μ - 20T
Multirange
DC to 10kHz
20ppm/°C

3MH6 Digital Teslameter Future functionality

- LAN and wireless connection to PC / HTML interface in browser
- Enhanced digital filtering
- FFT spectrum analysis
- Alarm functions
- Relay outputs
- Interchangeable probes
- Selectable range values

SENIS
magnetic & current measurement

3 axis
100x100μm
2ppm RES
50ppm ACC
2μ - 20T
Multirange
DC to 10kHz
20ppm/°C

3MH6 Digital Teslameter Application

- Calibration Laboratory
  - Fast calibration
  - High spatial resolution
  - Directional measurements

- R&D of MRI, NMR systems
  - High resolution mapping
  - Magic angle determination

33

3MH6 Digital Teslameter Application

- Light sources & plasma containment
  - High spatial resolution mapping
  - 3 axis field measurements and magnetic angle

34

SENIS
magnetic & current measurement

Application ASG
Measuring the ITER Tokamak

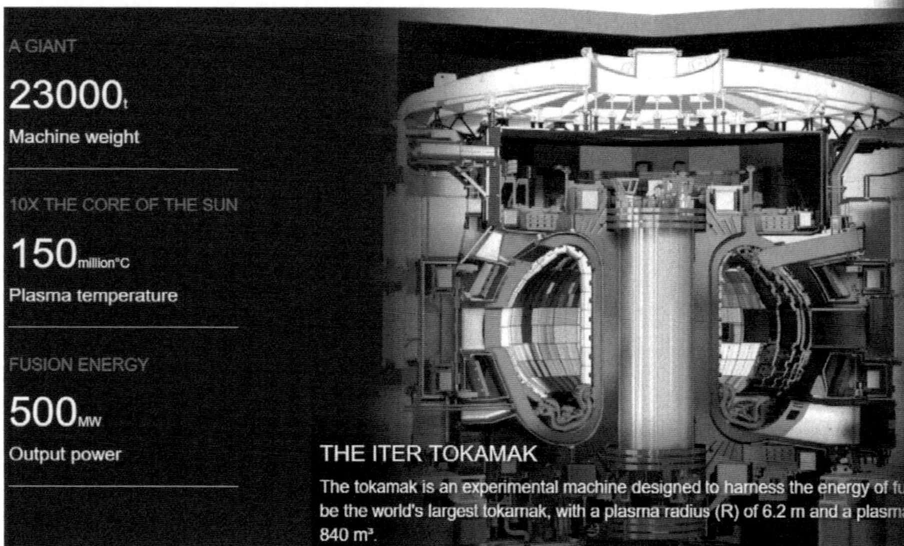

Nuclear fusion reactor

150 Mio °C Plasma

Confined in a Tokamak

Superconducting coils

SENIS
magnetic & current measurement

Application ASG
Measuring the ITER Tokamak

Nuclear fusion reactor

150 Mio °C Plasma

Confined in a Tokamak

Superconducting coils

SENIS
magnetic & current measurement

Application ASG
Measuring the ITER Tokamak

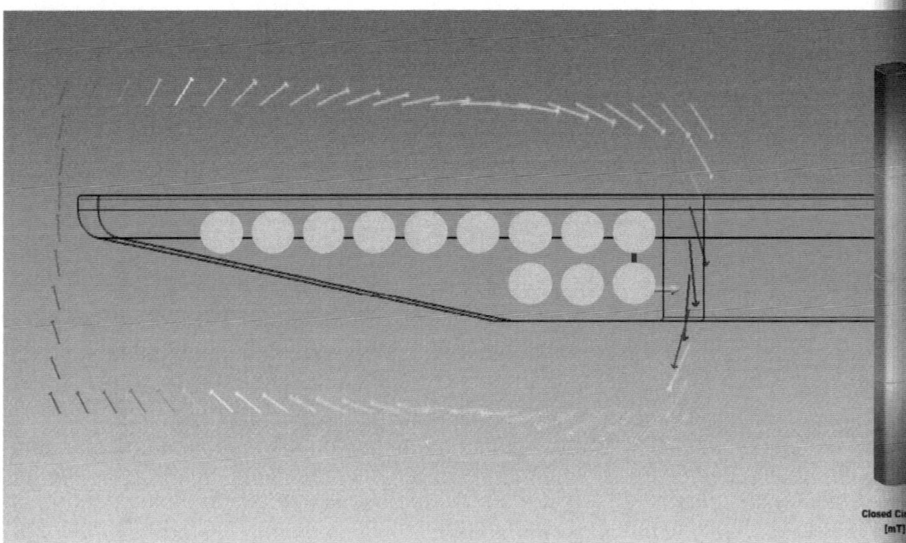

Nuclear fusion reactor

150 Mio °C Plasma

Confined in a Tokamak

Superconducting coils

SENIS
magnetic & current measurement

Application ASG
Measuring the ITER Tokamak

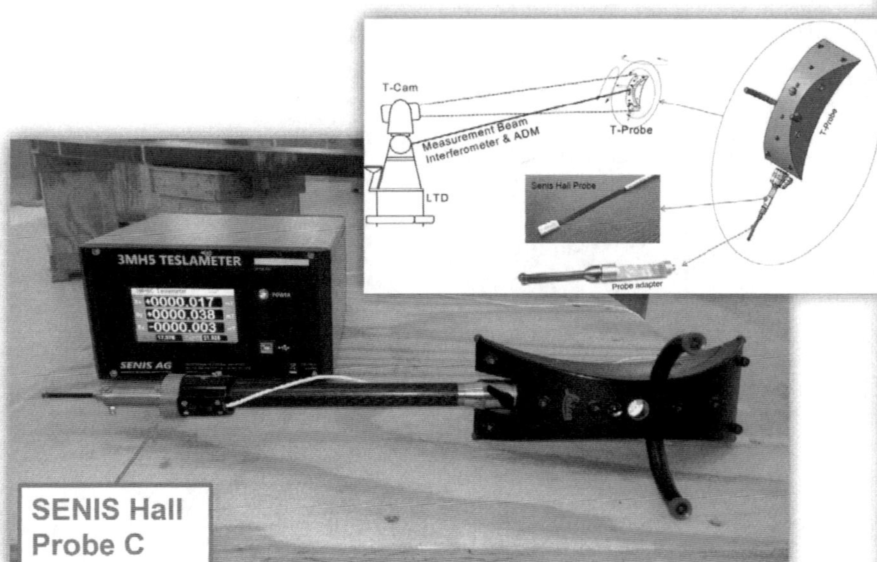

Verify simulation

3MH5 + Leica Laser Tracking System

Magnetic field

Magnetic angle

High spatial resolution

Application ASG
Measuring the ITER Tokamak

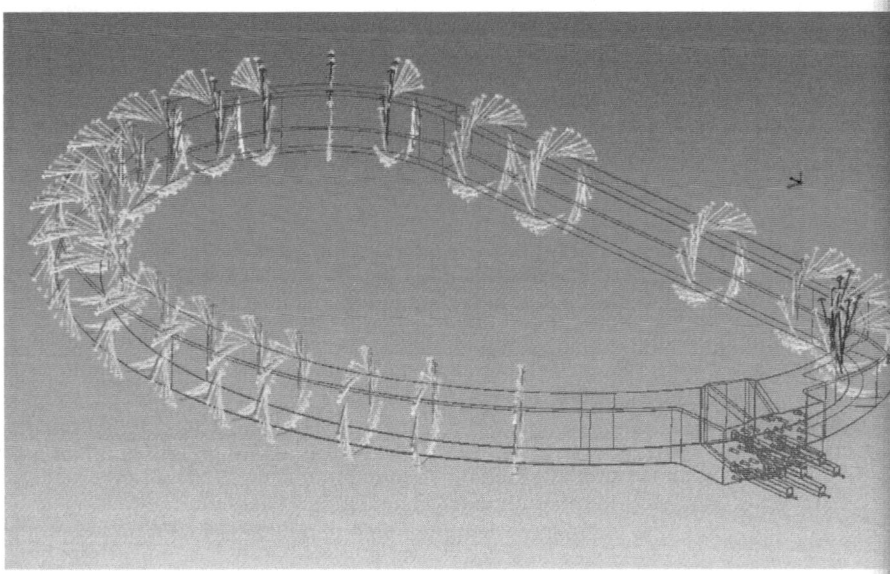

SENIS
magnetic & current measurement

- Verify simulation
- 3MH5 + Leica Laser Tracking System
- Magnetic field
- Magnetic angle
- High spatial resolution

3MH6 Digital Teslameter

40

3MH6 Digital Teslameter

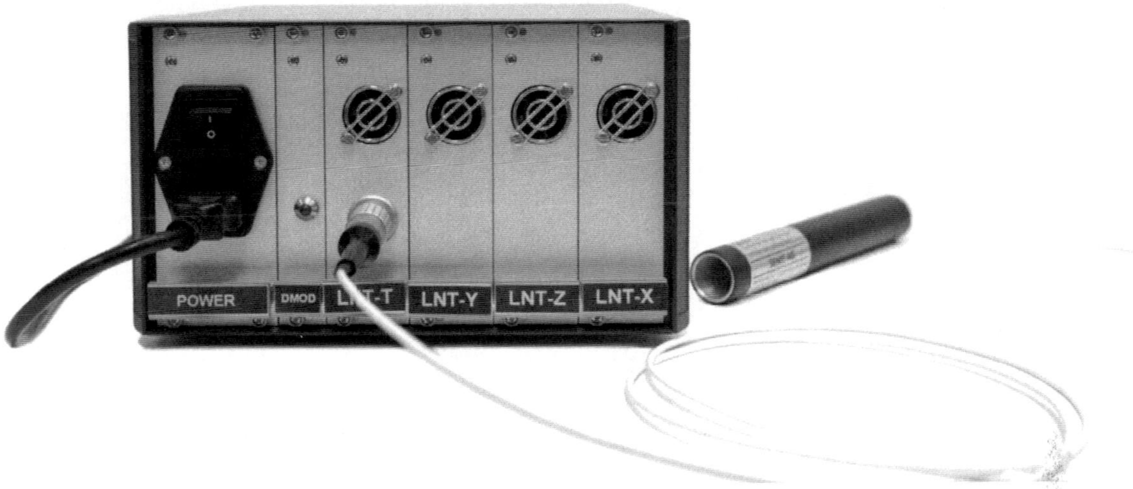

41

SENIS
magnetic & current measurement

GMW Associates

Visit us at GMW booth 308

Thank you for your attention!

TORNGAT

Supplying the rare earths needed for electric vehicles and for clean technologies

Rare Earth Recycling to Increase Supply Security

Orlando January 24 2019

Dirk Naumann

Rare earth sources, demand and supply

TORNGAT

Rare earth are critical in modern society and life
  consumer electronics, automotive, defense, chemical-petrochemical industries

About 80% of the rare earth produced today come from China
  government managing supply and export

Demand rising
  driven by electric cars and wind power

Environmental issues

Recycling required to alleviate supply crunch in future

Torngat Metals will offer a low-cost and sustainable recycling path

torngatmetals.com 2

Electric Vehicle Forecasts

TORNGAT

There is a growing consensus that EV production will grow exponentially

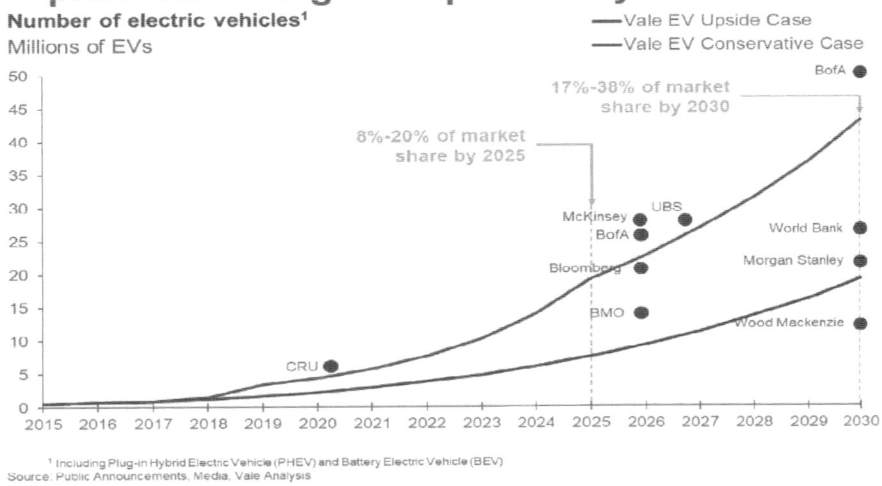

Source: VALE, Platts conference, October 2018

New rare earth supply is needed to meet the high growth demand for permanent magnets

TORNGAT

Projected life of EVs 10 years and generators 20 years plus

Within next 10 years economic and sustainable recycling has to be established.

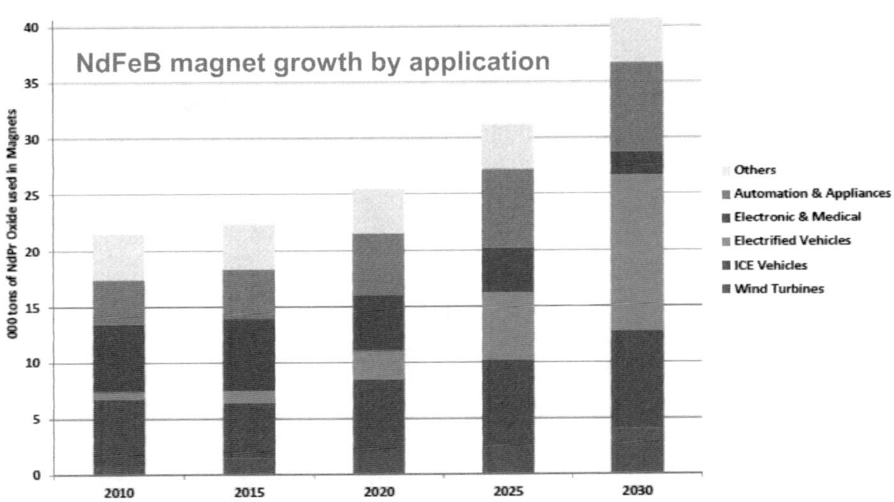

Source: Lynas at Argus conference, April 2018

China dominates rare earth supply

TORNGAT

Supply security risks

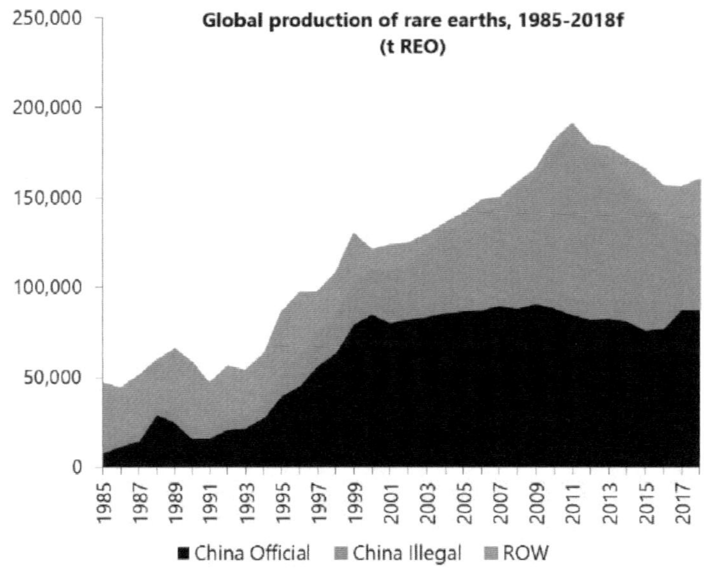

Source: Roskill, Metal Events Rare Earth conference November 2018

Rare earth recycling feed – not just magnets, but all rare earth applications are working on this

TORNGAT

What makes economic sense?

What are the barriers to recycling?

− Electronic waste - low concentration, multiple other valuable metals, other potentially hazardous compounds, difficult to separate REE

+ FCC catalyst - recycling in part already established

O+ Industrial process residue – polishing powder, magnet manufacturing residue, catalyst residue

O Fluorescent lamps, LEDs - declining market, LED little REE

− Batteries – La mischmetal, but Ni and Co of higher value

++ Magnets –Nd, Pr, Dy, Tb, residue from manufacturing, recycling from motors and generators

Potential for recycling for e.g. Nd

TORNGAT

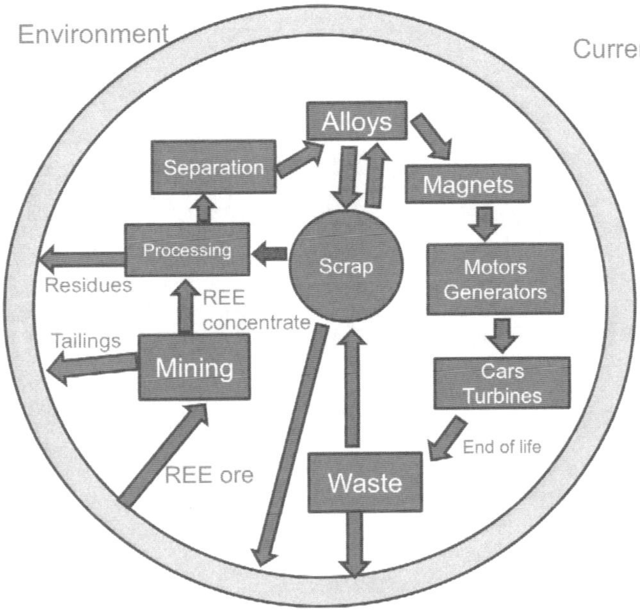

Current recycling rate:
<1%

Adapted from
Jowitt, Werner, Weng, Mudd
Sustainable Chemistry, Oct. 2018

torngatmetals.com 7

Torngat's Strange Lake Project – Start-up 2022/23

TORNGAT

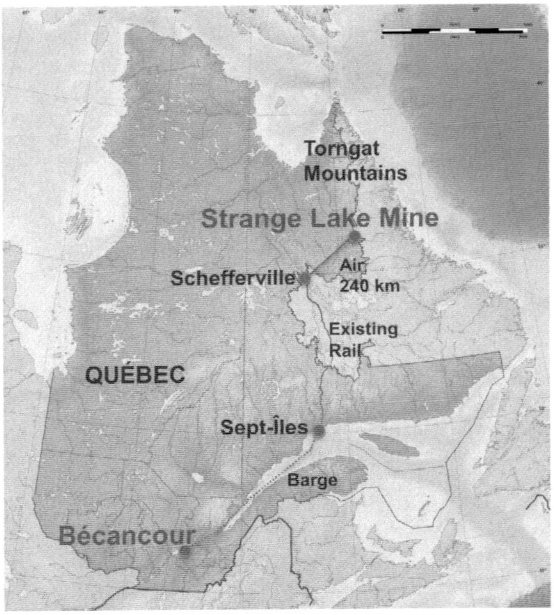

- The Strange Lake NYF-REE miarolitic pegmatite deposit is located in northern Québec on the border of Newfoundland and Labrador
- An open pit mine and onsite beneficiation at Strange Lake
- Flotation concentrate will be shipped from mine site to Schefferville by Lockheed Martin's new Hybrid Airships
- Transport from Schefferville to new processing plant at Bécancour by existing rail and port infrastructure
- Seen as one of the leading rare earth projects due to large deposit size, right rare earth mix, low costs, small environmental footprint and high geopolitical stability

torngatmetals.com 8

A Simple, Low Cost, Industrial Process

TORNGAT

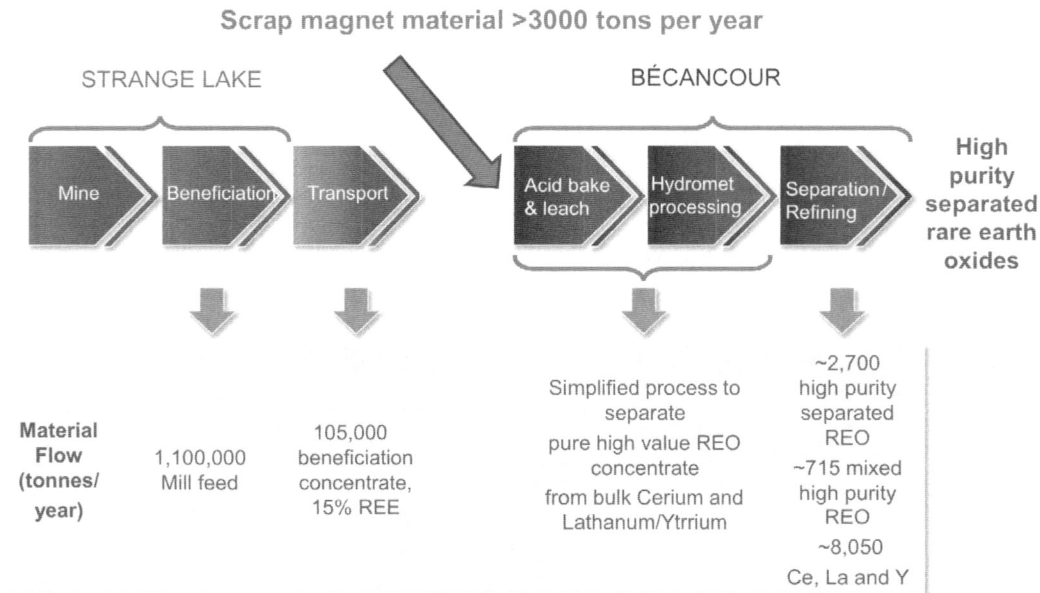

Chemistry of recycling process

TORNGAT

Scrap containing magnets: rare earth, iron, boron

Scrap contaminated with aluminum, copper, zinc, nickel, ...

Dissolve all metals in sulphuric acid
- in acid digester separately and add to ore concentrate
- add scrap directly to ore concentrate

In sulphation process all metals from ore and scrap convert to sulphate salts at 280C
- metal + H_2SO_4 → metals sulphate

All metal sulphates convert to insoluble metal oxides at 600C

Except rare earth sulphates!

Rare earth sulphates only decompose above 800C

Leach rare earth sulphates with water, purify and separate

Recycling of rare earth - conclusions

TORNGAT

Feed scrap into ore processing facility and process together with ore

Sulphation process can tolerate at least 10 % additional rare earth from scrap

→ more than 3000 tons of magnets

Torngat facility can process scrap from automotive and wind power industry for many years after start-up

Leverage an existing processing plant rather than another purpose-built facility for recycling

Cost:
Collection of magnet material
Processing: sulphation, purification and separation about 5 -7 $/kg REO

torngatmetals.com 11

Contact Details

TORNGAT

Contact details

Dirk Naumann – President
Tel: 514.220.2087
Email: dirk.naumann@torngatmetals.com

Christine Burow – VP Marketing
Tel: 519.501.7280
Email: Christine.burow@torngatmetals.com

torngatmetals.com 12

AUTHOR INDEX

Constantinides, S. 31
Devine, M. 1
Furmanczyk, K. 147
Holzhey, R. 16
Liu, J. 130
Miller, M. 186
Narasimhan, S. 89
Naumann, D. 230
Ohm, M. 173
Ormerod, J. 59
Parker, D. 115
Schliesch, T. 155
Ughini, R. 209
Whalen, J. 46